Brew Your Business

Brew Your Business

The Ultimate Craft Beer Playbook

Karen McGrath, Regina Luttrell,
M. Todd Luttrell, and Sean McGrath

Rowman & Littlefield
Lanham • Boulder • New York • London

Published by Rowman & Littlefield
A wholly owned subsidiary of The Rowman & Littlefield Publishing Group, Inc.
4501 Forbes Boulevard, Suite 200, Lanham, Maryland 20706
www.rowman.com

Unit A, Whitacre Mews, 26-34 Stannary Street, London SE11 4AB

British Library Cataloguing in Publication Information Available

Library of Congress Cataloging-in-Publication Data

Names: McGrath, Karen, 1965– editor.
Title: Brew your business : the ultimate craft beer playbook / [edited by]
   Karen McGrath, Regina Luttrell, M. Todd Luttrell and Sean McGrath.
Description: Lanham : Rowman & Littlefield, a wholly owned subsidiary of The
   Rowman & Littlefield Publishing Group, Inc., [2017] | Includes
   bibliographical references and index.
Identifiers: LCCN 2017030928 (print) | LCCN 2017032972 (ebook) | ISBN
   9781442266834 (electronic) | ISBN 9781442266827 (cloth : alk. paper)
Subjects: LCSH: Beer—United States. | Beer industry—United
   States—Management. | Entrepreneurship. | Brewers—United States.
Classification: LCC TP577 (ebook) | LCC TP577 .B739 2017 (print) | DDC
   663/.30973—dc23
LC record available at https://lccn.loc.gov/2017030928

♾™ The paper used in this publication meets the minimum requirements of
American National Standard for Information Sciences—Permanence of Paper
for Printed Library Materials, ANSI/NISO Z39.48-1992.

Printed in the United States of America

CONTENTS

CONTENTS

FOREWORD

Virtually everyone that I speak with who is a homebrewer or a craft beer aficionado has at some point wondered what it would be like to "go pro" and be involved, in some capacity, with a brewery or brewpub. If you have been brewing beer at home for a long time (for me over twenty years before I took the plunge) or if you enjoy today's fine craft beers, the following thought has probably crossed your mind: "Imagine if we had our own brewery? How great would it be having people drinking *our* beer and really enjoying it?"

With *Brew Your Business: The Ultimate Craft Beer Playbook*, almost every area of the business of brewing beer is addressed. Through various interviews with industry professionals, the people who are making their dream a successful reality on a daily basis, you can actually learn the dos and don'ts from experienced people who have gone through the entire process of a brewery from concept to opening day and on to present day.

When I decided to "give it a shot" and open my brewery, Helderberg Mountain Brewing Company in East Berne, New York, I didn't have a "playbook" to give me insight on such a variety of subjects that are part of running a professional brewery. It's a lot more than just brewing beer. A lot more—trust me!

The beer does outshine all else; don't get me wrong. If you don't brew good beer, you can forget about everything else. That is, after all, why people are at your door. For craft breweries, fresh beer crafted using locally sourced ingredients and brewed by local people is what excites beer drinkers nowadays. This has become something that more and more people are seeking out. When my friends and I started brewing beer at home, we quickly realized that we could produce a pretty good product with the flavors we desired. It was somewhat addicting, I must admit, when we were enhancing the flavors, aromas, or mouthfeel qualities of a beer that we liked or toning down things we didn't. Most of all, "the addiction" was rooted in the anticipation of tasting the beer when it was ready! Sometimes it worked out, and sometimes it didn't, but that was what kept us coming back for more. Of course, while sitting around and having a few of our handcrafted brews, the phrase "imagine if we had our own brewery" was spoken in many conversations. Winning "Best of Show" several times in local homebrew competitions only enhanced our thoughts and dreams. Today, brewing professionally, I still approach each brew day and beer with the same level of excitement! The goal is brewing quality beer which is full of flavor and using as many local ingredients as possible; and this sentiment is shared and executed on a daily basis by craft brewers. In my opinion, this is why the craft beer industry is so successful and growing exponentially.

It is the craft brewers and the craft beer industry that amaze me, especially the "brotherhood" among brewers in the professional community. I could pick up my phone and call almost all local brewers with a question or a request for an ingredient I may not have and they would go out of their way to assist me as best they could. We are all in the same business but all are working together to achieve the same goal: quality beer. I don't know of another industry in which this sort of camaraderie occurs.

Helderberg Mountain Brewing Company has been part of many collaboration beers with other breweries and we have many more planned. Having several breweries joining together to produce a beer is becoming very popular and provides insights not achieved by merely brewing alone. Each brewer has his or her unique set of ideas or brewing techniques and collaborating on beers from time to time helps to spread these ideas and brewing techniques, as well as additional knowledge between and among brewers. This knowledge sharing helps make everyone better at the craft. And, consumers are also winners, because a lot of these collaboration beers are unique offerings that the breweries themselves do not produce on a regular basis; they may be "one-offs." I personally believe that the networking and collaboration between and among breweries is a major reason for the success of the craft brewing industry. There are so many incredible beers brewed by very talented people. Spreading this brewing knowledge and working together to achieve the common goal of producing flavorful, high-quality local beer makes everyone better, for sure!

So, about the authors, Karen and Sean McGrath and Regina (Gina) and M. Todd (Todd) Luttrell, and why I support their efforts. Karen and Gina are professors of communications at the College of Saint Rose in Albany, New York, and Syracuse University respectively, and, together, they have authored professional articles, chapters, and one other book. I can honestly say that they are thorough and detailed when it comes to researching material for each project. In this case, a good portion of the research had to do with visiting many successful breweries and conducting interviews with industry experts. These informative interviews and subsequent morsels of knowledge from the pros are interspersed throughout this book. In addition, Karen and Gina did have able-bodied assistants who were more than willing to help out with the research required for the book, their husbands, Sean and Todd. Sean was adamant about dedicating as much time as was necessary to make the book extremely informative; it is a book about beer after all. Sean not only assists me at my brewery on many brew days but also attends brew festivals or local tastings with me, pouring samples, talking beer, and more. I believe this experience qualifies him as an "able-bodied assistant." Todd has a background in business administration, science, and biochemistry and likes to try new beers, all of which enhanced the chapters through his expertise in each area. He too is an "able-bodied assistant."

Overall, this book is a great resource, and each chapter delves into the many different areas of knowledge required for you to be in the business of brewing beer. As I have found out, you have to be a "jack-of-all-trades" to be successful in this industry. From topics such as the history and culture of craft beer to brewing basics and ingredients, business plans, law, small business management, marketing your brand, and offering resources and recipes, this book has it all covered. While no book can teach you everything, this one will get you well on your way as you get closer to your dream of professional brewing.

In conclusion, I am brewing professionally for a number of reasons. First, starting a brew day with sacks of grain, bags of hops, kettles of water, and yeast that is raring to go, and then arriving at the final product that hopefully mimics my original concept a few weeks later is the primary reason. Second, to be able to control and influence each step in the process from the color to the aromas and flavors and on to the overall experience of drinking each beer is exciting. It is quite satisfying when a beer comes out just as I pictured it would weeks earlier. So, when asked to finish this sentence: "I brew because . . ." I have to say, "it's to have your customers seek out your beers and enjoy them; it's really the icing on the cake!" Cheers!

Mike Wenzel
Co-owner and brewer
Helderberg Mountain Brewing Company
East Berne, New York

PREFACE

Beer: It's more than just a breakfast drink . . . really!

B elieve it or not, many people, children included, have enjoyed beer for breakfast, in large part because the alcohol content often rendered the local water drinkable. As we shall see in this book, the beverage commonly referred to as beer has come a long way. From bread makers in Egypt to homebrewers now experimenting with the cloning of their favorite beers, the craft is here to stay and is becoming more unique than ever before.

To date, the popularity of beer has grown precipitously as a social beverage of choice. Yes, wine certainly has its followers and will continue to be a staple of the beverage industry for years to come. However, beer, especially craft beer created for niche audiences, is making a ruckus in the beverage industry. Big beer companies like Anheuser Busch/InBev (add SABMiller in late 2016) bring national and international brands to market and have the advertising reach to support their brands. In recent years, individuals around the world have started to brew beer for the pleasure of creating their own beverages, avoiding many of the larger national and international beer company trends. Homebrewing, a common replacement for purchasing beer, is providing an opportunity to open small craft breweries in a barn or small shed. These establishments often experience rapid growth, expanding from one barrel to three barrel to seven barrel systems, enabling brewers to supply local taverns and grow their customer base. The explosion that is occurring in the beer industry is similar to that of the dotcoms of the early 1990s, but in this case, craft brewing and brewers seem to be operating at a much more stable rate of expansion than those technology companies. Why, you might ask? Well, there are numerous reasons.

What feeds this growth?

In particular, one reason that the craft beer industry and its consumption have grown over the years can be seen in how it parallels the political and environmental scenes in the United States. As seen in social movements like "Occupy Wall Street," grassroots movements of every stripe, and popular "antiestablishment" sentiments, craft beer brewers and consumers have diverged from the big-business beer companies that dominate the markets, buy their breweries, and then commercialize the beer. Additionally, there is a push for differentiated legislation from homebrewers across the country, craft beer brewers, and consumers—all demanding something different, something local, and the experience that craft beers have carved out for their niche audiences.

Furthermore, over the past decade, consumers have increasingly sought organic, local products including farm-raised animals and organically grown fruits, vegetables, and grains. This shift has promoted a growing interest in Neighborhood Cooperative Markets where all-natural and organic products can be bought and sold, and where the owners are the consumers. Such collaboration is now a trademark of the craft beer culture, which has "community" as one of its lynchpins. Clearly, there appears to be continued momentum for the "Grow Local, Buy Local" movement and craft brewers are happily tossed in the mix. (Or should we say, "hoppily"!)

A second reason for the continued growth within this industry results from community building. As @TheBeerGoddess, Erin Peters,[1] tells us in a personal interview, she loves the craft beer industry because "it allows her to hang out with a lot of great people," not only other consumers, but also brewers and those in marketing and equipment sales. Mike Wenzel,[2] an Albany, New York, brewer from the Helderberg Mountain Brewing Company spoke positively of the brewing collaboration that happens all across the country, wherein local brewers get together to concoct and create a specialty beer. One such creation that he was a part of was called "Too Many Cooks" and included a Helderberg Mountain Brewing Company select beer, CH Evans Ale, and ten others. Not only was it well received and highly desired by the customer base, the brewers agreed to work together again in the future. Less than two months later, Helderberg Mountain Brewing Company and CH Evans were at it again. Not only do these breweries collaborate on new brews, but they also make themselves available to local enthusiasts, new brewers, and consumers for discussions specific to their beer and processes. In casual conversation, one brewer noted that answering the question, "What do you do?" with "I'm a brewmaster" is definitely a discussion opener. With an introduction like that, people magically want to talk about the beer, his job, the brewing process, and all things beer-related. These conversations are the first steps to community building.

However, upstate New York brewers are not alone in desire for collaborations. San Diego–based Stone Brewing has its own program called, "Union of Forward-Craft Thinking" wherein they collaborate with other brewers to experiment with beer ingredients and styles. They have been doing this since 2008. For years, Delaware's own Dogfish Head Craft Beer Ales, headed by Sam Calagione, has been collaborating with other brewers and crafters of all varieties. Oftentimes, the results from these partnerships are only available in-house, and not through distributors or growlers. In fact, not only does Sam Calagione collaborate with other brewers, he also partners with other organizations who may not want to see part of their own products go to waste. Such is the result of Maine's Grain Surfboard Company, where leftover cedar wood shavings are used for a unique craft beer experience, and led to the creation of "GraintoGlass" in 2010 and again in 2014.[3]

Of special note here is that these collaborations are equal opportunity in nature, with a growing number of women taking a larger stake. In addition to brewing collaborations, the pinkbootssociety.org arose to assist women, who now make up about 25 percent of the industry, to come together and build a strong community. Chicks for Beer, an assembly of women who wish to pair food with beer, has also established a presence via Ingrid Alvarez Cherney in San Diego (and has now blossomed elsewhere). Additionally, local towns and counties promote gatherings among beer enthusiasts in nearly every area, supported by competitions and festivals, allowing consumers to develop their palate and sip eclectic beers. For those of you who can't make it out of town, consider taking part in a craft beer week and raise your glass. In May 2016 (and years before), craft brewers and enthusiasts across the nation turned their attention to American Craft Beer Week, where homebrewers and consumers "shared" their beer at the "same time" in order to focus on a different type of collaboration: sharing in the experience, no matter the miles between them, and climaxing with a nationwide "toast" to the growing beer culture in the United States. For those IPA enthusiasts out there—don't be discouraged, as there is also an IPA Day to celebrate every August. These are just a few of the examples in which community building takes shape in the craft beer culture.

A third reason for the US craft beer explosion is tied to community building, but more focused on recreation and socialization. Recreation is supposed to be something that we do for fun and that we don't consider to be work or career related. However, many homebrewers can be spotted brewing beer for friends and family, which then turns into brewing beer for a local tavern or taproom. Recreation for brewers focuses more on the act of "re-creating" something for themselves and others, simply out of the love for the craft. Ultimately, once a good brew is created, the goal is to "re-create" it again and again, without discrepancy; in other words, consistency is great for a brand because it allows brand loyalists to reap what you have sown in the brewing process whenever your beverage is consumed. Since brewers don't necessarily brew for the sake of doing so, they want to share their beer and discuss the process and quality with others who also enjoy the beer experience. Additionally, homebrewers and craft brewers relish in sharing their stories regarding their beer and business ventures. Billy Pyatt of Catawba Brewing in Morgantown and Asheville, North Carolina[4] (now also in Charlotte, North Carolina, and Montgomery, Alabama), loves to share the tale of the first homebrewing kit that he received as a gift from his wife. This story continues throughout his corporate life at Corning to eventually co-owning his brewing company in his "retirement years" (quotes indicate work is still ongoing but the amount of work required to run a brewery far exceeds his corporate hours). In sharing stories like these with us, Billy Pyatt has another outlet to describe the passion required to be in the brewing industry and to grow a business. Stories are essential to the community building and socialization processes and critical for continued growth.

The socialization process that accompanies this culture has also been around for many years, from brothels and taverns to taprooms and basements. What makes beer a social experience is the ability to be with others in one place, much like the aforementioned "toast." However, with the advent of social media and other technologies, craft beer brewers and enthusiasts no longer have to be in the same physical space to collaborate or socialize; they simply have to be able to share their experiences with others, even if it is through Facebook, Twitter, Instagram, or the Untappd App. Sharing experiences with others by enjoying the quality and flavor (aroma, appearance, taste, and mouthfeel) of the beer is now far more important than the "drinking" that you may have been done in high school and college. Simply put, men and women alike just aren't seeking to get a "buzz" anymore; rather, many beer enthusiasts are seeking out great-tasting beer in a welcoming environment and the camaraderie that comes with it.

A final reason that the craft beer industry continues to grow is the inherent competition and experimentation involved in the science of brewing. Yes, there is collaboration and even camaraderie, but there is also a desire for people to like your beer. This is where competition comes in. Having the opportunity to enter your brew at a festival or beer conference is also contributing to the boom in this industry. For these events, you essentially create your best beer and allow judges with trained palettes to evaluate the aroma, appearance, taste, and mouthfeel of your beer to rate it in relation to similar styles. For some, winning is the only thing that matters. However, those who enter BBQ Competitions can offer some advice: What the judges want and what your niche audience wants may not be the same, but winning drives new people to your business, which allows you to compete again and further build your business. So, competition can be healthy for many brewers and for the industry as a whole.

With these rationales driving growth in the craft beer industry, this book provides the reader with an overview of the history, culture, brewing process, science, marketing, and experiences an interested enthusiast or brewer can expect and learn from the industry. We hope that whether you are a novice or expert, connoisseur or sampler, this book will assist you in better understanding the industry. Skip around the table of contents or read from beginning to end. Whatever you do, do so with your favorite beer. Cheers!

Talking from the Tap!

Interview with Sean McGrath,
Coauthor, Homebrewer, and Self-Proclaimed "Beer Aficionado"

1. *How long have you been brewing?*

I started brewing back in the 1990s for personal consumption mostly, then had a lull in homebrewing between 2003 and 2015. Now I am back to brewing more regularly and working with a local brewer to learn the brewing ropes on a larger scale. What's interesting is that I still have my personal notes from that first brew process; every beer matters, and I want to know what worked and what didn't.

2. *What do I need in order to homebrew?*

Consider the path of Dogfish Head Brewery's modest beginnings. A small studio apartment in New York City, where brews were shared with friends and then friends of friends. Not much space was needed, instead only a commitment to brewing a good beer and the willingness to share with others often leads the way. Of course, having some equipment and ingredients are necessary. But let's get real; most of us aren't Sam Calagione from Dogfish Head, who had inherent talent and focus for making good beer right out of the gate. He too suffered some beer loss in his early ventures, but he persevered and continues to experiment and collaborate with others today, while many of us have to experiment using prepared beer kits with simplified instructions, especially when starting out. Regardless of our brewing experience or expertise, there are some basic steps we all must take in order to brew our one- to two-gallon batches at home.

3. *How did you prepare for your first brew?*

I identified a local brewing supplier to access equipment and ingredients in the early days. Now, I can simply go online and do an Internet search to find the best deals and products. I also bought a notebook to record information and notes about the beer and the brewing process. Nowadays, my smartphone or tablet can serve that purpose. I then went to my local supplier for necessary equipment and ingredients. Of course, now I can simply order online and have it delivered to my front door. When starting out, one-gallon kits are hard to find, so five-gallon kits are preferable. Plus, you produce more beer for personal consumption!

To start my first brew experience, I used a starter kit because it included everything I needed:

- a bucket and lid for fermentation
- a bucket for bottling
- a bottle capper
- a siphon
- an airlock for the fermentation bucket
- a hydrometer
- a bottling wand

Later on, I purchased a thermometer strip (Fermometer) to assist in gauging the temperature to pitch my yeast. If it's too hot, then it will kill the yeast and if it's too cold, the yeast will remain dormant.

4. *What beer did you brew out of the gate?*

It's best to begin with an all-malt extract ingredient kit to make an amber ale, which is a red ale, or a blonde ale because they are relatively simple. Mine was an Irish red ale.

5. *What else did you have to purchase for this first brew besides the kit?*

Some sort of sanitizer, such as Star San™ and a stainless steel twenty-quart kettle, because stainless steel works better than aluminum. However, if you have a big aluminum stockpot or lobster kettle, that will work too. Then, you need a pair of scissors and a large spoon to stir the wort. The best spoon to use is one with a wooden handle to avoid burns or a fully wooden spoon only because you'll be stirring boiling liquid and heat will transfer to the spoon. It should be long enough to reach the bottom of your kettle without having your hands over the boiling liquid because "that burns."

6. *Where can I get bottles and how many do I need for a five-gallon brew?*

You need forty-eight to fifty-two clean, recappable, brown bottles (recycled or new, this is your choice). I use recycled for two reasons: first we get to drink *a lot* of beer before we even brew, and second, we are helping the environment. Avoid green and clear glass bottles because they allow too much light to penetrate, which can then lead to "skunk" beer. The bottle caps usually come with your ingredient kit, but once they are used, they should be "tossed" and never reused because they are now dirty and bent.

7. *You aren't known for your organizational prowess, so how did you focus on preparing your brewing space?*

You're right. I'm not known for my organizational skills, but I was capable of organizing my space to fit my brewing needs and make the process a smooth one. Much like Rachel Ray does when she cooks a thirty-minute meal, I cleaned and sanitized the area, including removing my cat from the sanitized area, and gathered all equipment and brewing material together into my brew space. Then, on brew day, I sanitized the fermentation bucket, siphon hoses, and airlock that came with the kit by following the instructions. A note of reference for other beginners, if you are using home bleach, the ratio is one tablespoon of bleach to one gallon of water, and you soak all equipment for at least twenty minutes and then rinse each item with boiling water. Since I didn't need my bottles and bottling bucket right away, I sanitized these items just before filling them on bottling day, about seven to ten days later. If you sanitize too early, then you will have to sanitize them again.

8. *What's the best tip you can give to a first-time homebrewer?*
There are timing points during the boil where hops are added and stirred, so be sure to read your instructions thoroughly *before* you begin the brew process. And, most importantly, *DON'T WALK AWAY FROM THE KETTLE WHEN ADDING HOPS* because "the hot break" will occur causing the kettle to rapidly overflow, much like when pasta suddenly overflows the pot. Simple stirring or a quick spritz from the faucet until a rolling boil appears on the surface will alleviate this condition. I learned that lesson the hard way.

9. *Any final brewing advice?*
There is nothing left to do but brew and brew some more! Once you familiarize yourself with the general brewing process, you can experiment with different recipes and styles of beer. For example, Karen's first homebrew was a blonde ale brewed with me and one of her work colleagues in September 2015. A user-friendly kit and a patient mentor, me, made this a drinkable and refreshing beer. Karen is now looking forward to experimenting with a stout recipe as her palette develops and her brewing confidence builds. For a quick look at how to brew, read and follow the instructions with your kit, which includes this basic rundown:
Begin

- Bring 2 gallons of water to a boil.

- While waiting, take the can of malt extract and place it in a small pot of hot water making the malt extract easier to pour. Much like maple syrup, warming the liquid in its can or bottle warms the syrup and allows pouring to occur more easily.

- Once the water is at boiling temperature, remove it from the heat source so that when you add the malt extract it won't sink to the bottom and burn the pot making cleanup more difficult.

- Stir thoroughly until malt and water is well mixed.

- Return pot to the heat source and bring to a rolling boil.

- Most beers require a 60-minute boil time, but be sure to follow the kit's instructions for any variations.

- There are also timing points during the boil where hops are added and stirred, so be sure to read your instructions thoroughly *before* you begin the brew process. And, as mentioned previously, don't walk away from the kettle when adding hops because a phenomenon known as "the hot break" will occur causing the kettle to rapidly overflow, much like when pasta suddenly overflows the pot. Simple stirring until a rolling boil appears on the surface will alleviate this condition.

- Repeat previous step until all hops have been added as per the instructions in your kit.

- Once the time is up, as per your instructions for the specific beer (e.g., 60 minutes), remove from heat, and briefly cool by immersing in an ice-water bath (fill sink with ice and water) but be careful, because as the wort cools, it is more susceptible to contamination, so don't splash dirty spoons, hands, or other items into the liquid. Sterilization is key here!

- Transfer the liquid using the siphon from your kit and try to leave behind any residue.

- Add makeup water (tap, bottled, spring, etc.; whatever you use for brewing) to the fermentor to just over the 5-gallon mark.

  o What is fermentation? How does it impact the process? For a detailed description of fermentation see chapter 5. But, for now, here's what you need to know: Fermentation is the process by which the sugars from the malts are converted by the yeast into alcohol when a specific temperature is reached based on the type of yeast and style of beer you are brewing. This is why using a kit is highly recommended for first-time brewers.

- You want the liquid temperature to be below 80 degrees Fahrenheit.

- At this time, you can take a sample for your Hydrometer to ascertain the original gravity of the beer, which is dependent upon your ingredient kit. This is used to determine when fermentation has been completed and can be used to calculate your alcohol by volume (ABV) in your finished product. This sample *must not* be returned to the fermentation bucket.

- Re-sanitize the spoon.

- Give the wort a vigorous stirring to help aerate the liquid. If your temperature is within the desired range for your yeast packet, sanitize the outside of the yeast packet and the scissors you will use to open the packet. Don't, under any circumstances, use your teeth!

- The yeast can now be sprinkled over the wort in the fermentation bucket.

- Place the sanitized lid on the fermentation bucket.

- Place your sanitized fermentation airlock into the lid as instructed on the kit. The airlock allows the CO_2 to escape the bucket without allowing contaminates to infiltrate the beer.

- Store the fermentation bucket in a stable temperature environment between 60 and 70 degrees Fahrenheit based on the types of yeast. Most ales work well between 60 and 70 degrees Fahrenheit.

- Now comes the waiting game.

  o Within 24 hours you should notice bubbling activity from your airlock. This means fermentation is occurring. If you notice that foam or the wort has entered the airlock, then you need to remove, re-sanitize, and replace the airlock, and monitor the beer for the next 4–5 days (expect bubbling but not foaming).

- At this time, take another gravity reading.

  o Re-sanitize the hoses and siphon *before* taking the gravity reading sample. Make note of the reading, and if bubbling stops within a day or so, then take another reading. If the reading decreases, then fermentation is still occurring. If the reading stays the same, then fermentation is complete. This is your final gravity reading.

- Get ready to bottle.

  o Sanitize all bottles, bottling bucket, bottling wand, hoses, and siphon. At this time, sanitize bottle caps separate from the other equipment by placing in a small boiling pot for about 10 minutes (no actual sanitizer is needed for the caps because the boiling water destroys bacteria). This ensures that the caps are all in one place.

  o At this time, sanitize a lid for a small pot and then heat 1 cup of water and 5 ounces of corn sugar, often called priming sugar (check kit), and bring solution to a slow rolling boil.

  o Cover with the sanitized lid and let cool.

  o Once cool, add mixture to the bottling bucket, but make sure the spigot is closed on the bottling bucket.

- Transfer the wort into the bottling bucket using the siphon, but being careful to leave behind what is now called the "Trube" (the residue consisting of the dead yeast cells and hops matter).

  o Raise the bottling bucket to a higher level to assist with gravity filling of the bottles.

  o Attach the sanitized bottling wand and tubing to the spigot.

  o Fill the sanitized brown bottles now.

    ■ If you fill to the very top of the bottle with the wand still inside, when you remove the wand, you will leave the same amount of airspace in each bottle to allow for proper carbonation.

  o The bottles can now be capped with the bottle capper and the sanitized bottle caps.

  o Store bottles in a dark, stable temperature location (60–70 degrees Fahrenheit) for 2–3 weeks.

o   At two weeks, place bottles in refrigerator. Once cool, open one to taste. If it seems flat, then wait another week before opening another bottle. The tasting bottle should not be re-capped, so drink it! After the third week, open a bottle for tasting. ENJOY!

o   As you progress over time, you may want to name your beer and/or share with friends. Just as you think you are down and ready to call it a day, your must pause and start your cleanup.

Cleanup

• All equipment must be cleaned. Wash and dry with warm water and dish soap, then store in an accessible place for the next brew.

• Please note this tale of caution: When cleaning plastic fermentation and bottling buckets *do not* use abrasive chemicals or scrubbers because they may cause scratching, which may then hold bacteria and other contaminates. Instead, use warm water and dish soap with a soft sponge or cloth. A commercial cleaner such as PBW™ (powdered brewery wash) may also be used and works exceptionally well.

Now there is nothing left to do but BREW again, so REPEAT all steps!

10. *What's it like to taste your first sip of homebrew? Describe that feeling.*

Imagine a moment filled with such anxiety that you are almost too giddy to open the bottle. You get that cap off and sniff it. Smells like beer. Now the true test: Does it taste like beer? Yes! It does. Relief coupled with exuberance, turns to a high-five with whoever is nearby. You sip that deliciousness, admire its head, follow each carbonated bubble to the top, and are sure not to spill a drop because each drop is a reminder of the attention you provided to each bottle of beer during your first brewing process. It may just be the best beer you ever tasted . . . for now! You soon realize you want to brew again.

11. *Is there any additional equipment I should consider if I decide to brew more often or in larger quantities?*

Replace buckets with glass carboys or new buckets for fermentation (primary and secondary fermentation); beers with more grain build more complexity as you brew more, but the process remains the same. All grain brewing requires a mash tun and larger brewing vessels. Bottle brushes of different sizes, jet cleaners, bottle drying rack, carboy brushes (large glass cleaners), and more.

12. How can I make connections with other homebrewers?

You can first check the app called "Untappd" which allows beer drinkers to earn "badges" and rate beer, and even post their own homebrews as well. You should also be sure to venture out to local breweries, chat with brewers and other imbibers to network with others. Check the Internet to see about homebrewing groups in your area. Invite friends over to try your beer and encourage them to take part in the brewing process. Go to beer festivals and visit chat rooms, blogs, and Facebook groups where homebrewers interact. Better yet, start your own local group, blog, or Facebook group to connect with local brewers. You won't be sorry. Take a class at a local homebrew supply center to meet other homebrewers. If you are feeling bold, then enter your beer in a local homebrewing contest.

13. How do you decide on creating your own recipes? When should I consider doing so?

If you identify a beer that you enjoy from other breweries or brewers and you have given yourself enough time to develop your brewing prowess, then you should begin experimenting. Research the beer, become more familiar with your hops, malts, sugars, and other additives, then brew small batches to focus on the quality and replication of the beer. When you feel truly ready you will know it is time to create your own recipes.

14. What else do we need to know about brewing from home?

Don't let one mistake spoil your interest. Part of homebrewing is learning from your mistakes. If you create a "skunky" beer, figure out where you went wrong, write in your notebook, and ask other brewers how to avoid that mistake again. Brewing is a process with successes and challenges. Sometimes it's the brewing itself that is most satisfying as you see a product through from conception to production, maybe even consumption. For others, though, it's the product itself that is most satisfying. Know your local, state, and federal laws related to homebrewing and put safety first. Have a fire extinguisher at the ready and take caution when children are scurrying around the brewing area.

Remember that federal law allows for home production without payment of tax for personal or family use as long as it does not exceed two hundred gallons per calendar year if there are two or more adults residing in the household or one hundred gallons if only one adult resides in the household.

15. *Finish this sentence: "I brew because . . ."*

"I can! And, I enjoy controlling my product versus allowing others to control it. But mostly, I enjoy sharing my craft beer with others because it makes me feel as though I have accomplished something."

Part I

UNDERSTANDING BEER CULTURE: NOT JUST FOR THE BREWING NOVICE

Sometimes when I reflect on all the beer I drink, I feel ashamed. Then I look into the glass and think about the workers in the brewery and all of their hopes and dreams. If I didn't drink this beer, they might be out of work and their dreams would be shattered. I think, "It is better to drink this beer and let their dreams come true than be selfish and worry about my liver."

—attributed to Babe Ruth
(actually written by Jay Maynard, comic writer)

CRAFT BEER HISTORY AND CULTURE
"What Can Knowledge Do for You?"

We know what you're thinking. "Don't tell me I have to learn about history . . . again." Well, the answer is: You don't have to, but you may want to. Why? The history of beer, even in its short form, is beneficial for understanding where beer is today. And, knowing where beer is today lends itself to what the craft beer culture is in the United States today as well. There are many great, thorough resources available at your local libraries and retailers, so we don't dare set out to reconstruct thousands of years of history in a small section of a single chapter. Instead, we provide some highlights, emphasizing the journey of beer over the years. Much like producer, actor, director, and comedian Mel Brooks, we seek to provide the history of beer in a few pages by offering a sort of Cliff's Notes, or a Beer History 101. So, here goes.

History

Day One—just kidding. The history of beer dates back thousands of years. Although we aren't historians, our research, inspired by those "in the know," indicates that Mesopotamia, with its fertile lands and abundant barley, was truly ripe for happiness and was certainly a gift from the gods. There is evidence of a five-thousand-year-old brewery in China as well.[1] Starting with the Uruks onto the Sumerians, who incidentally brewed nineteen different types of beer, to the Babylonians and Nubians, beer, accidental or not, was quite a hit, and women were often the primary brewers.[2] Some would argue that bread yeast fermented on its own when left outside in the rain and was deemed palatable by its drinkers. Women, also the primary bakers of the time, then honed the fermenting process and began to create this yeast-formed drink and share it with others. Soon it became the beverage of choice, especially when potable drinking water was already a rarity. The alcohol in the water from the yeast provided much needed water sanitization. In fact, children and adults alike would often have this yeasty beverage for breakfast in order to begin the day. Thus, beer began as a safer environmental choice than water, whereas its recreational and socialization values emerged much later.

For centuries, monks controlled brewing, and the church maintained a strong influence over its parishioners and its beer. But beer started to become a socializing factor of the culture,[3] and with alcohol also came rowdiness. Therefore, and quite sadly, beer began to be regulated. Some regulations, including ale standards, were part of the Magna Carta of 1215; it was the object of sin taxes in the early 1300s; and the German *Reinheitsgebot* purity standard in 1516 required these ingredients—water, malted barley, and hops (yeast had not yet been discovered as significant for brewers).[4]

As the art of brewing beer grew around the world, people were traveling far and wide (sometimes very slowly and with many dangers), and taverns and inns began to spring up along well-traveled paths, allowing travelers, mostly men, to take a break from the road, quench their thirst, and even sleep overnight. Granted, many taverns and inns focused on the selling of whiskey and even moonshine, but these institutions became a place for people to socialize and do business with the locals and others along the way. Women were legally barred from drinking in public, so private rooms were reserved for them to enjoy a beverage, if it was allowed at all. However, most of the women who frequented these taverns or inns were often there to appease men and offer them "the company of a woman" for the night . . . and a fee. Brothels were very successful during this time and were well known. On the other hand, some women who lived in town would often order alcohol and have it delivered to their home, and some even made it themselves. There were even some well-known women, such as Martha Jefferson at Monticello, who were purveyors of beer and brewed regularly with much "brand" loyalty from the locals. Seems like the Goddess of Beer should be admired for all of her guidance and work; "Thank you, Ninkasi!"[5]

As industrialization expanded in the mid- to late 1800s, the growler also emerged as a vessel for enjoying beer. During the late 1800s, men working industrial jobs would often send their children to the local "watering hole" with a metal container to have draught brought home. Rumor has it that the word "growler" emerged during this time when the containers would make a noise that sounded like a growl while in transport.[6] Regardless of how the term emerged, what is clear is that taverns would sell customers beer in these containers because advances had not yet been made in the bottling and packaging of beer.

Let us not forget that in the 1920s, prohibition became the law in the United States. Religious conservatism had sparked a public outcry over the consumption and sale of alcohol dating back to the early 1800s. This concern strengthened through the nineteenth century until it became law under the Volstead Act of 1920, where the production, transportation, and sale of alcohol were now considered illegal under the Eighteenth Amendment. However, personal possession and consumption of alcohol was not included in the prohibition. While alcohol was legally forbidden, many skirted the law and made their own moonshine, beer, and wine; often distributed at secretly located Speakeasies. In a sense, prohibition supported a rise in criminal activity, from bootlegging to other forms of organized crime, and it is commonly associated with yesteryear's version of NASCAR racing, where bootleggers needed fast cars to flee the police (and some still do) in the hills and rural areas of North Carolina and Tennessee. Eventually, the vise on alcohol prohibition loosened and it came to an end in 1933 with the repeal of the Volstead Act (aka, the Twenty-first Amendment), leaving behind several counties and towns that are still "dry" to this day. While many small breweries were local and successful in the 1800s, the number of breweries dropped from about thirty-two hundred in 1870 to just over four hundred in 1940, and to just over one hundred in 1980 due to the combined influence of the Prohibition, increased commercialization of beer, and advanced equipment and packaging in the industry by big brewing companies like Anheuser-Busch, Schlitz, Pabst, and others.[7] Today, the number of craft breweries is growing, with over four thousand craft brewers in the United States alone by the end of 2015. The future looks strong for continued growth, with women looking to play a larger role in sustaining this rise of popularity.

An Important Historical Note: Women Are Integral to the Beer Industry

When we think about beer, many images of men tend to spring to mind: Men at pubs, men running the industry, or men drinking beer. However, what we know is that women have historically played, and continue to play, an integral and leading role in the brewing of beer and in the industry. As previously noted, women have traditionally been the primary bread makers and bakers of the family, and now make up almost 32 percent of the craft beer drinkers.[8] They may have also been responsible for the discovery of how damp grains ferment and then subsequently learned how to use leftover mash to bring beer to life. As caretakers, they knew beer had medicinal and other benefits,[9] especially because quality water became sparse as populations grew. Beer became a breakfast drink, though with lower alcohol content, for all people, including women and children. Cereals also became popular during this time, as grains were a primary source of nourishment. Beer was a natural progression and a favored beverage for starting the day—orange juice came so much later!

So how do women remain relevant in today's craft-brew industry?[10] A quick search of Google, or even of the American Homebrewers Association, tells us that women play a prominent role in many areas of the modern-day brew business. Many times women perform the public relations, social media, and marketing roles, but there are also women who are the founders and brewer masters.[11] That's right! Many more women today than years before not only know brewing science, but also know a good beer when they taste it. Notice the word "science" used here; brewing has become more of a science in the industry, which is why we include the science of brewing in this book.

When we first chatted with Gwen Conley[12] of Lost Abbey in San Diego, it was clear that she exuded confidence and know-how on all topics in brewing, ranging from flavor profiles to trends in the industry. Conley made it clear that when she first started her brewing career at Coors, she was one of a small handful of women in the industry. Participating as a judge in her first beer competition, the Great American Beer festival, made her one of only seven female judges. Now, she says, women constitute about 25 percent of the judges and the number is growing. In a biological sense, women tend to have a more developed palette than men, so this number may continue to grow as more women enter the profession. In 1938, long before Gwen Conley arrived on the beer scene, Elise Miller John of Miller Brewing became the first woman to run a major brewing company. She did so for eight years.[13] While today's big five may still be male-dominated, breweries such as New Belgium Brewery in Colorado (cofounder Kim Jordan, 1991) and Stout's Brewing Company in Pennsylvania (Carol Stoudt, 1987) were started by women who are still involved in daily operations. In fact, the number of female executives and brewmasters continues to grow.[14] However, when most people think about craft beer (or brewing beer in general), they associate men with these roles. Consider the May 2016 *USA Today* article that expressed an interest in the role of women in craft beer, raising the ire of some Twitter followers when the author asked, "How do we bring women to craft beer?" which presumed that women weren't already a part of the industry.[15] A debate ensued when female-operated High Heel Brewing marketed beer toward women by focusing on stereotypes and other negative assumptions about women and beer.[16] What most beer drinking women seek is flavor, not the light beers or the marketing strategies aimed at "sexy" or "body image" or "simple attractiveness." Female consumers should not be considered "dainty" and subsequently pigeon-holed into enjoying a single type of beer; instead, they can be thought of as connoisseurs with highly developed palettes and talents that benefit the industry.[17] In short, readers, consumers, brewers, retailers, distributors, and others should not assume that women are not part of, or informed about, the beer or brewing industry.[18] Women have been, and will continue to be, major players in the industry at all levels, and have even organized their own associations to support women in the industry, such as the Pink Boots Society.[19] Now all the craft beer industry needs is more diversity.[20]

If you are interested in learning more about the history of beer and craft beer, consider reading some of the books included in the bibliography. There are many history book options available and ready to quench your history thirst.

Craft Beer Culture: Explosion and Growth of Craft Beer

As you are now keenly aware, beer has been a staple for humans for thousands of years (of course, today, much of the leftover mash is often fed to local cattle or shared through other sustainability programs). Although beer drinkers have socialized in many establishments throughout history, a new "culture" has emerged with the advent and prevalence of craft breweries throughout the world. Simply put, culture is something that is created and shared with others and provides meaning to people's choices, beliefs, and practices. Throughout our personal interviews with leaders within the industry, we asked if a craft beer culture exists. Our intuition was confirmed. Each interviewee, regardless of his or her position in the industry, readily noted that a craft beer culture does exist. We discovered that this culture is focused on learning, resulting from the experiences beer drinkers have together, thereby forming communities. We touched on this in the preface, but want to reiterate its importance.

First, beer emerged thousands of years ago and remains today as a uniting force in American culture. Big brewing companies like Anheuser-Busch, Coors, and InBev, have been around for some time, and many smaller, creative, "craft" brewing companies have also become well established (e.g., Boston Beer Company). Since the late 1990s, however, numerous craft breweries have exploded onto the scene from small towns to big cities. As noted previously, we now have over four thousand craft breweries legally operating and licensed in the United States, compared to just over one hundred in 1980.[21] So, what is behind this explosion and the growth of a craft beer culture?

The number of craft breweries in the United States during the early part of the 1980s would be considered relatively low; however, since that time, craft breweries began to make their mark in various locales across the nation. What is important to note is that the major beer companies dominated the beer market, and in some capacity, still do. In fact, mergers of large commercial beer companies continues today with SABMiller being bought out by Anheuser-Busch/InBev, placing most commercial beer in the hands of a few companies; much like what happened in the media world.[22] These large commercial beer companies have also felt an economic push, or perceived threat; though comparatively small in terms of the amount of money from beer sales across the nation, from craft brewers' success and are now eliminating much of the competition by buying them out. Examples include Goose Island of Illinois, Shock Top of Colorado, and Blue Point Brewing of Long Island, New York, among others. This is not a criticism of these breweries but, instead, a recognition that some breweries want to go bigger (volume) and broader (distribution) but need capital investment from these larger companies to do so. The ways in which these smaller businesses brew beer has not changed, but the debate rages on about what "counts" as a craft beer. According to the Brewers Association, there are four distinct market segments comprising the craft beer industry: microbreweries (brewing less than fifteen thousand barrels), brewpubs (more than 25 percent but up to 75 percent of the beer is brewed on-site), contract brewing company (one brewery/business asks another to brew or produce its beer), and regional craft brewery (an independent brewery with its majority of volume in "traditional" or "innovative" beers). A regional brewery can produce anywhere from

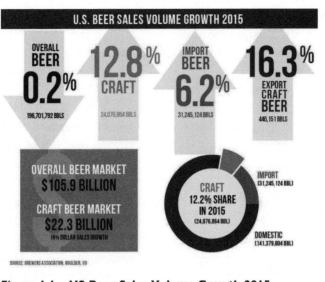

Figure 1.1. US Beer Sales Volume Growth 2015
Source: Brewers Association, Boulder, CO

fifteen thousand to six million barrels; however, once the brewery makes more than six million barrels per year, it is considered a large brewery.[23]

The Brewers Association also defines craft beer in a different way: beers that are brewed at small, independent, traditional breweries.[24] Other organizations weigh in on the definition as "brewed in limited quantities often using traditional methods" and focus on the beer itself and the goal in brewing that beer.[25] While the debate on defining a craft beer will continue as more mergers and acquisitions close, we focus on all types of traditionally brewed beers, whether homebrewed or not, and those identified as "local" beers in their geographic region. We do not, however, focus on larger mainstream beers, such as Coors, Budweiser, Sam Adams, or Heineken. While those companies have long-standing histories and brands, our goal is to assist those who want to learn more about the current shift in the beer industry toward homebrewers and those breweries that offer locally made, small, traditional, and even one-off brews.

As we reflect on the changes that are occurring in our country, it seems that the push to improve our health, be innovative, and save money may have actually contributed to the emergence of a craft beer culture. Since the dot-com era (1990s) both emerged and failed within a single decade, many people invested well and emerged from this era with greater financial security, while others were left broken and struggling. But this era of technological innovation may have sparked a thirst for entrepreneurialism; people wanted to make their own "stuff" and, with any luck, strike it rich. Individuals began making beer in their homes, sometimes in an effort to save money, other times because they believed they made a good product and liked to share it with others. Whatever the reason, homebrewers were instilled with a passion for making and drinking good beer, especially since the mid-1990s when growth in the industry began its resurgence that continues today.

Imagine for a moment stopping by a friend's house and in the dark, cramped space of a basement, garage, or kitchen tasting the maker's "first" brewed beer. Now fast forward several years and this same homebrewer has progressed to a one barrel (thirty-one-gallon) setup, and now is in business selling to a local bar. A story like this is exactly what craft beer is about. It is about growing your passion for a specialty product that you want to share with others. Sometimes brewers grow too quickly and can't keep up with demand, ultimately losing their business. Sometimes they grow even bigger than expected in a short period of time because the beer is that good—just ask Dogfish Head Brewery in Delaware or Treehouse Brewery in Massachusetts. What begins as a hobby and a love for beer can lead to growth and recognition, but it can also lead to your financial demise. The success rate of craft brewery startups was 66.2 percent in 2013, with 48.4 percent of brewery-restaurants opening since 1980 remaining in business.[26] The outlook for continued growth is promising.

As the 1980s closed and the decade turned to the 1990s, many cultural and technological changes were becoming mainstream. During this time, many early Generation-Xers (those born between 1965 and 1984) were increasingly becoming concerned with the environment, especially those Gen-Xers with young children. As a result, there was a surge in locally owned and operated food markets and co-ops, organically grown foods, other "buy local" products. This trend encouraged many people to leave corporate America, follow their dreams, and give back to the community: homebrewing and microbreweries were part of this vision for many.[27] Locally owned and operated breweries or taprooms became places where people could meet each other and build a community. Very often, consumers didn't go to a taproom or brewery to "get drunk"; rather, they were more interested in sharing a good beer with others (socializing), and some even share unique bonds over beer and open-heart surgery.[28] While there are still many beer drinkers whose goal is to drink their favorite beers to excess, the industry now increasingly trends more toward those who want a quality beverage (aroma, appearance, mouthfeel, and taste) with an equally satisfying experience.

Socialization and Recreation

As mentioned in the preface, two key characteristics of the craft beer culture are socialization and recreation. Both of these terms reflect the larger, all-inclusive "community" that is most prevalent in the industry.[29] So, let's examine the concept of "community." Community is about sharing and relationship building, both of which occur by communicating with others. It is the process of unique people coming together with an eye toward a common theme, experience, principle, or more. Historically, communities were created based on the close physical proximity of its people and often closely reflected the locations of neighborhoods. However, simply being physically present doesn't always make you a member of a community; something else has to happen. For example, we can live on a street with other families but never feel a sense of community. Many people from the craft beer industry that we spoke with for this book noted that community is the sharing of interests or passion for good beer, but it also entails what the brewery does for its employees and locality. In one case, Susanne Hackett,[30] Community Relations at New Belgium Brewery in Asheville, North Carolina, explained that she had worked with other local Asheville breweries and was invested in their success, so she felt like she was a part of something. Additionally, despite its size and history, New Belgium Brewery has demonstrated its commitment to the city of Asheville through events, coordinated use of lab space, and other types of collaborations with local breweries. Hackett feels like it's not only a community but a family, because the company is quite supportive of its employees. This sentiment was also expressed by Lauren Salazar[31] of New Belgium Brewery in Fort Collins, Colorado; so it seems as though New Belgium is doing something right in their business operations. Other industry people, such as Gwen Conley,[32] of Lost Abbey Brewing in San Diego; Billy Pyatt,[33] of Catawba Brewing Company in Asheville, North Carolina; and Mike Stevens,[34] of Founders Brewing Company in Grand Rapids, Michigan, also expressed appreciation for the camaraderie that people in the industry have for the beer and the industry's success, despite its competitive nature.

Being part of a beer community also means that you make time to socialize. Socialization is about personally spending time with other people who share your same passions or interests. Through socialization, whether you are a local or not, individuals are provided an opportunity to learn about the brewery, its beer, its owners, its history, and its customers. It is a chance to imbibe a frothy beverage in the company of others who are as appreciative of this beer experience as you are. It is also an opportunity for those of us who like the "buzz" of the taproom, brewery, or brewpub, to enjoy a good beer in the presence of others. Either way, being physically present makes this socialization worthwhile. Sometimes, socialization turns to collaboration, resulting in new one-off beers. For example, in the Capital Region of Albany, New York, twelve different local brewers banded together for a joint craft brew experiment. Despite the number of collaborators, a beer was born, brewed, and made available for sale in several of their own brewpubs or distribution areas. The "Too Many Cooks" brew was a success. No matter the size of these brewers' own systems, a collaborative beer was born and kegged for consumption. The beer was shared and embraced by beer lovers in the area. So why would brewers who compete for consumers in general want to collaborate? The questions for this group is actually, "Why wouldn't they?" Sharing expertise and insights is part of the craft brew culture, and working with other local brewers is a necessity that can enhance the localism inherent in the culture. Each brewer has his/her own flair and preferences, strengths and weaknesses. Being able to bring those elements together and demonstrate the collaborative and local feel of good beer is paramount for craft brewers as a whole. As with anything, not all brewing collaborations are successful, so sharing the cost and risk with others may actually benefit smaller brewers in the long run. In fact, there is a "wing" of craft brewers called "gypsy brewers" who move from brew site to brew site to create beer with brewmasters across the country. These gypsies may not have the money to build their own breweries, but some are well-touted in the beer community and can assist in bringing a one-off beer to fruition.

Another part of a beer community is recreation. Think about viewing this recreation as pursuing your interests after work; brewing is your playground. Here, you challenge yourself to use the brewing apparatus to achieve personal goals and have fun while doing it. You may assist local brewers because you enjoy the experience or you may brew your own beer so you can be an even more active participant in this form of recreation; you enjoy the process and its end result. Another way to think about recreation is with a hyphen: re-creation. You are not only interested in the process of making your own beer, but you also want to create good beer consistently, leading to a greater sense of pride in your product. In this sense, you strive to "re-create" the same beer because of its quality, and your friends and family may even come to expect it of you. Either way, recreation should provide a creative outlet for you. In fact, many brewery owners love the industry so much that when they retire from their *real jobs* and continue to work ten to twelve hours a day at their brewery, it doesn't *feel* like work; just ask Billy Pyatt of Catawba Brewing Company.

Ultimately, craft beer culture invites relationship building and collaboration and can evoke or sustain your passion or interest through your interactions with others, either as consumer, brewer, or both. As with any community, you must take time to experience your commonalties with others, or else you begin to feel isolation instead of socialization and recreation. There are many places where you can join craft beer communities. You can also check online for local beer guilds, festivals, and associations, and visit local breweries. You can even partake in the great homebrew day when people all across the country join "together" by sampling homebrew on the same night. Regardless, opportunities abound for socialization.

In the next chapter, we delve into some of the more important beer basics. If you believe that you already possess a firm grasp of the basics, feel free to peruse the next chapter at your leisure or move on to a different chapter regarding another important topic. Either way, you will discover more about beer . . . and, while you are at it, check to see if you need a refill on yours! Cheers!

Talking from the Tap!

Interview with Mike Stevens,[35]
Co-Owner of Founders Brewing Company

1. *When did you begin brewing and why?*
Homebrewing in 1992 out of curiosity and then it became a hobby. I also wanted to save money by brewing my own beer.

2. *How important is the history of beer and brewing to you?*
It's kind of odd. The foundation of beer history dating back to Egypt remains the same in America, but we shift to more discovery now. Take traditional elements, the fundamentals are still there, but recipes vary as ingredients vary. Things like coffee, chicken blood, chocolate, and more are used; this turns tradition upside down. Germans had the purity law, *Rein-*

heitsgebot, that said beer is made of these ingredients only: malt, water, and hops, but we, in America, do things differently. The American craft scene came on twenty to thirty years ago and there was much changing in society as well, such as food and wine industries.

3. *Is there a certain demographic in the industry?*

Drinking population is generally made of users between twenty-one and thirty-five but we see twenty-one to sixty-five, and it's more of the cultural shift, generational shift from a bland environment like light yellow fizzy beer and TV dinners to today's demands for more flavor in beer, food, and everything. This coincides with American craft beer. It's not about consumption as quantity; it's about quality and even the backstory.

4. *Would you say there is a craft beer culture in the United States? Describe a craft beer culture.*

Craft beer is about belonging to something with more substance than what's on the surface. It's that generational shift I mentioned. We have seen a cultural shift where consumers want to know more, like the backstories, they want to be intimate with it, they want to know the stories about how the brewery started, where do ingredients come from, how do cascade hops smell and more; they want to be educated about it. There is a lot of creativity in the industry, so craft beer is not just about the beer.

5. *Are craft brewers a close knit group? Do they share knowledge?*

Yes, it's very friendly but we still have competition. A large camaraderie exists. Craft breweries are at about 14 percent of the total number in the beer industry and that number appears to be growing.

6. *Where is the industry going?*

I've been in industry for twenty-three years now. Once it caught hold it hasn't slowed down. It's possible to double the market share; this seems possible and reasonable. It filled a need and people took hold, such that Budweiser or Coors could never really change it now by throwing money at it; money isn't the solution, product is.

This group of brewers and drinkers is looking to belong to something important; be a part of something. The goal is to educate and discover uniqueness and part of education includes the close-knit, sharing community that has arisen, where brewers are friendly yet competitive.

7. How do you take the step from homebrewing to opening a brewery?

Tenacity and ability to communicate are important; network and fall in love with your ideas. You don't have to be college-educated but you do have to commit to it.

8. How much do you need to know about local, state, and federal laws? Hurdles?

I think it is more about personality traits; I look at them as things to do, not as hurdles. I have to get them done. Despite obstacles, you have to keep moving forward. You just go through it and folks at the agencies seem to be quite helpful. It's not difficult; you just have to educate yourself on how to fill out the forms. You can't have a way out. Don't have a way out, because if you have it, chances are you will take it. Now we have regulatory staff and lawyers to assist with all of that.

9. What financial resources are needed to take the next step to open a brewery?

Forty million dollars [*laughter*]; it depends. If you open a small boutique-size brewery, maybe a couple of hundred thousand dollars. But if you create a bottling line and engage in distribution while leasing property, closer to about $1 million. You have to get investors to buy-in. For example, we may have, at one time, owned 1 percent at one point in our history, and then we buy back shares from investors once cash increases. At one point we had about thirty investors and we would sell off stock to keep going. A successful businessman in town explained how long it would take; he said about seven to ten years cleaning up the mess you are making, but that it may take fifteen to twenty years to be truly profitable.

10. Some of your beers have won awards. Which are you most proud of and why?

Probably the significance of Dirty Bastard because it is one we always look at as defining us as Founders. Our first slogan was "Brew for Us" and Dirty Bastard was the first with a new slogan that we still use today: "Beer we want to drink."

11. How do you get the names of these beers?

Creative juices flow and they emerge.

12. How did you settle on the name "Founders"?

Our corporate name is actually "Canal Street Brewing Company" because the building we are located in on Monroe Street, which used to be

Canal Street in Grand Rapids, housed brewers in the 1860s. We have a black-and-white photo of the four original brewers from Europe who settled here in Grand Rapids on our wall, and we put the title "Founders" above the photo. Customers would look at the photo and ask about who these founders were. Soon after, consumers would refer to us as "Founders" for short, and here we are today.

13. *Any advice for up and coming brewers?*

Yes, growth is still available even if the ability to start today and develop a large brewery is more difficult because the window of opportunity to do so is closed. There will still be a few shining stars on a large scale. But, there is room for local and regional growth for breweries. There are about forty-two hundred-plus breweries in business today. So, be practical: Differentiate your brew from other brews by doing different things; find a new path in a world full of similar beers.

14. *Finish this statement: "I brew because . . ."*

I brew because I love to; it's a way of life. I can't imagine working for a living [*laughs*].

BEER BASICS
What Do I Need to Know?

What Beer and Brewing Knowledge and Skills Do I Need to Hone?

W hether a novice or full-fledged beer enthusiast, the first step toward embracing the craft beer movement is to actually drink some beer, or at least sip it. One of the authors of this text is actually quite new to the concept of "enjoying" beer, but also has a deep interest in the culture and the passion it creates in others. Just recently, she began to sip others' beer to determine what worked and what didn't for her palette and general liking. What was once a low tolerance for even light beer has now turned to a deep interest in darker, heavier stouts and porters with vanilla, coffee, chocolate, or other additives. We beer lovers should strive to find time to enjoy the fullness of each beer or flight, seek to develop our palettes, make friends, learn from others—and pay attention to IBUs and ABVs or we will require an Uber or a taxi number or the transportation "911."

What are IBUs and ABVs you ask? Well, this a great question to address here. Most commercial beers are made for bulk consumption. Just go to any sports bar or keg party and the beer is usually low alcohol by volume (ABV) hovering between 3 and 6 percent. The lower the ABV, the more you can usually consume before becoming intoxicated. The higher the ABV, the less you can imbibe and still function or remain sober. The actual volume that you can drink before feeling tipsy will also depend on your weight and/or medical conditions. Some beers with higher ABVs can average 12–14 percent, which means that two beers will most likely impair your abilities more than three beers at low ABV measurements. Knowing the ABV can help frame the beer's impact on your general abilities. Just imagine what might happen if you drink one Brewmeister 2013 Snake Venom at 67.5 percent ABV![1]

Besides ABVs, we must also consider the international bitterness units (IBUs). These determine the "hoppyness" of the beer and are scaled within a range of 1 to 100. Double IPAs, for example, tend to fall around 70 on that scale. Some have even described a very "hoppy" beer as "chewy," so the IBU rating may be even higher in some cases. "Hoppyness" is a personal preference and not a condition or an indication of alcohol content, so venture out and taste a variety of beers with different IBUs before making your final decision on whether you like/dislike hoppy beers.

SRM, another beer acronym, stands for "standard regulation method" and is specific to the color of the beer, usually related to its appearance. The color is typically associated with the style of beer and the country in which it is brewed. Besides acronyms such as these, having a general understanding of the various types of beer is also helpful. Believe it or not, there are two general categories of beer: ale (yeast ferments at warmer temperatures) and lager (yeast ferments at the cooler temperatures), with a growing mix of beers called "specialty beers" emerging regularly.[2] The Beer Academy and the Beer Advocate,[3] online resources, tell us this:

- *Ales*—beers that are generally straw-colored to dark black (e.g., Guinness Stout), fermented at higher temperatures, and typically fruitier and full of flavor. Beers may include sours, stouts, and porters, as well as sessions and IPAs among others.

- *Lagers*—beers that tend to be gold, are fermented cold, and are often less bitter, fuller flavored. Examples include pilsner, bock, steen beer, and others.

- *Special Beers*—beers that have a range of flavors and colors including wheat, Wit, Weiss, or even bolder beers like those made with flowers, ginger, honey, chocolate, and other ingredients. These beers, usually ales, also range in ABV (alcohol by volume), aroma, texture, and SRM (color). Readers can find a sample SRM Chart at the Beer Judge Certificate Program.[4]

While numerous other beer varieties are available (and possible), being able to distinguish between the two primary categories (ale and lager) will benefit you in the long run, especially as beer tasting and enjoyment turns to conversation and debate. So, let's refer back to a few other relevant pieces of information that are important to beer consumers and brewing novices alike.

What about hops? What's all the fuss over "hoppyness"?

While you don't need to grow your own hops or even have a firm grasp of what hops are or how they are grown, some knowledge of this ingredient is paramount to develop an appropriate craft beer base. For example, did you know that there was a significant New York State "Hops Belt" that ran across the state many years ago? This area of the state is experiencing resurgence within the wine and distillery areas of the Finger Lakes Region due to the climate. However, not all beer ingredients are properly supported via New York State legislation. For example, New York State does not offer farm insurance for barley growers; however, they do for other grains grown in the state. These regulations can drive or inhibit craft beer growth in your area, so do some research if you plan on "going bigger" or growing your own hops in bulk.

What are we, Champagne? Why must craft beers have basic ingredients to be called "beer"?

As noted, beers are a product of four essential ingredients (prior to any additional experimentation): hops, malt (barley), yeast, and water. However, we recently learned in an informal conversation with a Massachusetts brewer that in England many years ago, malt was not readily available, so it was often excluded from beer brewed in that region. Nowadays, malt is much more readily available and is added to many English beers that are often labeled "Extra Special Bitter" because the added malt changes the flavor and bitterness of the beer. The letters "ESB" provide a "heads up" (no pun intended) to beer drinkers. Historically speaking, only three of the four ingredients were abundant in much of the world, which led to differentiation from those beers that were produced in England. For example, in Germany, the *Reinheitsgebot* of 1516 was a law whereby beer could only be brewed from water, hops, and malt.[5]

Hops—an ingredient introduced by the Germans around 822 CE. The hops not only impact the beer's bitterness and aroma, but also the process and final product. Specifically, hops (*Humulus lupulus*) are climbing plants that grow vertically, generally around wire and strings, and branch outward.

Hop plants can grow up to eight inches on a perfect summer day, but they should be regularly harvested in order to reap the benefits for many years. Designated as the flower of the plant, hops can grow almost anywhere if farmed properly, but they thrive in certain regions of North America far better than others. More about hops will be introduced in a later chapter, but for now, just know that hops are considered a primary beer ingredient and contribute to the aroma (essential oils) and bitterness (alpha acids, because beta acids contribute to aroma). For example, sometimes you pick up an India Pale Ale (IPA) and you immediately notice the aroma. While some beer enthusiasts use aroma as a guide and note that "hoppyness isn't my thing," others love "hoppy beers." Think of this as your hot sauce meter: some hot sauces are mild, medium, hot, and hotter (burn your esophagus-type sauces). The more hops used within the brewing process, including residence time while boiling (minutes), the "hoppier" the beer becomes. The number of "minutes" in an IPA determine the level of bitterness, which is defined by the Alpha Acid Table. For example, Amarillo hops have an average of 9.5 while Chinook has an average of 13; the higher the average, the more bittering potential per ounce.[6]

Grain—malt, or malted barley. Not all malted beverages are considered to be (or are even identified as) "beer." See *Brew Your Own*'s website for a thorough update on grains and adjuncts where "L" stands for "degrees Lovibond" and "G" stands for "Gravity."[7] Figure 2.1 is a sample table[8] from their website.

Yeast—"Oh, the yeast!" These are actually living organisms with an unforgiving temperament. They have "minds" of their own and relationships must be developed and massaged for best results. Laura Zeidler[9] of Ballast Point Brewing and Devon Hamilton[10] of Paradox Brewery shared some familiar stories resulting from their work with yeast. Both brewers noted that the process of cultivating yeast is quite important and takes a tender hand. You have to know "what they like" and "how they respond" so that they are "happy." Yeast is personified by many a brewer; yeast need to be nurtured, like children, to yield good results. If not properly cared for, yeast will absolutely wreak havoc on you and your beer.

Water—seems simple, right? Water is a key ingredient for beer; however, some places are known to have better water than others. For example, Beer City, USA (Asheville, North Carolina) is legendary for its water, which has resulted in exponential growth in the beer industry, including larger breweries like New Belgium Brewing, Oskar Blues, and Sierra Nevada coming to the region. The western part of North Carolina has an abundance of quality

American Grains			
Malt	**L**	**G**	**Description**
Black Barley	525°	1.023-1.027	Imparts dryness. Unmalted; use in porters and dry stouts.
Black Patent Malt	500°	1.026	Provides color and sharp flavor in stouts and porters.
Chocolate Malt	350°	1.034	Use in all types to adjust color and add nutty, toasted flavor. Chocolate flavor.
Crystal Malt	40°	1.033-1.035	Sweet, mild caramel flavor and a golden color. Use in light lagers and light ales.
Crystal Malt	90°	1.033-1.035	Pronounced caramel flavor and a red color. For stouts, porters and black beers.
Crystal Malt	60°	1.033-1.035	Sweet caramel flavor, deep golden to red color. For dark amber and brown ales.
Crystal Malt	30°	1.033-1.035	Sweet, mild caramel flavor and a golden color. Use in light lagers and light ales.
Crystal Malt	20°	1.033-1.035	Sweet, mild caramel flavor and a golden color. Use in light lagers and light ales.
Crystal Malt	120°	1.033-1.035	Pronounced caramel flavor and a red color. For stouts, porters and black beers.
Crystal Malt	10°	1.033-1.035	Sweet, mild caramel flavor and a golden color. Use in light lagers and light ales.
Crystal Malt	80°	1.033-1.035	Sweet, smooth caramel flavor and a red to deep red color. For porters, old ales.
Dextrin Malt (carapils)	1.5°	1.033	Balances body and flavor without adding color, aids in head retention. For any beer.
Munich Malt	10°	1.034	Sweet, toasted flavor and aroma. For Oktoberfests and malty styles.

Figure 2.1. American Grains Chart
Source: *Brewer's Friend*

water, removing many a headache for those interested in brewing. Other areas of the country, like Colorado, also offer quality water supplies. In contrast, locations like the Helderbergs of New York have the water, but it requires additional treatment and filtration in order to produce quality beer. It makes sense that Roanoke, Virginia, is another hotspot where many West Coast breweries set up East Coast shops—water, water, everywhere!

So, now I know the ingredients necessary for beer, but how are craft brews sold or shared when not in the store? And, are there any specific production limitations?

As you might expect, there are a variety of geographically specific restrictions and limitations that dictate the practice of brewing (see chapter 7 for more details). For now, it may be smart to locate and contact brewers in your area, see if there is a local beer alliance or organization, and join a state or national brewers association. In a later chapter we offer a comparison of some state guidelines and regulations from both New York and Michigan. Ultimately, it is the responsibility of each brewer, small, medium, or large, to understand the federal and state laws and regulations when brewing and sharing home, farm, nano, and microbrews. With that behind us, let's take a look at the types of brewing that are available.

Homebrewing is described as using one's own residence to brew small amounts of beer for personal consumption. Homebrewers are entitled to brew a limited number of gallons per year and per person of legal drinking age (twenty-one) on their property without permits, taxes, and licensing of any sort. The exact quantity that is allowed does vary by state.

Farm brewing occurs when regulated percentages of beer ingredients make up the brew. For example, New York passed a farm brewing law in 2012, whereby brewers interested in a Farm Brewery license must make beer primarily from locally grown farm products. The schedule for this type of license is as follows:

- Until the end of 2018, at least 20 percent of the hops and 20 percent of all other ingredients must be grown in New York State.

- From January 1, 2019, to December 31, 2023, no less than 60 percent of the hops and 60 percent of all other ingredients must be grown in New York State.

- From January 1, 2024, no less than 90 percent of the hops and 90 percent of all other ingredients must be grown in New York State.[11]

Nano brewing—These breweries are intentionally kept very small (about one hundred gallons or three barrels a year), usually don't brew more than one batch at a time, and don't desire to see their beer served at bars across the country.[12]

Microbrewing—A brewery that produces less than 15,000 barrels (17,600 hectoliters) of beer per year with 75 percent or more of its beer sold off-site and to the public.[13] Notice how some of these descriptions of brewing vary by volume produced.

Taproom—Typically located adjacent to a brewpub, the taproom serves minimal food, as per state requirements, but provides opportunities for consumers to enjoy beer without the expectation of restaurant-quality food. Beer is available to consumers via growlers, crowlers, or cans (as per state legislation), and generally these establishments produce less than 250,000 barrels a year.

Tavern/brewpub—Often used synonymously, a brewpub can serve up to 3,500 barrels a year of its own beer on-site, *must* serve restaurant-quality food, and can sell other beer, wine, and spirits. However, they may not sell their beer to other retailers.[14]

What Does It Take to Be a Good Brewer?

Developing a palette—Believe it or not, science shows that women generally have more discriminating palettes than their male counterparts. Additionally, the number of female Beer Judges has grown to almost 25 percent over the past fifteen years, and continues to grow. Before you set out to become a homebrewer, you may want to first identify the beers that you like and examine/understand what exactly it is about them that you like.

Perfecting the ol' sniffer—As wine enthusiasts will tell you, spending time "experiencing" the aroma is a key component of wine tasting, so why should beer be any different? Well, it really isn't. While we may not sniff a mass-produced ale from a large brewery each time we drink one, we should always engage the nose when tasting small-batch brews from any maker; our noses know what they like. Sniffing the beer and identifying the aromas heightens the taste of the beer for most consumers. For example, developing your nose to distinguish a preference for some melon-containing beers over others, and or to distinguish certain types of hops and pick up on other flavors in the taste of the beer is an important skill.

Sipping, not guzzling—While there are times when a good guzzle is necessary, such as on a hot day at the beach, for the most part, small-batch beers are really meant to be sipped. Why rush a good thing? Sipping allows for the taste of the beer to emerge and for the sipper to determine mouthfeel and aftertaste. Just like sommeliers, beer enthusiasts, also called "cicerones," should enjoy every last sip of a small-batch beer and appreciate its uniqueness.[15]

Learning some history—Don't learn thousands of years of history, but familiarize yourself with your local scene and how your town, county, or state supports homebrewers. Knowing something about beer can aid in general conversation and the process of cultivating brewing communities.

Knowing hops—Read up on the various types of hops and how each responds to the brewing process. Visit a hop farm, talk to others about their favorites, and see what's readily available to you in your area. And, for goodness sake, sample beers with different hops varieties to develop your palette.

Creating recipes—Be adventurous; start with a kit then hone those skills and experiment with recipes and all varieties of beer. (See the last chapter of this book for some recipes.) Ask others for some suggestions, read brewing magazines and websites, and take a few risks as you perfect the brewing process. However, if the beer is bad, don't hesitate to discard it; no one likes a bad beer, and it has lasting effects on tastings in the future!

Working knowledge of chemistry—Through trial and error and a bit of reading, you can get started with chemistry. Homebrew kits are great starters for understanding the brewing process. Over time, you will begin to learn about alpha acids, gravity, color, and more.

Testing your water—Get a home water testing kit to see if your water needs filtering or additives. Your local beer equipment shop can be a great resource if you are interested in learning more. Additionally, it is good practice to research the water standards that tend to lead to the better-tasting beers.

Creating a space—Whether it's the kitchen, basement, garage, shed, or somewhere else, you must make room for storage and sanitation of beer equipment. It doesn't take much space, but it does need to be a well-prepared and clean space.

Allotting brewing time—Don't expect to brew in an hour. The process, whether one gallon batches or a multi-barrel system, takes several hours just to brew, not including sanitizing, prepping, cleaning up, and bottling.

Developing patience—You want to drink your beer when it is ready, but not too soon. Don't rush the brewing process. You don't simply want to brew average beer; you want "good," or even "great," beer.

Maintaining virtue (throwing a beer away)—Focus on quality and consistency. If a batch doesn't taste good or is not the quality you expect, then feel free to throw it out. Making quality beer on a regular basis is always better for you and for those with whom you share.

Spending money wisely—You don't need thousands of dollars to get started. Basic homebrew kits supply most of what you need. A large stockpot, a large spoon, and empty bottles (sanitized used beer bottles work well) may be all you need with your prepared kit. As you advance and commit to the brewing process, purchase additional equipment.

Chat with Other Brewers in Your Area

Now that you have some advice, knowledge, and skills, here are some starter questions to use during conversations with other brewers when you visit their establishment or home, and chat with *them* while drinking *their* beer:

- How did you get started?

- What have been your biggest challenges to date?

- When did you realize you wanted to brew beer? Branch out?

- How do you create recipes?

- How important are the hops? Do you prefer certain hops to others? Why?

- What knowledge and skills do potential brewers need to have to get started?

- How did you get up and running?

- How do you get people on board with your idea?

- How do you know if the product is inadequate?

- How did you come up with the name of your company?

- How do you name your beers?

- How big do you expect to grow?

- Do you collaborate with other brewers?

- What advice can you give me?

Remember that socialization and recreation are part of what makes this industry a community. If you don't ask for assistance, then others may not know you need it.

Since the beer basics are now completed, remember that new information will emerge as the industry continues to grow, and you will be adding knowledge and skills to this newly formed baseline. The next chapter focuses on brewing basics for the novice. It's a step-by-step guide for you to consider when beginning the brewing process. How's your beer now? Need a refill? Remember the ABVs in the beer or you may soon feel tipsy! Cheers!

CHAPTER TWO

Talking from the Tap!

Interview with Lauren Zeidler,[16]
Director of Quality for Ballast Point Brewery

1. *How did you get involved in the beer industry?*

While in college, I would try different beers. As a science major, beer was a passion because it is scientific; evolutionary genetics are involved. I then moved to San Diego and wanted to know more about the industry and brewing so I e-mailed breweries to learn more. Ballast Point answered and I began in the lab. I was always interested in the quality of the beer and so I worked my way up. I started in 2012 as a lab assistant and now lead lab growth as director of quality for six locations, including four breweries, two of which are large scale, plus a new, large production facility in Daleville, Virginia.

2. *Do you have a favorite beer or style?*

IPAs because as a beer scientist I assess its quality. IPAs are the hallmark of San Diego craft beers; it is a very dynamic style and can have many flavors while still being hop-focused. Scientifically, there is still a lot of mystery behind the style.

3. *What is most important in quality control of beer?*

Yeast management. You have to treat them well. Happy yeast are important to the quality of the beer: You have to treat them like family. Our main production beers use several different yeast strains, while daily checks of cell count viability and vitality make for good beer.

4. *Is there a craft beer culture?*

Yes, but craft is difficult to define when some breweries are being bought out by larger companies and the landscape of non-macrobreweries is changing! For me, craft means being innovative. And part of the culture includes being part of something larger. For example, at Ballast Point, we are family. As a woman in this industry, I think that there are stigmas, assumptions, and stereotypes that women encounter in some breweries or the public sphere, but here, I was accepted based on my skill set and didn't experience some of the challenges other women may have experienced.

5. Where do you think the industry is headed?

It's growing. For example, in a part of downtown San Diego called "Little Italy" on the outskirts of town, we opened a brewery—Ballast Point Little Italy, which ultimately extended the downtown area's boundaries, specifically the borders of Little Italy. Pretty soon there were more breweries located in the area, which continues to expand the downtown map. In a sense, we are seeing "a brewery in every neighborhood," which is a goal in Portland, Oregon. But, quality and consistency are still keys to success.

6. Complete this sentence: "I brew because . . ."

"I like the beer industry" and its "culture and scientific aspects."

CHAPTER THREE
BREWIN' UP SOME BEER
Barely Gettin' Started

S o, now you think you are ready to brew?[1] Well, ask yourself the following questions:

Do I like beer?
Do I want to make my own beer?
Can I set aside half a day to prepare the appropriate space?
Do I have another half a day to actually brew the beer?
In a few weeks' time, can I set aside another hour to bottle the beer?
Have I researched or read enough to begin the brewing process?

If you answered "yes" to each of these questions, then you are prepared to brew. If you answered "no" to any of the questions, then reflect on what you need in order to change your answer to a "yes" and then brew away. Why do you need to commit the time to support these questions, you ask? Well, any hobby that you engage in must be one you actually like. Why brew beer if you know you don't like beer? Would you crochet something if you don't like crocheting? Would you shoot videos if you really didn't like viewing them after they are done? Of course not! The primary reason to brew beer is because you enjoy beer. However, just because you like beer doesn't mean you want to make your own beer. So building your passion for brewing is a necessity for you to get started.

As you may be aware, time is something that most of us feel that we simply do not have enough of. We often envision retirement or vacations as the times we can spend on something we want to do. So, you have to set aside enough time to read, prepare your brewing area (arrange ingredients, get all equipment and materials set up, sanitize everything), and then ultimately brew the beer. Once the beer is ready to bottle (about two weeks later if all goes well) you will also need time to complete that process and then sanitize the used equipment. So, the last question you should ask may be: "Do I have the patience required to complete this process and react appropriately if something goes wrong?" Patience is a virtue, and brewing certainly requires patience.

Steps for Brewing Success

Step 1—Read

As a great first action, you need to locate and identify materials, whether books or online resources, to gather information about the process of brewing beer. The bibliography included in this book offers many resources that you can use to get started. Additionally, you can also seek out other homebrewers and experts in your area for more information. Visiting a local homebrew shop or even attending a Brewing 101 class may be a useful venture. For easy access to the basics, try Marty Nachel's *Homebrewing for Dummies* or John J. Palmer's *How to Brew: Everything You Need to Know to Brew Beer Right the First Time* (4th ed.). Consider connecting with other homebrewers using social media or other outlets in order to establish a support network of experts or enthusiasts. Always ask questions, don't hesitate or assume something is accurate—confirm information.

Step 2—Prepare

This is where things begin to get real. You must start by decluttering your brew space; clean it and clear out all unwelcome (temporary or not) infiltrators (animals and children included). If the space becomes "infiltrated" then you may need to repeat the sanitization protocol—not fun. As you learn the process of sanitizing both equipment and space, and know why it is important, you can then introduce the area to pets (who often become mascots) or children (who want to learn along with you).

Next, you will need to locate the appropriate brewing equipment. Even if you decide to purchase your first beer kit online or in person at the nearest brew shop, you will still need a large stock pot, large brew spoon for mixing, scissors for opening sanitized packages, and a sanitized area to begin brewing, such as the kitchen, basement, or garage. Proper sanitization can make or break your first brew, so if you know you aren't "into" cleaning, this is your chance to "master" the skill set in the name of beer.

Once you have sanitized your equipment, you can begin to set up the ingredients by either following the steps offered in your beer kit or by doing it yourself. Either way, a little bit of cash is required to get you started. For example, a one-gallon small batch brew kit from a well-known supplier such as Northern Brewers Homebrew Supply may set you back a minimum of $50, in addition to the two-gallon kettle and clean, empty beer bottles. Nonetheless, you may consider brewing your first batch before digging your heels in and purchasing more equipment and ingredients.

All introductory brewers need a brew pot (two-plus gallons [perhaps larger for future brewing]) to boil the wort, a container to ferment the beer (such as a fermenting bucket or glass carboy), an airlock for the fermentor, and clean, empty beer bottles (new or used). However, keep in mind that the fermenting container must have a carbon dioxide release and be airtight (use an airlock), and the bottles will need appropriately secured caps (you may also need a bottle capper). If you notice, the list of necessities is already growing and you haven't actually even started brewing your first batch. If you brew regularly, you may want more efficient equipment, which then costs a bit more money. Necessary items for regular brewing may also include bottle brush, bottle rinser, bottling tube with a spring-loaded valve, bottling bucket with spigot, thermometer, hydrometer that measures gravity/liquid density (used to calculate alcohol by volume [ABV]), and a drilled rubber stopper for the airlock.[2] John Palmer, renowned beer author, recommends a glass measuring cup that can hold boiling water and plastic wrap or aluminum foil for keeping items "clean and sanitized."[3]

Now that you have your equipment and your space is prepared, you need ingredients. If you bought a prepackaged beer kit, the ingredients were included. If you are supplying your own ingredients, you will need yeast, hops, malt, and water. Seems simple enough, but ratios do matter. You may not need to be a chemist or microbiologist, but you will need to follow directions on the kit or research the combination of ingredients *before* beginning the brewing process. Your due diligence is of paramount importance!

Step 3—Sanitize

Anyone who has been on a cruise ship the last few years may already know that the word "sanitize" can be overused, but in the case of brewing, it is an essential part of the process and is rarely overused. Every beer kit comes with its own sanitization packet and you must be sure to always follow the instructions or you may "anger" the yeast and spoil the beer. Every piece of equipment and surrounding surface area must be sanitized. You can use bleach, but it may leave an unwanted flavor in the beer. Instead, consider using StarSan™ or Final Step™, both of which were specifically "developed for sanitizing brewing equipment."[4] Follow the instructions for all sanitization.

Step 4—Assess Water Quality

The majority of brewers will not have to initially worry about the water source, especially those who receive city or town water. However, for anyone using wells, it is necessary to also think about the additional chemicals that may be present in the drinking water. Since water is one of the four essential ingredients for making beer, if the water has too much chlorine or other additive it can leave an unwanted flavor on equipment as previously mentioned. For example, those individuals living in Flint, Michigan, or Hoosick Falls, New York, who have made national headlines related to their contaminated drinking water, it may be a good idea to secure potable drinking waters in five-gallon jugs or bottles for use in brewing. Others who live in areas with highly alkaline water would also benefit from more potable water. You can also try to dechlorinate your water, use charcoal filters or water softeners, or even chloramine tablets.[5] The bottom line is this: make sure your water tastes good, and take any and all precautions for treating the water to make great beer.

Step 5—Understand the Importance of the Three Other Vital Beer Ingredients: Hops, Yeast, and Grains

Hops come in many varieties and can influence a beer in so many ways. The "Science of Brewing" (chapter 5) will provide more insight into the role of hops, but for now, beginner brewers should know that hops impact the bitterness of the beer. Specifically, hops need to be measured appropriately in order to provide the most information about Alpha Acid Units (AAU), bitterness going into the boil, or International Bittering Units (IBU).[6] The higher the IBU, the more "hoppy" the beer will be.

Yeast are what we call our "most easily agitated member" of the beer family. Yeast, which are microorganisms, turn out to be the only living part of the brew process, and their "happiness" is fundamental to good beer. What makes yeast happy? Proper sanitization is a great start. Ripping open a yeast packet with your teeth is not as sanitary as cutting open the yeast package with a sanitized pair of scissors. Using your teeth will agitate (anger) your yeast and potentially disrupt the brewing process. The type of yeast used, how it works with other ingredients, its temperature, and how well it is aerated also make a difference. Ultimately, the qualities of the yeast also impact flavor. But for now, let's just keep the yeast "happy." There is much more to be said in chapter 5 for those who want to learn more.

Malt extracts are typically derived from the malt sugars extracted from malted barley.[7] Malt is soaked in hot water to increase enzyme activity, which leads to a conversion of starch into fermentable sugars called "wort."[8] Beer kits typically come with an extract kit to assist new brewers in the brewing process. Just follow the instructions and you will be headed in the right direction. As you continue to develop your brewing expertise, you can venture into other areas of interest like the gravity of the beer and utilization. For now, leave that to the more experienced homebrewers.

Step 6—Boil the Water

And after it comes to a boil, *remove it from the heat source.* Otherwise, during the next step, the malt extract will settle on the bottom of your brew kettle, and it will start to burn if you are still on direct heat.

Step 7—Add Malt Extract

Dissolve the malt in the boiled water that has been removed from the heat source. Check your kit instructions for the exact amounts of malt needed for this step.

Step 8—Return the Dissolved Malt Extract to a Boil

The dissolved malt extract is now called "wort." The old adage "a watched pot never boils" should be totally ignored here. It will boil, and you must keep a focus on the boil. The mixture will begin to foam, which is good, but it can boil over if you aren't vigilant, which is bad. So prepare to lower the heat when necessary. When the boil has the appearance of "egg drop soup," the wort has reached its "hot break," and you are now ready to add the hops.[9]

Step 9—Add Hops to the "Hot Break"

At this point it is time to add your bittering hops and continue to boil for one hour. Make sure that all of the hops are wet, stir the mixture, and keep the wort at a rolling boil for the allotted time.

Add half of the finishing hops roughly 30 minutes into the Step 9 boil. At 45 minutes into the boil add the last half of finishing hops. At this time, also prepare a sink or tub with cold ice water. It will be used to cool the wort at the end of the 60-minute boiling period.

Add any remaining hops at the 55 minute mark.

Step 10—Cool the Wort

At the completion of the 60-minute boiling period, place a lid on the pot, and move the pot into the cold-water bath. Swirl the cold water around the pot, but be careful that water from the bath or the ice does NOT get into the pot and contaminate the wort. Use a sanitized thermometer to determine when the wort's temperature hits about 70°F or 21°C (usually around 30 minutes) or whatever temperature that your brew kit calls for when pitching the yeast.

Step 11—Begin Fermentation Process

Transfer the wort into the fermentor (a sterilized container that you will use for the greater part of the next two weeks). At the top of the fermentor, you will need to be sure to have a stopper and a release to control carbon dioxide (CO_2) buildup, often called an airlock. Controlling for gas buildup is critical in order to avoid an explosion (ultimately wasting your brew). At this point, take a small sample and fill your hydrometer tube. After taking the measurement, DO NOT return this sample to the fermentor, since it is most likely contaminated. Using the hydrometer, note the original gravity reading (OG) because you will compare this reading to the final gravity reading (FG) when fermentation is complete.

Step 11.1—Pitching the Yeast

Although there are several ways to pitch your yeast, most new home-brewers are encouraged to add the kit's yeast packet on top of the wort in your fermentor. Without the yeast, the fermentation process will not begin.

During the fermentation process, yeast (your best brewing friends or worst enemies) absorb oxygen and then convert the sugars into alcohol, and subsequently carbon dioxide (CO_2). An interesting fact about yeast is that the total number of yeast cells present in the wort roughly doubles every day.[10] At the completion of the "yeast feast," very little oxygen remains, fermentable sugars are low, and the yeast sinks and settles to the bottom. Of course, fermentation time varies based on temperature, the amount of yeast pitched (added), how healthy that yeast was at the start, and the amount of fermentable sugars available during the process. More details about this process can be found in chapter 5. But, for now, your brew kit should provide you with fermentation basics so that you can prepare for bottling over the next two weeks. Be sure to check the fermentation process every other day to avoid mishaps. When you notice the bubbling action in your airlock has been greatly reduced, use your hydrometer to take a second gravity reading and compare this reading to the FG expected in your brew kit.[11] In two days, do a third hydrometer sample and if the gravity is the same as the second reading, then fermentation is complete. If this reading falls below that gravity reading, then the process must continue and you have to check it again in two days. Once you have two consecutive readings, then this becomes your FG for the beer. Now you are ready to bottle!

Step 12—Bottling Your Beer

As you prepare for bottling, be sure to locate and sanitize darker bottles rather than clear or green bottles. Why? Well, the darker the bottles the less potential damage that will occur to your beer; darker bottles refract the light better! Also, as you are locating or buying bottles, be sure to avoid the screw-cap bottles, because threaded bottles can't be capped. It is important to note that it is *not* necessary to purchase new bottles; recycle your older beer bottles or visit your bottle return areas of your local beer retailers, then sanitize each bottle for about thirty minutes. You will need to have about fifty-four 12 oz bottles to fully account for a 5-gallon brew. For a great bottling calculator, visit the Brewer's Friend (brewersfriend.com) where you can estimate the number of bottles, kegs, growlers, and more needed for your brew.[12]

Clean each bottle using a bottling brush and bottle washer, and then with a sanitizing agent. Additionally, sanitize your bottling tube (filler), plastic hose, bottling bucket, bottle caps, and drying rack if not using a manufactured bottling rack. There are YouTube videos that are a helpful resource for the full bottling process from priming to capping; one of many in a brewing video series by the Brewers Association.[13]

Once you have completed the bottling process, and the tasting or sampling has confirmed your beer is at least consumable, you will need to allow the beer to carbonate and settle for about two to three weeks before refrigerating; if it is refrigerated too soon, it will slow the carbonation process. During the conditioning phase, keep the beer in a cool and dark area with a stable temperature, usually between 70°F and 75°F. Now, don't get too excited and leave cleanup for later; instead, sanitizing and cleaning the equipment with hot water *now* sets you up for brewing success on your next batch. No one enjoys the process of cleaning up, but it must be done properly to ensure the quality of your beer.

Step 13—Ahh! Drinking Your Beer

After two weeks, chill a couple of bottles of beer for sampling. Once the beer is thoroughly chilled, open and pour into a glass. Verify that the carbonation is strong and prepare for the tasting. The best part of this entire process is the ability to actually drink *your* beer. Don't chug it! Savor it! Smell it, look at it, taste it, assess its aftertaste, and reflect on that experience. If the beer seemed a bit flat, condition it for another week and repeat the conditioning process. When the beer is truly ready, enjoy the moment and your success, and perhaps even share with a friend or family member. Remember that sharing stories and beer are quite important to the brewing culture.

Although the beer basics may seem easy, remember that science rules the roost. There are many places where your brewing process can falter. Having a successful brew is a wonderful experience, each and every time. Remember to be patient and focused, and plan accordingly for continued brewing success. As novice homebrewer Michael Young says, "I brew because it makes me happy."[14] So, be happy and start brewing. That's what Devon Hamilton of Paradox Brewery did, as he explains in the "Talking from the Tap" interview below. Cheers!

Talking from the Tap!

Interview with Devon Hamilton,[15] Head Brewer, Paradox Brewery

1. *How did you get into brewing?*

Started homebrewing as a hobby and overdid my homebrew setup. I was in school for history but didn't stick with it because I was interested in brewing, so I dropped out of college and went to Adirondack Brewery, where I was scrubbing floors, cleaning floors, cleaning tanks, and so on. Then I went to a startup brewery in South Carolina, but my whole family is here, so I stayed there for a year. Then I found this job and have been here for two years.

I went to the Siebel Institute, oldest beer program in the country, and all course work was online. I completed that program while working at Adirondack. That program doesn't have a required lab component like other programs. It's more beer theory, like yeast metabolism and sanitation.

2. How much science and chemistry did you need to know?

It's good to have, but I had some basic science from school. I didn't know everything related to brewing. But, I needed a foot in the door to get in the brewery industry. So that's why I got into Adirondack. I know about cell replication cycle but not all I need to know about alpha acids and hops isomerization. You really need to be well-rounded.

3. How did you find this job at Paradox?

Paul (of Paradox) had a listing on a Pro Brewer website for people looking for work and for those breweries looking for brewers. I had also met him while I was working at Adirondack. That site is growing and getting more information as time goes on.

4. Do you think knowing history has helped you at all?

No, I am interested in historical beer styles, but it doesn't inform what I do. I don't brew those types of beers.

5. What challenges do you face?

We are in a 10-Barrel system and are almost at capacity. We have 110 barrels of fermentation space. We are trying to keep it up. Keeping ingredients here and overcoming daily issues is key. I lived on Excel for three months to keep things organized. We have plans for expansion, but it takes time. I do data entry and paperwork while the beer is fermenting. I would be brewing more if we had a larger system. I also have a quality-control director and a greenhorn, cellar man, and they are great.

6. How do you decide what to brew next and where do you send it?

We have a series of one-offs every month. Our distributors go from the Canadian border (north) and into Orange County, New York (south). I would like to go broader in New York. We go to TAP NY and bring two barrels (62 gallons), when we go to NYS Brewers Association in Utica, we bring six kegs.

7. *Did you have to know about laws and regulations?*
No, I'm getting educated as time goes on, but I am not doing that. Others do that. I do some taxes but I'm still learning.

8. *Do you do any collaborations?*
I would like to do an upstate-downstate collaboration. But I haven't done any yet. We might occasionally have sales guys or distributors come in and brew with us. If homebrewers are here, then I like to bring them in and have them look around.

9. *Is there a craft beer culture?*
Yes. It's friendly and collaborative; beer is about bringing people together. Being social, being together, getting people loose, and having conversations. Being local and smaller helps that, but craft beers are going more and more corporate. It needs to grow up at some point so smaller breweries are going to have to grow and acknowledge the assistance from larger breweries.

10. *Why did craft beer explode and where is it heading?*
It happens with everything. People wanted small-batch brews and local goods. Farmers markets exploded. People want something that makes them feel special; they want to differentiate themselves. I also don't think my age group (Millennials) doesn't think about craft beer as beer. They aren't always mainstream in their choices because they grew up with many options. Craft beer was considered a movement; and, people can be part of a movement and come together.

11. *What about Untappd (the app)? What role, if any, does that play?*
I think brewers use that app. It's a good resource for brewers to see how others feel about their beers. You might look at the ratings and ask questions. It can get a little crazy too!

12. *Where do you see yourself in five years?*
Here, at Paradox, but with a bigger system, bigger crew, and more experimental beers. I'm looking for new ideas. For example, fruit and oat, or which fruits go together. When I started I was into hops, and now I think we have that under control. Maybe in a few years it won't be fruits it may

be other things I am reading about. I also go to conferences and festivals, like the Great American Beer Festival, and trade shows, and I network with other brewers here and elsewhere.

13. *What's it like to throw out a batch?*
I'm over it now. The first one was tough. But if the beer isn't right, you don't send it out. The reality is I don't want a bad beer out there. Don't save it. Fix it if you can but if it's fundamentally wrong, don't keep it.

14. *Do you ever enter beer into contests?*
Yes, seven in the past year. We are entering wild ales and anything that is bottle-conditioned will be entered into the Great American Beer Festival in 2016. Last year, 2015, we were in medal contention for Saison. We hope this year is our year.

15. *How do you name your beer?*
I don't. Sales and marketing folks do that. I do some work on the bottle labels but they do the bulk of that other work. I usually have a clear aesthetic in mind for that bottle audience. Bottles may run more expensive, but the label and its description help beer drinkers make decisions. Those who buy cans may need a bit more hand holding.

16. *Do you have a favorite beer?*
It's a moving target. I like Belgian beers and Saisons on the whole, but not one in particular. It's because of the yeast, not the mouthfeel, which is why I like the wild ales.

17. *Any advice for homebrewers?*
Just do it. Start homebrewing and read. Start with a kit. You can teach yourself to brew and it doesn't cost much to take the risk, maybe $30.

18. *Paths to the industry?*
Go to school, because it gets your foot in the door. It lets others know you are serious. Be willing to start at the bottom. Work your ass off and work your way up. You'll be better off for it in the long run, so if the keg washer calls in sick, you can do that too.

19. *Finish this sentence: "I brew because . . ."*
"I don't know what else I would do, honestly. It's all I have ever professionally done. I'd be lost. It's all I think about."

Part II

BUILDING MORE BEER KNOWLEDGE AND SKILLS: THE COMPLEXITIES OF BEER AND BREWING

Craft breweries are a significant sector in out agricultural and tourism industries, and when they do well, our economy does well. I encourage New Yorkers to sample all of what our craft brewers have to offer.

—Governor Andrew Cuomo

CHAPTER FOUR
MORE ABOUT PRIMARY BEER INGREDIENTS

As mentioned in previous chapters, there are four primary ingredients in beer: hops, malt (or other grains), water, and yeast. We spent some time in an earlier chapter discussing the importance of water, and, with the recent 500-year anniversary of *Reinheitsgebot* in Germany, now we offer more details on the other primary ingredients.

Hip Hops, Hooray!

Hops abound in very specific climates in the United States and elsewhere, and they are part of the cannabis family. Hops grow especially well in the Northwest United States, and other areas of the United States are now developing their own crops, including the East Coast, but there are many obstacles, a few of which are discussed here. Hops are responsible for the bitterness of a beer and relate to what are called "alpha acids," which provide part of the aroma and mouthfeel of a beer.

Currently, in New York, "A statewide effort is underway to expand the production of hops. Cornell researchers are evaluating thirty varieties of hops to determine which are best suited for growing in the region. Working with the Northeast Hops Alliance, Cornell researchers helped brew a beer from hops grown entirely in New York State—perhaps for the first time in more than half a century."[1]

In Michigan, hops production has increased over the past few years and has given rise to more breweries on the horizon. Michigan has become a "hop-bed" (pun intended) of activity for locally produced and consumed hops for hop growers, brewers, and consumers alike. Michigan's extension programs, such as Michigan State University's, are similar to New York's Cornell Extensions, and they too can offer a wealth of insight and resources to assist craft beer-related businesses begin, sustain, and increase hop production for more homegrown beers in the state.

There are currently over two hundred types of hops which must be nurtured well to produce results and to continue to produce for years to come. New varieties are introduced each year and others disappear from market. Some grow better on the West Coast than the East, some better North than South, with only about thirty varieties doing well on the East Coast.

Hop Threats—Climate, Insects, and Diseases

According to the National Oceanic and Atmospheric Administration (NOAA), climate change is one of the most prevalent dangers to hops growers, especially since 97 percent of the country's hops are grown in three states: Washington, Oregon, and Idaho.[2] Although some among us believe climate change is a myth started by the Chinese, many of us who are interested in the present and future development of the craft beer industry take climate change seriously. In the summer of 2016, upstate New York experienced some of its worst drought conditions in decades; if there isn't water, there isn't beer. Now is the time to be concerned for hops growing and even more so when farm brewing is defined by the percentage of ingredients grown in a state and used in a farm brew. If the Northeast produces less than 1 percent now, how can farm breweries be sustained under current regulations? This was one concern raised during the Fourth Annual Hudson Valley Economic Development Conference for Beer, Wine, and Cider.[3] Here, questions were raised about sustainability and growth of hops farms when New York laws currently use rising percentages of locally grown beer ingredients for labeling some breweries as farm breweries. What is now a low percentage will rise in 2019 until 2023 to 60 percent of hops and 60 percent of other ingredients from the state, which make farm breweries hard to sustain. As the number of breweries, meaderies, and wineries grows, so does the demand for the limited supply, which indicates costs will indeed rise for these farm breweries. Imagine what will happen in 2024 when the percentages hit 90 percent!

In addition to climate change, insects are another *bugger* (pun intended). Many of us have heard about the Japanese beetle and the damage it does to so many gardens and hops fields. But they aren't the only insects to wreak havoc: Other bugs, including parasitic wasps and flies, predator mites, assassin bugs, and more, spread disease and can kill hops and other necessary grains (i.e., malt).[4] Then, add in rising temperatures and humidity, and the case for mold's devastating impact grows exponentially. Knowing which hops are resistant to which molds (e.g., Downy or Powdery) is key to your initial success.[5] We need to pay more attention to what is happening in the farming business to prepare ourselves for coming changes so be sure to identify your local farm bureau or cooperative extension. Much of their research yields many new resources for farmers of all types. For example, the Cornell Cooperative Extension in Madison County, New York, publishes a yearly guide to Integrated Hops Production in the state and it sells for about $28 on the Cornell Store's website.[6]

Disease in hops also varies across the country, so it is best to contact some hop farmers before diving into production. However, some diseases are quite common across all regions. For example, Black Root Rot develops when standing water envelops the hops due to poor drainage or overwatering; roots become too soft, leaves turn black, and hops die. Additionally, nutrient deficiencies can also impact growth and so it is best to begin with proper soil preparation from the start.[7]

To avoid all sorts of problems, visit hop farms, talk to hop growers, and start small. Nurture and develop the hop growing area and be sure to pay attention to risks in your area as well as harvesting, which is always time dependent. And, know some of the basics.

Hop Basics

Although there are many hop aspects to consider, we offer the following to begin creating your knowledgebase:

Rhizomes—some think these are the same as roots, but they aren't. Plants usually have two sections called root mass and vegetative mass, whereas rhizomes have those two plus a third, a stem that acts like an energy source for the vegetative mass.[8] These stems are quite sensitive too, which comes as no surprise since they produce the temperamental hops we spoke about earlier. Sunlight, drainage, depth of planting, and a soil pH between 6 and 8 are some of the details growers must understand. It seems easy, but takes lots of nurturing from beginning to end.

Bines vs. Vines—both are climbing plants, but vines use tendrils or suckers to clamp onto their support systems while bines use hairs along the stem. Whether they grow counterclockwise or clockwise depends on which hemisphere you are in: Northern hemisphere grows clockwise and Southern hemisphere, counterclockwise. With bines, you must train them to climb to produce strong crops.

Female vs. Male Hop Plants—since we use words like "strong," "hairs," "climbing," and "beer," we may automatically assume that hops are male. Yet, when it comes to hops (and beer), female hops are the *better* sex. How many female readers just breathed a sigh of relief for the power of the female hop? Conversely, how many male readers thought to themselves, "Oh, jeez! Even hop plants are feminists?!" Whatever your beliefs about human males and females, hops plants that have cones with seeds are male and those that produce cones without seeds are female. And, we want to use hops without seeds to avoid reducing alpha acids or imparting other negative effects on our product. This means female hop plants are actually better-suited for brewing beer.[9] Once you get past the male/female debate, remember that male hop plants do pollinate but that their seeds can damage the quality of the hops they pollinate. It is best to keep them separated and focus on the quality and growth of the female hop plants, much like we separated the boys from the girls in middle school! Once the hops are grown, they are now ready for harvesting and timing is essential.

Hop Harvesting

Your hops have survived and now they are ready for harvest. Many homebrewers may harvest by hand, but as the size of the hop fields grow and time becomes a primary factor, machine harvesting is coming of age for breweries. Laura Ten Eyck and Dietrich Gehring provide hop growers an essential guide for small-scale production.[10] In their book they discuss their shift from hand to machine harvesting. Despite the fact that their hop field is relatively small, the amount of time and energy it took to harvest that field by hand took more time than they had, and when hops are ready for harvest, they are ready NOW, not in two days or two weeks . . . NOW! But, let's say you want to harvest your hops by hand. Let's look at what you will need to do to get the job done right and *on time*.

Steve Miller from the Cornell Cooperative Extension in Madison County, New York, tells us hand-picking is not feasible for anything more than an acre or so.[11] A stationary Wolf 140 or 170 harvester will cost in the range of $30–$35,000 but is not easy to find in the United States, so shipping from Europe is necessary. NEHA has one located at Morrisville College that is available for members to use and there are fifteen more of these privately owned around the state. Keep in mind that the harvester you use needs to be within an hour of your farm because of transportation time and costs. Growers are developing small scale machines and several types may be available soon. Larry Fisher of Foothill Hops has built his own and will be sharing the plans; there are also plans from University of Vermont, in Burlington, for a harvester they designed and built with funds from SARE (a government grant program focused on agricultural productivity), as well as for a small-scale kiln and baler; growers have used the plans to build one.[12] Laura Ten Eyck and Dietrich Gehrich would agree with him, as they harvested their first two seasons of their one-acre plot by hand then finally purchased a small hop harvesting machine, only to find out from fellow hops grower Danny Hallman of Emerald Hop Ranches in Sunnyside, Washington, that their small machine with rubber fingers would not work as effectively as one with metal fingers, which is more likely to pick the hops from the bine correctly.[13] Again, we emphasize, that visiting other hop growers and asking their advice on growing hops in your region is paramount; it is better to know what is necessary *before* preparing your hops for production.

In addition to choosing the right machine or hand-picking, you will need to set aside time between late August and mid-September, no matter where you are in the United States. This is a short window for harvesting your hops and once they are ready, they need your immediate attention; procrastinators will not make the best hop growers! And, hop growers need not only a harvesting plan or machine, but also space for effectively drying these hops.

Hop Drying—It's Now or Never!

Space is the key to success for the harvested hops. Drying them requires separating the varieties; start with early-maturing varieties and work toward the later-maturing ones for best results.[14] Some suggested drying methods for small batch hops include:

Food dehydrator—Using a food dehydrator is the easiest way to dry out your hops as it ensures air movement but does not get excessively hot.

Well-ventilated oven—You can use your oven to dry your hops by
spreading them out on a pan. You will need to make sure that
you get adequate air flow through the oven, watching closely by
checking on them at least every twenty minutes. The temperature should never exceed 140°F (60°C).

Hop drying screen—If you have a small amount of hops to dry, the
easiest way to do so is spread them out over a window screen or
a house air filter. Place them in a warm, dry location. You can
use landscape fabric over the top to keep them in the dark and
occasionally fluff the hops so moist inner cones are brought to
the outside of the pile. Leave them for a few days with a fan
under or next to them to maintain air flow. You will also want
to elevate the screen to improve air flow.

The hops need a moisture content of 8–10 percent by weight to prevent
molding. To see if they are dry enough, try breaking the central stem of
the cone; it should be brittle enough to snap in half. When dry, the yellow
powdery lupulin should easily fall from the cone and the leaves should have a
papery and springy texture. If your hops aren't properly dried before storage,
they could become moldy, wilted, or rancid.[15]

As for larger hop-growing operations, consider the following from the
USA Hops Organization's website:

Harvest begins in the field as the hop vines are mechanically cut at the
ground and at the overhead support wires, and fall into a trailer or truck
bed. The hop-laden vines are transported to stationary picking machines
on each farm which are capable of picking 8 acres in a single 10–12 hour
shift, or 15 acres if picking runs round the clock.

The vines are hung upside down on hooks and carried into the picking machine, where hops and leaves are stripped from the vine and sent
through a series of cleaning devices to remove leaves and other debris.
The stripped vines and other debris are chopped and spread back onto
fields to improve the soil.

Cleaned cones are immediately transported by conveyor belt to the hop
kilns. Kiln floors are each approximately 32' × 32', and hold some 15,000
pounds of hop cones. Cones are spread to a depth of about 32 inches.
Once the kiln is filled, drying occurs when oil or gas burners are fired
and hot air (140°Fahrenheit) is forced indirectly through the bed of green
hops. Drying requires about 9 hours, reducing the hops to 30% of the

green weight, with 8–9% moisture content. Hops are removed from the kiln floor and cooled for 24 hours. After cooling the hops are compressed into 200lb bales, wrapped in burlap and subjected to quality inspection. At this point they leave the individual farm operation and are transported to cold storage warehouses.[16]

Ultimately, no matter the size of the hop growing field, harvesters must take special care of the hops throughout the process. And if you have a favorite dog mascot, be aware that hops are toxic to them. Clearly, as we learned in earlier chapters, hops are crucial to great beer production and they need to be nurtured throughout their lives; their temperament must be actively monitored and you must be the *alpha* (pun intended!) throughout. There is so much to learn about horticulture, so be sure to visit your state's Department of Agriculture and Markets to access all available resources and regulations guiding your region.

Pellets, Plugs, Whole Leaf, or Liquids: What Should I Choose for Brewing?

If you have now decided to not grow your own hops, then as a brewer you must decide which hop type you will use in the brewing process. Knowing the impact of each type and its impact on the end product, the beer, are important for the success of your brew.

Choosing your type of hop depends on how much beer you want to brew, what space you have, and how good you are with conversions when brewing. For example, pellets are highly processed (hammer milled[17]), created from finely powdered hop cones compressed into pea-sized tablets that are 20–30 percent stronger than loose varieties and generally cost more per ounce,[18] while plugs are whole flowers dried and compressed into plugs and are reported to impart a better aroma and flavor.[19] Depending on the quantity needed, either of these would be less likely to take up as much room as air-drying hops in your own space. But, if you want to use whole leaf hops, the flowers are kept whole and dried but are less efficient for bittering and you need a larger quantity for bittering compared to pellets.[20] Also, some brewers think whole hops are less harsh than pellets, but there doesn't seem to be empirical evidence to back this up.[21] For convenience, some brewers use hop extracts because they come in liquid form and don't require as much physical space for storage. However, it may be best to mix pellets that do a large part of the bittering work and save the whole hops for the more delicate operations in the brew (later).[22]

Dry Hopping vs. Wet (Fresh) Hopping

Although the words seem to offer a clear distinction, they can also be deceiving; the distinction is clear between these two phrases once you know one is a process (dry) and the other is a descriptor (wet). Dry hops are used regularly during the boil and added to the wort at different times to "impart different aspects of the hops via oils and resins."[23] Wet hops are straight off the bine (not vine); when added, they offer a mellower hop bitterness and you will need roughly ten times the amount of the dry hops.[24] Let's take a closer look at bitterness.

Bitterness: IBU Range

To understand bitterness in beer you must know its association with these three letters: IBU. "The strict definition is simple: An IBU is an empirical measurement, measured in parts-per-million (ppm) of isohumulone (which is the main chemical compound derived from hops that makes your beer taste bitter) in a given volume of beer. Isohumulone is created when the alpha acids in hops *isomerize* (basically dissolve or breakdown) in the boil. That's it. That's literally what an IBU is."[25] But this may still sound complicated. What's important is to determine the desired amount of bitterness you want to achieve.

Tyler Barber of the Homebrewers Organization tells us how to determine IBUs by using Fred Eckhardt's quick formula for determining IBUs:

> For a 5 gallon batch of homebrew, you take Ounces × Alpha Acid × Percentage Utilization (boil time) divided by 7.25. Example—we have a Pale Ale using Cascade hops with 6% alpha acid, it would look like this:
>
> > 1 Ounce (Boiling Hops) × 6% (Alpha Acid) × 30% (Utilization) divided by 7.25 = 24.8 IBUs
> >
> > 1.5 Ounces (Flavor Hops) × 6% (Alpha Acid) × 15.3% (Utilization) divided by 7.25 =15.8 IBUs
> >
> > 1 Ounce (Aroma Hops) × 6% (Alpha Acid) × 5% (Utilization) divided by 7.25 = 4.1 IBUs
> >
> > 24.8 IBUs + 15.8 IBUs + 4.1 IBUs = 44.7 IBUs. This beer would have 44.7 IBUs.[26]

Since hops require awareness of alpha acids and beta acids, we offer this to our readers. These acids don't provide bitterness until they are engaged in the boiling process, where they become iso-alpha acids. Alpha acids are known for adding the bitterness to the beer. While there are five alpha acids, two are primarily the focus for brewers: humulone and cohumolone, and it is best to keep high on the former and low on the latter when brewing.[27] Beta acids used to be the "ugly step sister" of acids, but they are coming a long way and can also impact beer in positives ways. There are three types of beta acids: lupulone, colululone, and adlupulone, and they dissolve over time in the process and can change the profile of the beer, especially when it is aged or lagered; most hops have an alpha to beta acid ratio of 2:1, except for noble hops which are 1:1.[28] So, while we don't often hear a lot about beta acids, they too are important to include when discussing the hoppyness of a beer. If you want a thorough assessment and understanding of hops, then read Stan Hieronymus's *For the Love of Hops*.[29] But, recognize that besides hops, there are also other ingredients to consider when brewing.

"I Got Grain . . . and Fungi!"

Grains, usually malt (barley) but sometimes wheat, corn, rice, rye, and other cereal-type grains are a significant part of the brewing process and its result. While some geographic regions didn't have access to malt and have trouble growing it today, others had more malt than they knew what to do with, so beer became a natural use for this grain.

Malt (barley) was one of the primary ingredients the Germans included in the *Reinheitsgebot*. Malt has been a staple of the beer industry because it was sustainable and produced or even naturally available across the country in vast quantities. There are several broad categories: base malts, which provide much of the protein; specialty malts, which can increase body, improve head retention, and add color, aroma, and flavor; and, malted barley, which offers a rich, grainy character.[30] Check out Figure 4.1 as well as *Brew Your Own*'s website to access more charts on grains and adjuncts.[31]

Next, we have corn. Take a look around some states, and corn is highly prevalent. Stalks grow unencumbered in many climates and need little care taking from planting to harvest. Some brewers are using corn in their brewing; critics say it is a cheap fix for managing costs while others embrace its utility. Corn can be converted to sugars, which can then add to ABV and can change the bitterness level as well. It can provide a smooth sweetness, lighten a beer's body, and decrease haziness;[32] it's not just a filler anymore.[33]

American Grains			
Malt	L	G	Description
Black Barley	525°	1.023-1.027	Imparts dryness. Unmalted; use in porters and dry stouts.
Black Patent Malt	500°	1.026	Provides color and sharp flavor in stouts and porters.
Chocolate Malt	350°	1.034	Use in all types to adjust color and add nutty, toasted flavor. Chocolate flavor.
Crystal Malt	40°	1.033-1.035	Sweet, mild caramel flavor and a golden color. Use in light lagers and light ales.
Crystal Malt	90°	1.033-1.035	Pronounced caramel flavor and a red color. For stouts, porters and black beers.
Crystal Malt	60°	1.033-1.035	Sweet caramel flavor, deep golden to red color. For dark amber and brown ales.
Crystal Malt	30°	1.033-1.035	Sweet, mild caramel flavor and a golden color. Use in light lagers and light ales.
Crystal Malt	20°	1.033-1.035	Sweet, mild caramel flavor and a golden color. Use in light lagers and light ales.
Crystal Malt	120°	1.033-1.035	Pronounced caramel flavor and a red color. For stouts, porters and black beers.
Crystal Malt	10°	1.033-1.035	Sweet, mild caramel flavor and a golden color. Use in light lagers and light ales.
Crystal Malt	80°	1.033-1.035	Sweet, smooth caramel flavor and a red to deep red color. For porters, old ales.
Dextrin Malt (carapils)	1.5°	1.033	Balances body and flavor without adding color, aids in head retention. For any beer.
Munich Malt	10°	1.034	Sweet, toasted flavor and aroma. For Oktoberfests and malty styles.

Figure 4.1. Malt
Source: *Brew Your Own*

Rice is also used by some brewers because it imparts little to no discernible taste but it does provide snappy flavors and a dry profile while lightening the beer's body. Rye, however, while working in conjunction with barley, can sharpen flavors while adding crispness and some subtle spiciness.[34]

Wheat also works well with barley; it complements it nicely and is present in such beers as Hefeweizen, Lambic, Gose, and others. Flavors are drawn from the yeast and esters and can yield more sharpness based on whether the wheat is malted or not.[35] Moreover, wheat can also create a fuller body and mouthfeel, as well as "a foamy head as thick and lasting as Cool Whip."[36]

And, if you like creamy, then work with oat(meal), which adds smooth, rich, enjoyable textures to stouts, giving a "thicker" mouthfeel, and creating a creamy full-bodied brew.[37] Oatmeal stouts are on the rise and just may make breakfast more enjoyable . . . again!

Ready to funk it up a bit? Try mushrooms or fungi . . . not only in your skillet but also in your brew kettle to add body and richness, along with "the mystical fifth taste: umami"; umami is derived from free amino acids and MSG-like elements.[38] But, the type of mushrooms, and their cost, often determine the outcome of the beer-fungus collaboration. Some mushrooms lead to gritty, dirt-like products, while others nuance the beer in ways that highlight some of its features, such as chanterelles, which bring about a light apricot taste.[39] The mushroom's more sophisticated cousin, the truffle, is also in play for some brewers.[40] But, despite its psychedelic appeal, mushrooms and truffles can change the flavor and offer a unique beer experience.

Fruit also adds to the beer experience; blueberries, elderberries, strawberries, and other berries are used alone or with pears, oranges, kiwis, apples, and more to offer distinctness in beer and expand the drinking audience. Some beers are sweet, others more tart or sour. Regardless, fruits have become a go-to resource for many brewers. And, since many meaderies and breweries coexist and collaborate as needed, fruit and honey-based beers make sense.

Finally, why not go way out on a limb and make other unique beers. Some include the use of sheep dung, bull testicles, beard (hairs), Sriracha sauce, margarita pizza, peanut butter, chocolate, maple bacon, coffee, and even hornet's abdomen and more.[41] Experiments are unlimited; some are tasty, others not so much. Unique beer styles also emerge, as was the case with Braggot, Gruit, Gose, and more.[42] New beers or beer styles appear weekly, if not daily, worldwide, and your palette is the ultimate decision maker; what you like, I may dislike. Regardless, the world is your oyster (which is also used in beer).

Yeast Rules, Oxygen Drools

Prior to the fermentation step, oxygen can be quite helpful to the brewing process. However, once fermentation begins, the presence of oxygen can often contribute to the creation of off-flavors and beer that spoils before its time; worse, it can damage flavor stability, thereby making consistency and quality of your product difficult to manage.[43] So, this is why we say, "yeast rules." As a living organism, yeast consumes oxygen before to promote growth and expansion; however, during the fermentation, oxygen becomes a real nuisance! Let's take a quick look at the fermentation process.

Fermentation

The essence of brewing relies on the process of converting starch into sugar, which then leads alcohol. The transformation of starch into sugar takes place during the mashing stage, with further conversion of sugar to alcohol completed during fermentation.[44] Furthermore, fermentation is impacted by yeast during two of its processes: attenuation and flocculation.

Attenuation is the degree to which yeast ferments the sugar in a wort and if you have 50 percent attenuation it means that 50 percent of the sugars have been converted into alcohol and CO_2 by yeast; if you have 100 percent attenuation, all of the sugars have been consumed by yeast. This means that beer fermented with normal brewer's yeast will never have 100 percent attenuation. This is important because it can help predict the final gravity and alcohol content of a beer. A yeast with low attenuation will leave a beer with more sugar and more body than a yeast with high attenuation. This can also be very helpful when selecting a yeast strain for a recipe.[45]

Flocculation is a desirable and important characteristic that is unique to brewer's yeast. When brewer's yeast nears the end of fermentation, single yeast cells aggregate into clumps of thousands of cells and drop to the bottom of the fermentor, leaving clear beer behind. If yeast flocculate too early, the beer will be under attenuated and sweet. If yeast do not flocculate, the beer will be cloudy and have a yeasty taste.[46]

Both of these processes must be controlled as much as possible to produce good beer. Knowing more about the yeast strains or types and how they react during the brewing process can yield positive results and keep the yeast "happy." The following provides some additional information regarding yeast and even some basic science related to fermentation.

Yeast Types

There are literally hundreds of varieties and strains of yeast. Historically, brewers have preferred using two types of beer yeast: ale yeast (the "top-fermenting" type, *Saccharomyces cerevisiae*) and lager yeast (the "bottom-fermenting" type, *Saccharomyces uvarum*, formerly known as *Saccharomyces carlsbergensis*). The varieties of both of these yeast categories vary widely, as well. Use the *Brew Your Own* website to locate a homebrew yeast guide.[47] Familiarizing yourself with these yeast strains will help you bring more aroma, flavor, and mouthfeel to your beer.

Pitching Rates

Do note, however, that not all yeast can be pitched in the same ways.[48] Northern Brewer offers a clear explanation of pitching rates and their relation to gravity. In short, it's the amount of yeast added to cooled wort and

Name & Number	Type	Lab	Floc.	Atten.	Temp.	Description
American Ale 1056	L	Wyeast	Low/Med	73-77%	60-72°	Well balanced. Ferments dry, finishes soft.
American Ale BRY 96	L	Siebel Inst.	Medium	High	64-72°	Clean ale strain
American Ale II 1272	L	Wyeast	Medium	72-76%	60-72°	Slightly nutty, soft, clean and tart finish.
American Ale Yeast Blend WLP060	L	White Labs	Medium	72-80%	68-72°	Blend celebrates the strengths of California ale strains.
American West Coast Ale BRY-97	D	Lallemand	Medium	Medium	63°	Very clean ale flavor.
Brewferm Top	D	Brewferm	Med/High	NA	64-77°	Universal top-fermenting beer yeast.
California Ale V WLP051	L	White Labs	Med/High	70-75%	66-70°	Produces a fruity, full-bodied beer.
California Ale WLP001	L	White Labs	Medium	73-80%	68-73°	Clean flavors accentuate hops; very versatile.
CBC-1 (Cask and Bottle Conditioning)	D	Lallemand	Low/Med	NA	59-77°	Valued for its refermentation ability.
Coopers Pure Brewers' Yeast	D	Coopers	High	High	68-80°	Clean, round flavor profile.
Denny's Favorite 50 1450	L	Wyeast	Low	Medium	60-70°	Can be used for almost any beer style. Accentuates malt, caramel, or fruit character.

Figure 4.2. Amber and Pale Ale
Source: Home Brew Yeast Strain Chart—*Brew Your Own*

is usually measured in millions of yeast cells per milliliter of wort. And the amount of yeast necessary is highly dependent on the original gravity of your beer and the fermentation temperature. Simply, the higher the original gravity or the cooler the temperature during fermentation, the more yeast you will need. Most calculations of pitching rate are based on a different system of gravity called "degrees Plato (°P)." Using a low pitch rate usually results in a higher finishing gravity, lots of fruity character, and increase in off-flavors, while a high pitch rate usually results in lack of mouthfeel, yeasty flavors, and lack of fruity characters. Brewer's Friend offers a quick yeast pitch rate and starter calculator to assist you in being precise.[49]

So, if we get into the habit of paying closer attention to the ingredients used to brew, the resulting chemistry becomes more relevant and brewing beer can become quite complex. Chapter 5 offers a more detailed and formulaic perspective on the science behind beer and the brewing process. Now might be a great time to refill your beer. But first, read how one commercial horticulturalist discusses beer ingredients and the role of farming in the industry in the "Talking from the Tap" below. Cheers!

Talking from the Tap!

Lily Calderwood, PhD[50] (University of Vermont),
Commercial Horticulturalist at Cornell Cooperative Extension

1. *Where are hops mostly grown in the United States?*

Pacific Northwest in places like Washington, Oregon, and Idaho. But there are disease problems here and elsewhere. A group of fifty farmers out in Washington, Oregon, Idaho do most of the growing and up until eight years ago they were growing all the hops and are still growing the most now. They share how they grow hops with others in states like New York, Vermont, and Michigan, but they are also cautious.

2. *How did you decide to be in agriculture or pest management?*

I grew up in rural Massachusetts and always had an interest in biology. So I started to work for Massachusetts Audubon. I wanted to involve the community with biology and science and then worked with a nonprofit called EarthWatch. Agricultural projects were most interesting because they involved the farmers, the food systems, and their visitors. I went on an insect project via Cornell Extension and went to Costa Rica. Then I applied to UVM (University of Vermont) and worked with Heather in the Soil Department who was also affiliated with Cornell Extension. She studies hops, barley, beans, and more. She is a great resource for farmers.

3. *What can you tell us about the hops and the hops industry?*

Out west, they are growing for big brewing companies like Coors and Miller. The Anheuser-Busch/InBev merger with SABMiller throws off the hop industry because channels will vary. Farms that are fifteen hundred acres may grow one variety of hops. Best to grow one variety in one field. They mature differently.

Hops are particular and brewers are particular about the hops they use. Biochemists are very good about telling about hops. *Hops*, *Water*, and *Yeast*, and *Barley* books by John Palmer. Every brewer reads them; great place to start.

Brewers out west are also looking for proprietary varieties. They have a patent from the United States Department of Agriculture (USDA). Cascade is very popular here in New York. It is mildly resistant to a disease called downy mildew. It's always a good yielder and grows fast even though it is the slowest of the hops varieties. We can only grow commercial varieties.

4. *What are the concerns about growing hops here in New York?*

Pest issues make things difficult. We are on a learning curve, such that 90 percent of the hops growers in the region are new to hops or farming. A lot of people are treating it like a hobby after work, but hops growing is a full-time job. You will break even if you can put in five acres, so growing a bit more you can make a profit. We have mechanized the labor and instituted cultural controls for eliminating weeding, such as black plastic to assist growers.

5. *Is there an anticipated hops shortage?*

In some ways there are big breweries who are using more hops now than ever. But demand has gone up, and especially for the proprietary varieties, but we can't grow those here. Cost per local hops is higher. They charge a premium for local hops, $15–$30 per pound for dry hops. It is going to be difficult to sustain farm breweries with the state laws currently in place. They will have to change the laws. We have to grow barley, but crop insurance is an issue for many specialty crops, such as hops. That also means they don't have crop insurance because they don't get federal monies for specialty crops. Wheat and barley for flour is just coming under control. But with malted barley we have lost the varieties that were prominent in the "bread basket" of the East. So, we get some varieties from Canada and are still trying to breed varieties for this area. Malting barley is behind the wheat and flour grains. Some roast their own barley—Andrea at Valley Malt in western Massachusetts, she is a maltster. They were one of the first to do it. Every farm is its own microclimate, so place matters.

6. *What area are you responsible for here in the upstate New York?*

Hops don't fall under my jurisdiction anymore, but I know so much about them I still help the growers if they reach out. I cover six counties in upstate New York: Albany, Rensselaer, Greene, Columbia, Washington, and Schenectady, and I'm on a regional agriculture team. I do ornamental horticulture like flowers and Christmas trees, but my title is commercial horticulture, herbs and edible crops but not vegetables and fruits. Hops are also beautiful to look at, have a strong aroma, and offer an ornamental feature too.

7. *What is considered a good yield for hops?*

A good yield is between fifteen hundred and twenty-five hundred pounds per acre in the West but here it's about fifteen hundred. We are still learning here.

8. *Will we see the learning curve expand for areas that don't normally grow?*

Yes, they are already doing it. Microbreweries are driving the demand. Once we improve the curve, the problem areas will change as we continue our research and educate people. We are still tailoring nitrogen utility, how to train and when to train varieties here.

Education has also expanded to SUNY Cobleskill, where they do some hops work and SUNY Morrisville has a brewing school, Middlebury, Vermont (Drop In Brewing) has a brewing program, Schenectady County Community College, and Paul Smith's College.

9. *Are there farming incentives?*

The farm brewery law in New York has helped hops acreage increase. It triggered acreage for growth. Barley hasn't quite caught up, but I think it will. There are no real restrictions for bringing across state lines. Farmers grow from plugs or rhizomes (roots) they get from a nursery or farmer. Rhizomes have more energy and may grow better. But they aren't regulated in terms of virus and disease management, so the USDA regulates crops and who can grow them. The Clean Plant Network is USDA approved and scans every mother plant to be used for propagation for a number of diseases and viruses.

10. *Do farmers share growing secrets?*

Oh yes, especially in this region; it helps everyone try to make a high-quality product.

11. *Can you distinguish the types of beers or hops when drinking beer?*

Somewhat but not like professionals. I can tell Cascade from Citra but not other hops sometimes in the same group.

12. *Anything else you would like to share?*

Quality measures are alpha and beta acids, hops storage index (HSI), and essential oils. Take a sample from the hop cones before harvesting to know when to harvest. Four days to one week makes a difference in harvesting. There are labs in Vermont, Michigan, and Washington where we send our samples for assessment. Also, researchers at the extension formed a group to serve the region east of the Mississippi to help educate farmers, and Steve Miller (Cornell Extension) is a Hops Specialist in New York.

YOU DON'T NEED TO BE EINSTEIN
The Science behind a Good Brew

I n its simplest form, the wonderfully refreshing, foamy, anytime beverage that we call beer can be broken down into four essential building blocks that fulfill the needs of the brewing process. But what does "malt" or barley really contribute to the end product? How can adding ingredients like yeast or hops lead to the delightfully frothy brew that has been enjoyed for centuries? The process of brewing beer is truly captivating, and yet simple in nature, wherein we experience the transformation of malt, grains, yeast, and water into a wonderfully complex, yet refreshing final product. The science behind the brewing process itself is of particular interest, as the basic principles have remained relatively unchanged since its origins nearly five thousand years ago.[1] However, the process of brewing beer should not be oversimplified into merely mixing a certain amount of ingredients together and by noon you are enjoying your creation. Rather, within the larger system a number of necessary intricate biochemical reactions associated with the individual transformations of each component ultimately lead to the final product. For instance, barley, or malted barley, will need to be converted into starch and subsequently into sugars, while yeast will help to convert these sugars into alcohol. As we will see, within the process of brewing beer, each ingredient has a role to play.

Principles of Brewing

In its broadest sense, the process of brewing beer leads to a fermented beverage that is produced from a source of starch.[2] As is common with other types of alcohol-containing libations, the composition of beer can vary, with water comprising up to 95 percent of the final product.[3] With this in mind, the selection of an appropriate water source is incredibly important to the overall quality of the final product; a topic that we will specifically discuss later in the chapter. It is also important to note that there are a large number of other minor components that can each leave their individual mark on the final flavor, color, and alcohol content if not controlled for appropriately.[4]

As mentioned, the composition of beer can be traced back to four main ingredients: malt, grains, yeast, and water. Each is important in its own way and contributes to the overall bitterness, aroma, flavor, stability, and other attributes of the beer. For instance, an appropriate level of bitterness is essential in order to balance the sweet flavor of the malt in the beer. Changes in aroma can result from many ingredients, but may result from the oils extracted from hops or from the amount of caramel. Hops can contribute to the flavor and complexity of the beer, as well as influence the overall stability as their beta acids aid in deterring any contaminations resulting from bacteria.

Additionally, variations in both the ingredients and process, including temperature, fermentation time, and more, are important to understand, as they can lead to different varieties of beer all together. For instance, the type of yeast that is used can have an obvious influence on the type of beer that results at the end of the process (ale yeast, lager yeast, or wild yeast). Let's take a quick look at a number of common beer types/styles and associated characteristics available in today's marketplace (table 5.1).

To build on the concept of beer characteristics, the properties of a beer result from the particular components. Many common properties associated with beer include:

- Body—dependent upon the levels of extracts (albumoses, peptones, amides)
- Life—dependent on carbonic acid
- Color—dependent on the level of caramel
- Brilliance—dependent on the level of particles in suspension; consisting of organic matter. Inorganic matter contributes to turbidity.
- Taste—bitterness depends on the level of hop resin present; sweet depends on the level of sugar and maltodextrin; tart depends on

Table 5.1. Common Beer Styles

Beer Style	Characteristics
Bavarian	This type of lager consists of a dark color, malt flavor, and sweet taste. The aroma and hoppy taste are little pronounced.
Bohemian	This type of lager is light in color, has a pronounced hop aroma, and a bitter taste.
American	This type of lager beer is light in color and also has a pronounced hop aroma. It is less bitter than a Bohemian lager, and generally has a high degree of brilliancy.
Ale	This variety of beer is generally light in color with a very pronounced hop aroma and bitter taste (tart if aged). Ales tend to have a higher percentage of alcohol.
Stout	Very dark in color with a malt-like flavor and sweet taste. Generally stronger than an ale, but less alcohol content than an ale.
Weiss Beer	Very light in color with no pronounced malt or hops flavor. Typically, quite tart and turbid.
Common Beer	Light in color with very little hop aroma or bitterness.

the level of lactic acid; while a refreshing taste would depend on the level of carbonic acid

- Foam—dependent on carbonic acid gas content, in addition to the extracts associated with Body

- Hop Flavor—dependent on the level of hop-oil

So how do we take all of this information and the associated variables and actually brew some beer? For starters, there are three main phases in brewing, comprised of eight basic steps. These phases include malting the barley, mashing the grains, and numerous subsequent fermentation steps (wort separation, boiling, chilling, fermenting, conditioning, and finally packaging). Let's take a deeper look at each of these steps in order to better understand the science behind the beer.

The Biochemistry of Beer

As with any intricate system of transformations, brewing involves a series of complex biochemical reactions at each stage of the process. Although the majority of these activities are desirable, the presence of other side reactions can lead to an unwelcome dip in quality of the final product. Unlocking the desired characteristics requires a delicate balance and a basic understanding of the journey that each compound takes to support the end product. So let's take a closer look at some of the interesting chemical conversions that occur during the process of brewing beer; beginning with the building block responsible for many of the necessary compounds that are important to beer—the carbohydrate.

By definition, carbohydrates consist of any large group of organic compounds that are present in foods and living tissues; inclusive of sugars, starch, and other various fibers. Simply put, carbohydrates make up one of the four basic food groups and are extremely important to our health and well-being.[5] If you recall, there are numerous steps involved in brewing, with the first contributing to the release of carbohydrates in order to make these components available for further transformations. As simple as it may sound, the process of milling and mashing is extremely important in setting up the end product for success.

Milling, Mashing, and Separating

The practice of brewing beer begins with a mixing of barley malt (comprised of approximately 15–20 percent sugars and starch) and water (mash), which is then heated. This process is designed to convert the starches into sugars in about one hour.[6] However, it is important to understand that the starches that are contained within the barley (or other grains) need to be made available for transformation in order to kick-start this process. To promote this "unlocking" of sugars and starches, the barley is milled, or crushed, by being pushed through metal rollers or smashed using a hammer-style press. Ideally, you are looking to crush the grains in a controlled manner so that the starchy center of the barley seed is exposed and so the grain hulls that encase them are not damaged. If the grains are not crushed enough, there will not be enough starch available for conversion to fermentable sugars. On the contrary, if the grains are crushed too fine, then the husks, a component that will also act as a filter bed for the brew, could be damaged, often leading to gummy and unusable brew.[7]

Once the milling step is complete (often unnecessary if brewing from a kit), the crushed grains (grist) are mixed with hot water. This concoction is often referred to as "mash." It is during this process where science takes over as the heated water activates the enzymes hidden within the barley (grains), and the starches contained within the exposed husks are converted into a mixture of sugars, peptides, and other amino acids (known as amylases which are converted later into ethanol and carbon dioxide). It should be noted that there are various types of enzymes that are present in barley, each of which

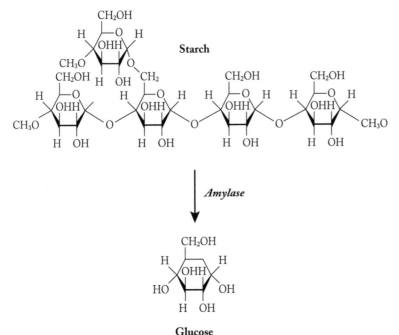

Figure 5.1. Starch Conversion to Sugar (Glucose)

has an ideal working temperature. By closely controlling the temperature of the mash, it is possible to control the types of sugars produced by the enzymes. Lower temperatures (140°F/60°C) lead to highly fermentable sugars and can result in dry beers. At higher temperatures (158°F/70°C), sugars are not as yeast friendly (at later steps), and can lead to a sweeter, more full-bodied end product. This conversion of starches to sugars[8] completes the first chemical transformation of the brewing process (figure 5.1).

At the point where there is no additional starch conversion to sugars from the crushed grain husks (grist), the sugar-laden liquid (wort—pronounced wert) needs to be separated from the solids. This process is either referred to as wort separation or lautering.[9] Brewers typically mash and lauter (separate) within the same piece of equipment, called a mash-lauter tun, containing a false bottom, and a particle screen (for collection of the solids).[10] The clear wort is then filtered through the screen and into a separate container, with the remaining solids washed with hot water to ensure that any remaining sugars are collected. This process is known as sparging.[11] This collection is typically followed by a prolonged boil, wherein hops can be introduced to the mixture, and other contaminants can be removed. As this step is not the focus of this chapter, we will leave a further explanation of this step to later. However, we will take some time to discuss the next important chemical transformation, which turns sugars into alcohol (ethanol); a product resulting from fermentation.

Yeast and Fermentation

In its simplest form, fermentation is the process of converting the sugars contained in the wort into an alcohol-containing beverage that is widely enjoyed. During fermentation, the yeast consume the wort sugars, ultimately discarding the highly prized ethanol as a waste product from this internal biochemical processes.[12] The chemical reaction that takes place in this step changes the sugars that were produced in the mashing process largely into ethanol and carbon dioxide (among other products). Therefore, on a scientific level, fermentation resembles the following (just know that there are a number of other complex, intermediate steps and products that are formed during this process (see figure 5.2).

It is also important to understand that the general character of a beer is largely influenced by the chosen method of yeast fermentation. For example, yeasts associated with top-fermentation (ale yeasts), are widely considered the best choice for brewing ales, porters, stouts, and wheat beers. These yeasts are regarded as top-fermenting because they tend to rise to the surface during the process of fermentation. This type of yeast thrives when left between 50°F and 77°F (10°C–25°C) and produces a beer higher in esters (another chemical compound that adds to the character of these types of beer).[13] Fermentation using top-fermenting yeast can be completed in as few as a couple of days. On the contrary, yeast considered bottom-fermenting (lager yeasts) are larger in size and most efficient when left to "work" at temperatures ranging from 45°F to 59°F (7°C–15°C). These yeast grow less rapidly and settle out at the bottom of the fermentor once the fermentation

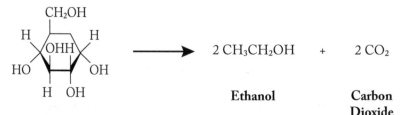

Figure 5.2. Fermentation by Yeast

process approaches completion. Bottom fermentation can typically take eight to sixteen days for completion. Common lager style beers that are brewed using bottom-fermenting yeasts include pilsners, bocks, and American malt liquors.[14]

The Chemistry of Flavor

Regardless of your preference, remember that the selection of yeast can influence the character of the beer in numerous ways that you may not necessarily think about. While the type of malt, hops, and water that you select impact the flavor, the other by-products from the fermentation process do as well. In addition to the desirable products of this biochemical process, ethanol and carbon dioxide, other compounds responsible for flavor are also produced during fermentation and can add to the complexity of the final product (table 5.2).[15]

It is also important to understand the effect of light during the entire beer brewing process. Experts recommend that homebrewers store fermenting beer in a temperature- and light-controlled environment. Selecting the appropriate color bottle for storage of the end product is paramount (brown is best). As you may be aware, beer that has been exposed to light can sometimes take on a foul odor and flavor; often referred to as "skunky" beer or lightstruck. On a scientific level, let's take a look at the responsible party for this undesirable outcome.

The compound that is inexplicably connected to "skunk" beer is none other than 3-MBT (3-methylbut-2-ene-1-thiol; see figure 5.3). This by-

Table 5.2. Fermentation By-Products and Associated Flavors

Fermentation By-Product	Chemical Structure	Flavor/Aroma
Acetaldehyde		Green apple
Diacetyl		Butterscotch
Dimethyl Sulfide		Sweet corn, cooked vegetables
Clove	Various	Spicy
Esters (fruity)		Banana, strawberry, apples, other fruits
Phenolic	Various	Medicinal, plastic, Band-Aids, smoke
Sulfur	S_2	Rotten eggs/burnt matches

Figure 5.3. 3-methylbut-2-ene-1-thiol

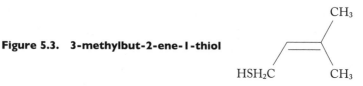

product is one of the most potent flavor contributors in beer, and only takes a small amount (four parts-per-trillion) to impact your brew.[16]

When beer is exposed to light, during fermentation or even during the course of drinking, compounds that may only be present in trace amounts can decompose as a result of a catalysis reaction (meaning that only trace amounts are necessary). While there are various other biochemical transformations that occur during this process, the sequence concludes by reacting with a sulfur-containing amino acid, to create 3-MBT. It is the sulfur component (thiol) of this compound that is responsible for the "skunky" flavor.[17]

The presence of oxygen (O_2) can also have an impact on the final flavor profile if not managed appropriately. The overall stability of a final beer product can be directly influenced by oxygen and is a reason why brewers take such care to exclude it as rigorously as possible. On an elemental level, oxygen (in its atomic or reactive form) can participate in a number of oxidation/reduction reactions, each of which can contribute to the larger impurity and taste profile. Taking the time to exclude oxygen (as best as possible) from the earliest stages of the process, such as milling or mashing, can minimize some potential unwanted flavors present in the bottled product.[18]

The Role of Water in Brewing

In taking a closer look at the entire brewing process, including the preparation of equipment to the final end product, it should be obvious that the choice of water can have differing degrees of impact on your beer. Are there specific water sources that are better for brewing specific styles of beer? How can water ultimately affect a brew? Luckily, these questions are pretty straightforward to answer.

Water selection can influence the beer in multiple ways. Initially, the pH (acidity or basicity) of the beer can vary, which directly correlates to how each flavor is received by your taste buds. However, the pH of the water doesn't necessarily dictate the outcome; the pH of the mash and wort is what is important. For example, the combination of grains like barley, malts, and more that are selected can influence the pH of the mash. Choosing dark-roasted malts as part of the mash can help neutralize the alkalinity (basicity) of water to achieve promote a proper mash pH.[19] Ultimately, both carbonate (CO_3^{2-}) and bicarbonate (HCO_3^-) ions are largely responsible for the basicity of the final product. Additionally, the presence of chloride (Cl^-) and other anions (negatively charged components) can contribute to a fuller and sweeter beer as well; assuming these are present in the appropriate ratio. It is important to understand that chloride ions should not be confused with chlorine, a common disinfectant, and that the concentrations of each component are distinctly unrelated to the other.[20]

Water can also contribute to the presence of many off-flavors from minerals, chlorine, or other unwanted bandit compounds. Generally speaking, the water source that is selected for brewing should be free of odor and have low-to-moderate alkalinity (basicity). Water choices can range anywhere from distilled water to using rain water (and everywhere in between). The following water sources are available for consideration and use in the brewing process:[21]

- *Distilled water* is typically considered a poor choice for brewing simply because all impurities have been removed, including important minerals, and can adversely affect the beer.

- *Tap water* is another available water choice; however, depending on geographic location, a number of additives (chlorine, stabilizers, etc.) can be present, which can also influence the final product.

- *Purified (filtered) drinking water* (or mountain spring water) is generally a great choice, as this water is largely free of minerals, allowing brewers the freedom to add various mineral salts.

- *Rainwater* typically contains all sorts of pollutants and other contaminants. Any compounds found in the atmosphere, including carbon monoxide, can be present in rainwater. Unless filtered appropriately, it may be best to steer clear from rainwater.

Keep in mind that beers originating from different geographic regions of the world can exhibit characteristic chemical profiles that may not necessarily be available where you live. With that being said, it may be necessary to add a combination of salts, chloride compounds, or carbonate sources (CO_3^{2-}, HCO_3^-).[22]

If you remember nothing else that we have touched on previously, the selection of an appropriate water source is critically important to the final product of your brewing experience!

Knowledge Is Powerful!

Whether you are a first-time brewer, or a seasoned veteran of the craft, it is important to gain a basic understanding of the overall brewing process and chemical transformations that occur in order to raise your chances for a successful brew. Simple decisions related to available water sources, varieties of yeast, and types of grains can lead to an ever-changing profile of characteristics and by-products, some which are good and can add to the final flavor profile, and others that can lead to a spoiled brew. Take your newfound scientific knowledge of the brewing process and build on it by doing a little more research on any of the topics that have been introduced. We encourage you to experiment often at every step of the brewing process, and confidently "wow" your friends and family with your keen understanding (although simplistic) of the journey that carbohydrates initiate to support the fermentation process and conversion of sugars to alcohol (ethanol). Having the ability to create a delicious beverage that can be shared with a community of beer lovers contributes to the overall draw of brewing that has become synonymous with the craft. Use your knowledge wisely, enjoy the journey . . . and read the next "Talking from the Tap," but fill your beer first! Cheers!

Talking from the Tap!

Interview with Gwen Conley,[23]
Director Production/Quality, Lost Abbey/Port Brewing

1. *How did you get into the beer business?*
I grew up in Maryland and worked at Flying Dog Brewery. Then I went to California State–Fullerton and was working on my degree, and just before finishing, my husband and I moved to Colorado and I finished my degree at University of Colorado, Boulder.

2. *In the 1990s, was craft beer as big as it is now?*
Yes, wow; 1992 was a big introduction to craft beer. I was introduced to Odell Brewing, Avery Brewing, and New Belgium, and five miles from the house was Coors. I began there as what I call a "grunt" microbiologist where

I wandered the bowels of Coors and collected microbiological samples and sent them out for testing. This then led me into Ball Corporation, where I ran the flavor panel for about ten years. This included eighteen months of sensory training, one hour a day every day; I did six months food, six months beer, six months packaging off-notes, and then some wine tasting too. This allows me to teach sensory courses now. I was deconstructing everything. When profiling beer, we start with ketchup and pick apart and deconstruct the order of ingredients as they pop up. At Ball we might do mayonnaise, ketchup, and then work up to chocolate. I can't eat mayonnaise or potato chips to this day. I just can't help but deconstruct them.

3. *How did you get your Twitter handle or nickname, "Sensory Goddess"?*
"Baron von Marketing" at Flying Dog Brewery in Maryland gave me the nickname "Sensory Goddess." Everyone had to have a funny name or title; it just stuck.

4. *Can you describe your job now?*
No, but I can describe my roles, as I see myself, as Mom or Brewery Warden. I schedule everything that has to be brewed and packaged, and do yeast management, and all the quality. I need to be sure that yeast and beers are happy healthy "babies." When they are out of our control (leave the brewery), I want to know if they behave the way they are supposed to. I anthropomorphize the yeast because this living entity is in beer, and if you packaged it and raised it well, then it should behave as it is supposed to unless it is stored in somebody's trunk; if so, they should be punished [*laughter*]. I'm also in charge of the nursery school and barrel program. I grow all the bacteria and wild yeast, and I decide what goes into what barrels. Recently we had a Framboise tasting where we organized fifty-three barrels and picked out forty-eight that will get blended and some will be dumped. The barrels being kept get resealed and the cultures pulled out, and we decide what goes back into the barrels. I am often responsible for one-off beers too. This year we are celebrating an anniversary, so I am creating a one-off (black berry sour with some vanilla beans). All of that falls under my "hat" or "hats." I also teach at UCSD (University of California, San Diego) in their certificate program; courses like sensory and beer styles, and beer-food pairing. I also teach microbiology and lab setup at American Brewers Guild (twice a year). And the barrel program incorporates beer, spirits, and wine.

5. *Why do you think the craft beer industry blossomed these past few years?*

The local piece is big. It's not just beer; craft overall is huge—things like cheese, chocolates, and bread have become craft. People are searching out flavor and you don't have to be a robot when buying local; you can be rogue. Listen to what your brain tells you, not what others tell you. At the (American Brewers) Guild, if you are making bad beer, do it consistently because someone likes it. Just do it consistently.

6. *What do you need to know about science, like chemistry or microbiology?*

You don't need to know these, but it gives you the whole picture. You need an understanding of how the pieces and parts work. My grandfather taught me from experience and observation of things in nature.

7. *How do you settle on which grains or hops to use?*

It depends on what you are looking for and when you are thinking about styles. We are doing a red, but okay, let's look at hops, yeast types for a fruity profile, and rye may give it a spice. It is just like cooking; it's experimentation. Malts are attributed to baked goods, hops are the fruits or herb, and yeast can create fruity esters, spicy thalamic, like clove, nutmeg, or even smoky. So it is super food-related.

8. *What role does local or regional climate play?*

Our vessels have a glycol system (refrigeration) that controls the beer as much as possible. The wild beers can be a challenge due to fluctuation in how yeast react. But we have a steady climate here in San Diego, so that helps.

9. *More beers are migrating toward nitrogen. How does this impact flavor profile?*

Mouthfeel, definitely. Flavor encompasses three areas: aroma, taste, and mouthfeel. Aroma is about 80–90 percent of beer, taste has five parts: sweet, sour, salty, bitter, and umami (savoriness), and mouthfeel includes both temperature and tactile-feel in the mouth. Nitrogen has tiny bubbles that create a creamy mouthfeel; a roundness is created in the beer. It's a milkshake-type of effect.

10. *Is that what makes a milk stout?*

No, milk stout is a style. If on nitrogen, it gets more creamy and it contains lactose. Not all milk stouts are nitrogen based and not all nitrogen-based beers are milk stouts.

11. *Is there a craft beer culture?*

Yeah. As an example, the Sam Adams representative in San Diego was saying that he has a hard time getting beers in local establishments because the zip code matters. The places want to carry the local brewery, whether here in San Diego, in Philly (Philadelphia), DC, or elsewhere. They are trying to concentrate on promoting craft beer (common) sense because you create community. People are looking for local products—locally grown, locally made.

12. *Do you network with others or do beer collaborations?*

Yes, with beer and sharing information, from insects to use of equipment and more. At Coors you were very closed-lip. Yes, knowledge is power, but it is only powerful when it is shared. Always be an honest taster, because you are only lying to yourself, which I learned from a mentor at Ball Company.

14. *Are there dangers with bigger companies moving in on the industry?*

I don't know. We are at the point where we don't know. Perhaps distribution. The positive pieces are that raw materials will be made available that weren't before, or craft breweries are going to be bought up. The distribution piece is big, product placement. Are they going to hoard space so we can't get our beer out? Is it craft or not? Who owns this small brewery now?

15. *Do you have a favorite brew?*

No. What time of year is it? Day? Weather? Eating? I can't drink some beers by themselves, but when pairing it can make a difference in what I like. And, where am I? East Coast? West Coast? And, what is the date on the bottle?

16. *Tell us about Lost Abbey?*

It's actually Lost Abbey, Port Brewing, and Hop Concept (three different brands), and all beers share the tanks. Lost Abbey is Belgian-style, boutique-like beers that have cork with wired cages over them and are bottle-conditioned, which means we add yeast and sugar to beer at bottling and look for natural CO_2 from that. Then port brewing includes Imperial Red, Double IPA, Double Chocolate Brown with crowns where we force-carbonate, and Hop Concept and Hop Freshener, which is seasonal IPAs, like "Dank and Sticky" or it tells you what the hops types are, like "Mosaic and Equinox" or "Tropical and Juicy"; it's the new thing. It definitely appeals to Millennials.

17. *What is the Confessional?*

It's our tasting room. Fits forty-five or so people, maximum. Right on the beach!

18. *What's it like to be a woman in the industry?*

I walk around with our plant manager (who actually works for me) and I ask a question; the others will talk to him, not me. "Are you seriously not going to make eye contact with me because I'm a woman?" The sales guys are in competition for bottling lines and they were asking why we chose that line and he asked me, "What exactly do you do for the brewery?" Because I am a woman there is this weird piece where people look for those in charge and when I introduce myself they still want to talk the person in charge. Can't believe that still happens.

19. *Do you have a network of women to work together?*

We do, but there are a lot of women in San Diego, and it is more accepted here. Facebook groups and festivals. In the first year, 107 judges and 7 were women. But recently it was 278 judges and a ton of women, about 25 percent at least, many of whom are brewers, such as Megan Parisi at Sam Adams or Highland Brewing's Holly Stevenson. So many women are just fantastic.

20. *Basic advice for those who want to enter the industry?*

Just do it. Keep doing it. I think of things as opportunities and try not to fear new things. If you "oil," you still earn and can keep moving on and lead to other things that are great. What's the worst that could happen?

21. *Do you need to know laws?*

Yes and no. There are some you may need to know, but learn as you go. For example, I did a seminar on Customer Complaints, but if you can compensate and don't take their complaint personally and seek their help in solving the issue . . . sort of like Beer Ambassadors, but there are monetary and state and federal laws in place that may prohibit this in some ways, such as shipping beer across state lines.

22. *Anything else you want to share?*

I call working in a brewery the "Rock Star Syndrome." You are a rock star because people around you will remind you of that; they think you have the best job, ever. Then there's that one day when you think, "I hate that guy," but then you share a beer with that person and that changes. Or when others look at what you do as the best job ever, but they don't really always know what it is that you do. But others are interested and that matters to us.

23. *Finish this sentence: "I'm in brewing because . . ."*

"Dumb luck and a gypsy career! Mother said that drinking beer would never get me anywhere, and boy, was she wrong! I wasn't afraid to take chances, and I drink and cuss a lot too!"

FROM EXTRACT TO GRAINS
Brewing Bigger!

Since many of you have been brewing one-to five-gallon batches for a while now, you may be interested in going bigger or from extract to whole grain. One author recently committed to going bigger, from one-gallon and five-gallon extract to up to ten-gallon all grain, and set up shop in the garage. Here is how that change happened.

Who Parks the Car in the Garage Anyway?

Before moving your setup be sure to have conversations with your partners, roommates, and other family members about the move because going all-grain usually means using more space, which is now a brewing commodity. Making a good argument is half the battle. For now, let's assume that conversations have gone your way and you are ready to make the move. Just as you did for your basement or kitchen space, you will need to prepare the area for more equipment and storage. So, review the earlier chapter on how to sterilize and prepare your space.

Now, the equipment you once used may not all be appropriate for this move. For example, fermentors and boiling pots will take on new sizes, as will other pieces of equipment, not to mention the number of bottles you will need. Below is a step-by-step example of how to prepare for your move.

What can I keep? We know you don't want to throw equipment away, so here is a list of what you can keep from the smaller batch process.

Testing equipment

- Thermometer—temperature still matters
- Hydrometer (reads gravity)—more important as the amount of beer brewed increases
- Scale—adjustments to ingredients have to be measured

Fermentation equipment

- Fermentation buckets or carboys
- Airlocks
- Siphons

Cleaning and sanitizing equipment

- Sanitizer (PBW™ and Starsan™)
- Bottle brushes
- Carboy brush

Bottling equipment

- Racking cane
- Bottles
- Caps
- Bottle capper

Brewing ingredients

- Yeast packets (not expired)
- Malt (not expired)
- Hops (not expired)

Miscellaneous

- Big spoon

- Mesh bags

- Mesh strainer

- Tubing

I have this equipment organized, but what should I buy? Well, you could go full tilt and purchase all equipment from suppliers or you can do it yourself (DIY) and scrape materials together while also purchasing other necessities to set up your system.

For example, Sean McGrath, one of the authors, just completed his own all-grain setup. Going to all-grain means moving to more and bigger equipment. Most brewers would rather spend money on ingredients instead of equipment; we are a frugal lot! First, to go bigger you will need to be able to boil full volumes of your batch and to do that requires more BTUs (heat source output) than you will get out of your stovetop. This means the addition of propane burners or some other heat source. Although it has been done, it isn't wise to boil more than five gallons of mash in your kitchen, especially with a propane burner indoors, unless you have the fire department on your 911. In addition to resizing the boiling kettle or vessel to handle your larger batch, you will need to purchase a mash tun.[1] You can purchase one for about $200 from a brewer supplier or make one yourself. To do that, here is what you do.

Making a Mash Tun Cooler: Thank You, Craigslist!

First, you need a gently used cooler, between ten and twenty gallons round, such as an orange Igloo sports cooler, or a rectangular cooler of forty-eight to fifty-two quarts. The round coolers provide you the benefit of being able to purchase a factory-built false bottom designed to fit the cooler, whereas the rectangular cooler will demand that you design your own manifold. A false bottom or manifold allows the grain bed to set and draw off a clean, clear wort without pulling bits of grain into your boil kettle. You must have this; it isn't optional.

Figure 6.1. Mash Tun
Courtesy of Sean McGrath

If you purchased the round cooler and installed the false bottom, then you are ready for the next step. However, if you bought a rectangular cooler, then you will need to make your own manifold system. This can be as simple as creating a braided steel screen filter or as complex as creating a copper or CPVC manifold (to handle heat). There are many online resources available for you to learn how to do this, or ask another local homebrewer for assistance.[2]

Next, you need to purchase and install a ball valve, usually a half inch, in your mash tun. Try using your local homebrew store (LHBS) to purchase a premade kit rather than fabricate your own. With some coolers you may use the drain plug already installed by the manufacturer, but on others you may have to drill your own hole which will require a drill as well. Follow the instructions that came with the kit or follow the instructions viewed online. Then connect the manifold to the ball valve in the mash tun (MT).

The next piece of equipment to be added is a hot liquor tank (HLT).[3] The tank provides the required hot water for mashing and sparging your grains. This can be a large cooler with a valve at the bottom or it can be a brew kettle and valve setup. There are two trains of thought when considering a whole grain setup. Most beginners use a multitier setup whereby

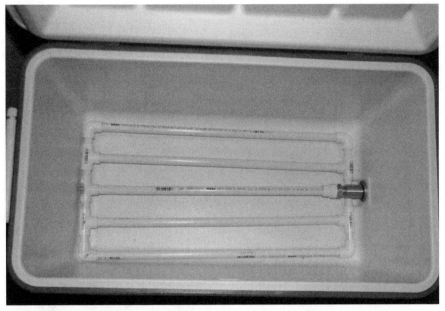

Figure 6.2. Manifold
Courtesy of Sean McGrath

they use gravity to bring the hot water to the mash tun and then from the mash tun to the boil kettle. If you are using a cooler for your hot liquor tank, then fill the tank with hot water and place on a high shelf or stand (higher than the top of your mash tun) so the hot water can flow with ease; gravity takes hold and the cost of pumps is eliminated. Remember, safety first; scalding water is being lifted so avoid rickety ladders and always seek assistance! For advanced brewers or those with great skills or a higher budget, all of your brewing can be completed at a safe height level with the addition of required pumps and hoses. This means that no heavy lifting is required, so much of the danger is removed since the process can be done at the same level as the mash tun. Each gallon of water weighs about eight pounds, so safety and ability are paramount; you also need to make sure the space is stable enough to hold this extra weight. Always ask yourself, "Do I want to lift that HLT each time or invest in a pump designed for homebrewing for about $100–$200?"[4]

After you have the HLT, you will also need to have a larger brew kettle. The twenty-quart brew pot used for extract is no longer an option. Your three options are to purchase a ready-to-go brew kettle sold for about $250 or more; turn a ten- to fifteen-gallon pot into a brew kettle by installing weldless fittings, including a thermometer port, valve, sight glass (tubes for water levels) for less than a full out purchase of a kettle; or, build your own "keggle" which is a brew kettle built from a repurposed keg. Here's how you can build your keggle.

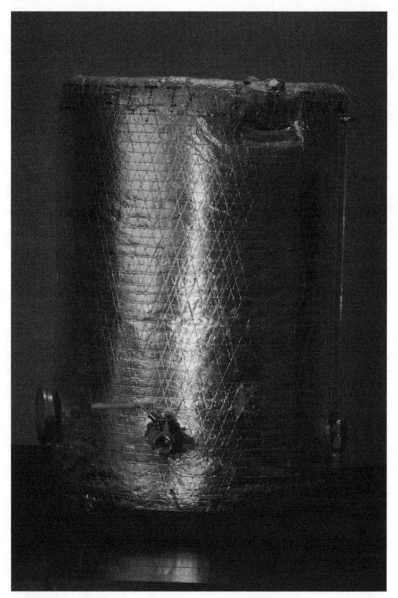

Figure 6.3. Keggel
Courtesy Sean McGrath

Building Keggles, Not Doing Kegels!

First, be aware of how the keg you are receiving came to you. For example, some may be "technically" stolen, since they weren't returned, but they can also be purchased as used kegs from brewery suppliers for about $100 or more; from other brewers it may cost you about $70. The keg should be 15.5 gallons or a half barrel (half-barrel keg). We aren't encouraging theft or the use of stolen property, so err on the side of caution and the law here.

Second, once you have your keg, install your fittings.[5] After verifying that pressure has been relieved from the keg, cut the top off so that you have a big opening to work through the brewing process. Then add your own bulkhead valves and fittings. Online videos describe this process, including YouTube. You can buy the whole shebang for about $400 from a supplier as well. Once this is completed, you now need to prepare a heat source.

A Heat Source Is Needed and It Isn't from Your Warm Personality![6]

Most homebrewers begin with a basic turkey fryer burner (e.g., Bayou Cooker), which can be purchased at your local Walmart or other retailers for about $50. Others purchase a burner specifically used for brew kettles from your LHBS or online supplier which will cost, on average, about $150 (e.g., Blichmann[7] or Edelmetall Bru[8]) and the brand is a personal preference. Some like Blichmann because of its warranty, but others like the Edelmetall Bru because it has four legs instead of three. When it comes to purchasing equipment, research the pros and cons using the forums or suppliers for reviews. Then make the choice best suited for you.

Since you are brewing larger volumes of wort now, you will also need a more efficient way to cool it down to fermenting temperatures. This can be done with immersion chillers, counter-flow chillers, or plate chillers.[9] Each of these uses a tap water system to remove the heat from your wort. The plate chillers are the most efficient but they also cost the most. Immersion chillers are the easiest and least expensive but not as efficient or practical for batches of more than five gallons. Counter-flow chillers can be home built if you are up to the task but soldering and brazing (welding) skills are needed. You can purchase one for about $200 if your cash flows in like you want your beer to flow out!

Now you have the necessary equipment required to brew and ferment your all-grain recipe. Many homebrewers will move to kegging versus bottling at this point in time.[10] Sanitizing and cleaning one keg is a lot less work than cleaning and sanitizing two and a half cases of bottles. If you invite friends over to assist in the brewing process, then they could clean and sanitize the bottles for you. But, you can also fabricate a keezer, which is home draft system for your kegged beer made from an old chest freezer.[11] It can also serve as a temperature-controlled fermentation chamber for those who live in an environment that experiences various climates, like upstate New York. Be sure to discuss this with roommates and partners because you may have more guests over to brew and drink than you anticipated!

With all-grain brewing, there are many associated fittings, hoses, and valves that facilitate the movement of liquids. Not all tubing is created equal, so purchase tubing that is rated to handle high temperatures generated while brewing; avoid general tubing found at local big box store (e.g., Lowe's or Home Depot).

Here We Go!: Let's Get Our All-Grain Batch Going

First, call friends over to assist.

Second, have beer ready for these friends; they may not work for money, but they will usually work for beer. However, be sure to complete the boiling process *before* drinking too much beer, or else you may be brewing while intoxicated (BWI), which can cause mishaps in measurements and other parts of the process.

Third, confirm your setup is ready to go; check that all areas are properly sanitized, all pieces of equipment are well-sealed, and all ingredients are measured and ready to go.

Because there are so many types of beer one could begin brewing, and so we don't complicate the process with too many recipes right now, we are going to explain how one recipe comes to be done as all-grain. Please note that the amount of grains and water needed will vary based on your final setup, so be sure to research the math and other tips for brewing in *your* special system.

Going Rogue: One Man's Mission for Brewing Beer!

Now you are prepared for the mashing process.

- Heat/Strike about 15 gallons of water in your hot liquor tank (HLT) to 175°F because you will lose 15–20°F when you add hot water to your grist, thus creating the mash.

- Based on the recipe and the grains you are using, you will have different absorption rates. Use a calculation chart for conversion of your grains and then mash the required amount into the pot.[12] "The volume of strike water for the mash is a function of the amount of grain and the desired mash thickness. The mash thickness can vary with the recipe, the mash tun configuration, the volume of any additional mash water infusions, the sparge water volume, and individual brewer preferences, but a value in the range of 1.0–1.5 quarts of water per pound of grain (2.1–3.1 liters per kilogram) is typical for homebrewers."[13]

- Add 3.5 gallons of the mashing water from the HLT to preheat your mash tun. Let it sit for about 5–10 minutes to stabilize the mash tun temperature.

- Slowly add your pre-weighed crushed grains to your mash tun and stir then in gently and efficiently to break up any dough balls that may be created. Be sure that everything in the mash tun is thoroughly moistened.

- Check your mash temperature and add a small amount of hot or cold water to adjust to desired resting temperature for your recipe.

- Close the lid and rest it for 60 minutes.

- Near the end of your 60-minute rest, bring the remaining water in your HLT back up to about 180°F (depending on recipe) and then begin batch sparging.[14]

- Slowly add 1 gallon of sparge water to your mash to heat your temperature to around 170°F. This step is called the mash-out. This will stop the enzymatic process and lock your sugar profile.

- Let it sit for about 10–15 minutes to prepare to set your grain bed.

- Set the grain bed by using a 2-quart pitcher to slowly drain your mash tun, watching for particles and husks from grain. Slowly return the water from the 2-quart pitcher back to the mash tun without disturbing the grain bed inside. Do this several times until the 2-quart pitcher reveals no particles or husks in its presence and it is now clarified; this step is called *Vorlaufing*.

- Now that the bed is set, drain your mash tun into your boil kettle. When draining is complete, close the valve and add your calculated amount of sparge water to the mash tun and repeat to remove all sugars.

- Slowly drain the remaining wort into your boil kettle. This is called batch sparging which is one drain after another to remove all fermentable sugars from the grains.

- If the boil kettle has not reached your pre-boil volume which is dependent on your environment and brewing setup, then you can add some remaining sparge water from the HLT. This is usually about 6.5 gallons.

- From this point forward, follow the same process as you would for extract brewing but pay special attention to the recipe and its requirements, and watch for the hot break (foam top) because excessive boiling may occur. See chapter 3 for more information on the boiling and fermentation processes that remain the same.

After the brewing and bottling/kegging process is fully complete, then prepare to enjoy your beer. Get the proper glass for the style of beer you brewed, and enjoy while reading the next "Talking from the Tap." Or, grab a craft brew and read the interview now. Cheers!

Talking from the Tap!

Interview with Emily Armstrong, Communications[15] and Spokesperson, and Jeff Joslin, Lead Brewer: Left Hand Brewing Co.

1. *What is the history behind the brewery?*

Emily: In 1993 two former Air Force officers, Dick Doore and Eric Wallace, were both familiar with quality beer, especially in Europe, and joined forces in the US. There was a microbrewery culture emerging here, so they wanted that to be the next step for them. They were living together, and Dick was showing Eric how to homebrew. At that time, there was not a whole lot of craft brew competition in the late nineties so they started a brewery. They wanted to be in northern Colorado, so they went with the better water quality and opened doors in 1994 at a former meat-packing plant in Longmont. The brews are now present in thirty-seven states and a handful of countries. We also created the first homogenized packaged beer.

2. *What challenges does the brewery encounter?*

Emily: Lots of ups and downs. Challenges are always there. They continue to evolve based on the time, industry, market, and size of business. Change in demand, big buyout in late 1990s, and we were almost there. Then late 2000s the craft beer renaissance emerged. Can we expand quick enough? And brewing is a huge capital investment and put demands on industry, including the equipment. Mo' money, mo' problems. As the industry matures, there is limited shelf space; competition is present, walking a fine line for access to ingredients, best people on your team, and more.

3. *What does it mean to be a craft brewer? Where is the industry heading?*

Emily: I was reading about what it means to be a craft brewer. Ownership is intent. Do you intend to be owned by a global firm or be entrepreneurial? The Brewers Association doesn't want to punish resounding success, so they don't want to cut you out from the collective. It's going to go through a cycle, both consumer interests and financial. Much more pressure and commitment to beer quality with so many options available; marketing and sales perspectives to make unique connections with consumers to affirm our brand. But beyond that, any time a market churns, buckle down on your financials.

Jeff: If I knew five years out, I'd be rich.

4. *Do you have to know about science and chemistry to be a good brewer?*

Emily: Yes. My college degree is in English. I was bartending for a few years and eventually networked in the industry in the Pacific Northwest. I got into an entry-level position and moved my way up. I am into year two now and have been here for two and a half years. I am able to use my interests every day; it does help to know about yeast, elevation impacts, and more. You have to be better at the mental game as you move up. Many people liken brewing in a kitchen. But the bigger you get the more you have in common with General Motors.

When you enter the higher levels of brewer management, it's incredibly challenging. You need to know what is happening at a biological and chemical level and you have to be an artist in some way by understanding flavor and what makes a good beer, flavor profile, what hops work well with which ingredients, troubleshoot equipment, and so on. A well-rounded education to put all elements into play and solve problems with what is going on in all facets of the industry. Recipe-development is a group project; mediocrity is not an option.

5. *How do you decide to go with recipes?*
Emily: Sales and marketing as well as brewing team's feedback. There is a seven-barrel trial system in place to experiment with recipes. One department can't do everything by itself; it's a melded harmony.

6. *What's your favorite brew? Why?*
Emily: Here—Smoked Imperial Porter is my personal preference. They are smoked here on-site and the brewers add that to their workload (time). If it's a Grosch beer, then Munich Malt had to be made because it wasn't available. But that is what makes it unique.

7. *Marketing efforts and creativity put into labels?*
Emily: We do all of our art in house except for the original design that is made in Boulder, Colorado, that specializes in food and beverage packaging. And, it is a collaborative endeavor. We give them information, and they in turn give the illustrative equivalent. We get artwork back and the designer takes and turns it into our packaging and merchandising.
Craft brewing is about the beer and the fan base. It is the connection we are making elsewhere in our marketing efforts. Social media helps. People are interested in all aspects, from smoking the wood or winning medals; digital media are outreach. We can interact with our fan base, we host five unique events here every year, and perhaps the country's only Nitro Beer Festival. Digital media and large sales team. We send our beer out to many places, so having people on the ground to educate and hold unique events and visit retail places; brand ambassadors. Merchandise is a huge operation. People love beer T-shirts. When e-commerce took off, many breweries didn't offer merchandise online, but you have to give the people what they want.

8. *What is the meaning of Left Hand?*
Emily: Named after southern Arapahoe Chief Niwot, who wintered his Navajo tribes in Boulder Valley in late 1800s, and his name means "left hand" in Navajo language. We try to incorporate some history into some

of our beers. It's present in some of the geography here as well. It's a local cultural reference.

9. *What is a craft brew culture?*

Emily: It has put American beer back on the dinner table. They took something that was not produced and had little differentiation in America prior to this time. They took that and took traditional styles in the last ten years in the US. Now the US is known for what is happening in the beer world, from styles, trends, and new hops. Willingness to do something different and dedication to flavor, quality, history, and innovation. A strong current of entrepreneurialism and tenacity; willingness to take a nitty-gritty occupation industry and fully commit themselves to it because they believe in this art form and the communities and culture that beer has built in Europe and beyond and bring that to their own hometowns. A different attitude about life and what it means to be a valuable and contributing member. It takes a lot. They are fully committed and are of a different fiber. Also, the people were ready for it. Our industry growth would not have happened if the people didn't want it.

10. *What role does collaboration play in the industry?*

Jeff: Yes. It happens quite a bit. I have done a few collaboration brews. From a marketing and sales standpoint, it is great because the consumers see us working together. From a brewer's perspective, we can kick ideas around and be with like-minded people. They are a field trip; they are phenomenal. If you are a guest brewer, they feed you beer and donuts. As for the broad collaborative efforts, we have an excellent lab staff and a few breweries come to ask for assistance; we are more than happy to help. We have also asked for help and readily received it. I see them in our tasting room and I visit theirs.

Emily: Survival of the fittest as a collective.

Jeff: Don't get me wrong, I still want my beer to be the best.

Emily: With hop shortages, there is power in numbers. When we stand as a collective then we can gain ground. From a legislative perspective, the Brewers Association helps and we thrive on relationships across the board.

11. *How do you take homebrewing to the next level?*

Jeff: Get a microscope [*laughter*].

Emily: You can do all the fancy things but our lead folks are in the science-based fields. You have to have respect for the science that is happening at every level.

12. *Laws and regulation?*

Emily: It's challenging because state laws and regulations vary across the board. But, from the early days of craft beer there is more acceptance legally and culturally.

13. *Finish this sentence: "I brew because . . ."*

Jeff: "It's a passion; you don't usually say, 'I do it for the spreadsheets!'"

Emily: "Yes, I agree. It's a passion; a labor of love. At the end of the day . . . there are a lot of functions of my job that are similar to other marketing jobs. But we love the product we make. . . . It's a privilege to have your hobbies and interests intertwine with your profession; you can live out your passion."

Part III

STARTING UP A BREWERY, BAR, OR TASTING ROOM: BREWIN' UP A BUSINESS

To have a man whose name is on the label showing such interest, commitment, and determination for the best is a wonderful thing. This is someone who will throw money at quality, who believes in being the best. Never knock it. Would you prefer to have a bean counter in corporate headquarters, someone who never comes near the brewery, making decisions solely on the basis of the bottom line and profit margins?

—Charles W. Bamforth, *Beer Is Proof God Loves Us* (2010)

"HOW DO I GET MY BUSINESS APPROVED?"

The Ever-Changing Landscape of the Beer Industry

Since the end of prohibition in 1933, the United States has made great strides for homebrewers and commercial brewers alike, but there is still a long way to go. Recent data from the Brewers Association confirms growth in the craft brew industry and the economic contributions the sector has provided, and will continue to provide, in the coming years.[1] If you have been homebrewing for a while now, then you may be ready to expand or "go bigger" and move from the basement or garage into your own brewing space in order to expand the capacity of your beer output. If this is the case, this chapter will help familiarize you with some of the legal basics. For more information, visit some of the websites cited in the notes to this chapter and also review some of the resources included in this chapter.

Federal, State, and Local Alcohol Beverage Laws

The most difficult aspect of these laws is that although federal laws apply across the nation, state and local laws can vary. This means that you have to thoroughly investigate the laws in your state and local area *before* brewing. Let's investigate a bit.

Do I Need a Permit?

We answer that question with one of our own: Do you want to brew beer to sell to others or do you just want to brew more beer in a larger system? Let's discuss how to go bigger without much pressure or visits from government officials.

Going bigger but not necessarily selling is less complicated legally than the act of selling your beer to others. As you are probably aware, there are specific regulations for the amount of beer that an individual may brew as a homebrewer, nano brewer, microbrewer, or however your operation is defined. The size of the brewery and its output capacity are limited, with tax penalties if you go beyond those limits. Homebrewing is legal in all fifty states (that's right, *all!*). While some were slower than others to come around (e.g., Alabama), many states were on the front lines leading the way (e.g., Colorado). Current federal law allows an adult homebrewer, defined as eighteen years old or older (check caveats in the law for those with a criminal past), to brew one hundred gallons a year. If there are two or more people in the homestead, then two hundred gallons may be brewed per year per homestead (not per person).[2] So, if you like to brew five-gallon batches each week and live alone, you would go over your *legal* amount of homebrew (5 × 52 = 260 gallons). While homebrewing is difficult to regulate on a large, local scale, you might consider getting a roommate, drinking less, or brewing less. Ultimately, you have the responsibility to keep up-to-date on the laws. But, let's say you want to expand your brewing and sell it to friends and other locals. Now, you are heading into new territory. There are a few key pieces of information for your consideration.

First, you cannot, under any circumstances, sell beer to anyone at any event without a license to sell in your state and in your country; this is forbidden in all fifty states. The Federal Alcohol Administration Act (1935), which has been amended over the years, is part of the Alcohol and Tobacco Tax and Trade Bureau (TTB) and "provides for regulation of those engaged in the alcohol beverage industry, and for protection of consumers."[3] TTB ensures that permits are required whether you are in the business of brewing as a producer, importer, or wholesaler; controls the right to suspend, revoke, and issues said permits; and, scrutinizes those who wish to embark in the industry to maintain the integrity of the industry and protect its consumers. Additionally, they also stipulate the regulations for labeling and advertising to further protect consumers. These regulations are always evolving, so staying current is important to your success. For example, in July 2016, new labeling restrictions were passed. Now, each beer label must include calorie information, complicating brewing for small-batch, one-off, nano, micro, and craft brewers because product samples will have to be sent to a lab (often delaying the beer's release date).

Second, you will need federal and state permits to sell beer to others and this process can be slowed by many factors, including, but not limited to, a backlog of applications, incomplete applications, lack of clarity on the application, or other specific reasons. The permit process may take weeks, months, or years, depending on the specifications of the request. Sometimes, you may receive state approval and wait on federal, or vice versa. Either way, patience is necessary. For example, Mike Wenzel, of Helderberg Mountain Brewing Company, had to wait almost a year to complete his permits at all levels. But, patience paid off, as did his perseverance, and he has been successfully up and running for over a year a now. The permit process requires completed applications, which can be found on state and federal websites. Be prepared to offer a name and location for your company.

Third, before embarking on the process, it is probably best to seek legal advice from an informed attorney or firm. While you might understand the basics, the nuances of the legal system may far exceed your understanding, and violations can stop you in your tracks. If you are on the West Coast, try seeking out Candace L. Moon,[4] a legal expert in the beer industry; for national recognition, try Lehrman Beverage Law, PLLC.[5] Otherwise, learning about the best ways to register and run your business in your area is certainly important to your success. Check your local chamber of commerce, research lawyers in your area, chat with other brewers, and visit the TTB website to find out more information about the legalities of the industry.

What's Next? A Briefing on the Law

You have your permits, so now you can begin selling *your* brewed beer on tap, in kegs, bottles, or cans. But, caution is needed when it comes to local, state, and federal laws and regulations. Variations are prominent across towns, counties, and states, so once again you must be familiar with your specific locale. Let's take a quick look at the federal laws for selling beer.

Federal Laws

Dating back to 1920, the US government heard the concerns raised by many factions, including those with strong religious beliefs, and took action by adopting the Eighteenth Amendment whereby Congress prohibited "the manufacture, transportation and sale of intoxicating liquors."[6] Much to the dismay of the government, organized crime and other social issues emerged with

93

bootleggers taking the reins in many regions. New venues, like the speakeasy, allowed people access to alcohol and appeared in every major city and town, and some still live on today (e.g., The Speakeasy on Howard Street, Albany, New York). This so-called noble experiment may have led Herbert Hoover and others to ratify the Eighteenth Amendment; however, citizens continued to discover many loopholes among the amended "fixes." It was not until December 1933 when thirty-six states ratified the Twenty-first Amendment, thereby lifting the ban throughout the country. To this day, some counties and towns, especially in the region commonly referred to as the "Bible Belt" (running as far west as Arkansas into Tennessee, the Carolinas, and farther south, including parts of Alabama, Mississippi, and Georgia), have many areas that are considered "dry," meaning that they don't sell alcohol. However, this does not, in many cases, prohibit citizens from purchasing alcohol across county, town, or state lines and transporting it into that region or even homebrewing within state guidelines. But, once again, check the laws in your state.

While alcohol regulation goes further back than 1920, our goal is to focus on legislation that is more recent, especially those laws and regulations that impact the beer industry and the craft beer industry more directly. As noted previously, the TTB regulates the amount of beer that someone can brew for personal use (per household), with the quantities clearly defined when it comes to the type of brewer you are or wish to be.[7] Additionally, strict labeling laws require federally mandated label warnings for alcoholic beverages. The warning statement that is required to be present on packaged products must read, "GOVERNMENT WARNING: (1) According to the Surgeon General, women should not drink alcoholic beverages during pregnancy because of the risk of birth defects. (2) Consumption of alcoholic beverages impairs your ability to drive a car or operate machinery, and may cause health problems."[8] Specifics and requirements on how/where the warning is to be placed must be adhered to via these guidelines, so be sure to read up on this. In addition, licenses must be secured *prior to* the sale of your brew. You must do *your research* via the TTB, and it is advised that you speak with an attorney who specializes in the industry and in your specific state too.

State Laws

Since space and time are limited, the authors provide a brief comparison of just a couple of state laws and regulations between two states they call "home": New York and Michigan.

New York—Currently, New York has a very supportive government as it relates to brewing; even providing a "hotline" of sorts via an active e-mail (craftbev@sla.ny.gov), that allows a "one stop craft beverage shop" for addressing various questions related to the craft beer industry.[9] In 2012, legislation was passed in the form of Program Bill #42, encouraging industry growth and creating incentives for non–New York brewers to build facilities and promote job creation. In 2013, Program Bill #17 passed, focusing on changes to labeling for brand label approval. In 2014, the Craft Beer Law was signed (Craft New York Act) reducing some of the legal pressures for producers of craft brewers and their marketers. According to the New York State governor's website, the governor, wanting to "develop the industry and raise the profile of New York's beverage producers . . . launched the Craft Beverage Grant Programs—a $2 million Craft Beverage Marketing and Promotion Grant Program and a $1 million Craft Beverage Industry Tourism Promotion Grant."[10] One resulting opportunity allowed for producers to conduct tastings with a reduced food requirement for such tastings. Additionally, the state government supports many alcohol producers, including an annual Wine, Beer, Spirits, and Cider Summit. In 2015, the governor expressed continued support for local businesses and identified $16 million in support of the craft beer industry via state actions, investments, and initiatives.[11] Through these annual summits and other website resources,[12] the governor and administration demonstrate their ongoing support and willingness to listen to those in the industry. Discussions from these summits have led to changes in the law and we hope they will continue to do so.

Similar to other states, New York also has a generous "growler" policy. A growler is a sixty-four-ounce glass, ceramic, or stainless steel vessel that allows consumers to have beer "on-the-go" or at home from their favorite brewers.[13] Not all states allow brewers to sell or fill growlers (their own or others'), and if they do, certain rules do apply. For example, in New York, growlers may be filled at breweries, beer shops, and even some pharmacies in New York City.[14] New York breweries, by law, can also fill growlers from breweries in neighboring Massachusetts. Interestingly, one writer noted how New Jersey also has strict growler fill laws but noticed how one innovative brewery devised paper-sticker versions of its own growler label and somehow bypasses the "inflexible" New Jersey laws.[15] According to the Brewers Association, the TTB's growler policy is often different depending on how the growler is defined by law: large glass or bottle; by definition, "glasses" can be filled by beer on tap and consumers can use their own growlers, whereas "bottles" are filled in advance of sale on brewpub premises.[16] Now, breweries and brewpubs often sell "growlets" (32 oz) or "crowlers" (on-site canned tap beer), which are ramping up sales across the country and may soon replace glass growlers because they can maintain the freshness and quality of the beer longer, up to six months in some instances.[17] Additionally, growlers serve a recycling purpose as well. Unbeknownst to many consumers, growlers are refundable if returned to the same brewery; however, many beer aficionados love them as souvenirs and physical, often refillable, reminders of their visits to local or faraway breweries.

Despite its openness to the industry, the one heavily regulated space is the brewpub, brewery, or taproom operated in New York. A brewpub must have an attached restaurant and at least 25 percent of its profits must come from the sale of non-alcoholic beer and food options. On the other hand, a brewery must serve or provide some food (which can be as little as a bowl of peanuts or pretzels). Many breweries, including Dogfish Head Brewing in Delaware and Catawba Brewing Company in North Carolina, have food trucks visit the premises to meet their state-mandated guidelines. Taprooms, where flights or tastings may occur, must also follow suit; some food, which may be as simple as a bowl of mixed snacks, is required, just like at bigger breweries.

As for taxes, New York is also on the more generous side for brewers. *Brew York* notes that while the state doesn't necessarily have the lowest excise tax, it ranks fourteenth-lowest at about fourteen cents per gallon across the state (New York City also adds its own excise tax of twelve cents per gallon). The state with the lowest excise tax is Wyoming, currently at two cents.[18] Licenses also have an applied fee, such that New York charges about $320 per year for small breweries (up to 75,000 barrels), whereas Wisconsin affirms its commitment to the industry by not charging a licensing fee. But, remember that the industry is always changing and new legislation is afoot each day throughout the country and state, so pay attention to your local, regional, and national political scene to keep abreast of any changes.

One other relevant law for brewers is the self-distribution law. Once again, states vary on their permissions for brewers to self-distribute. Many small breweries will endure the complex distribution process to ensure that their beer is being marketed and promoted rather than rely on contracts with distributors who may or may not work hard for your brand. As of 2015, New York allows self-distribution up to 75,000 barrels per year.[19] You'll certainly be busy if you take this route, but at least you know for sure that your beer is being marketed and promoted in positive ways.

Lastly, you may be asking, "If I don't provide my brew directly to a tap in a brewpub, brewery, or taproom, but I want to sell cans or bottles, then what legal guidelines do I have to consider for labeling?" Well, there are federal and state guidelines you must follow. In New York, when a brewer makes more than 1,500 barrels per year, labeling laws require the standard federal advisory statement, brand name, net contents, and class and type of alcoholic beverage.[20] Those brewers who make less than 1,500 barrels per year have an exemption on this regulation, but must file that exemption with the state. However, there is a recent legislative push for brewers, and others, to place nutritional information on the label as well, which would slow production and sales for small craft brewers who would have to send out samples for confirmation and preciseness to labs *before* they would be permitted to sell it. Ideally, it is important to ensure that you stay current with the changing legislation in your state. One misstep, intentional or not, could have devastating consequences, from fines to closure.

Michigan—Despite the water challenges seen in Flint, the state of Michigan also has some welcoming support for craft beer in its midst, including the governor and other administrators. For example, in 2013, Enrolled Senate Bill No. 27 was introduced and approved; this bill amended a 1998 act specifically related to vendors who sell alcohol, including brewers.[21] While changes were sometimes slow, big companies with long histories, such as Bell's Brewery or Founders Brewing Company, have brought much beer recognition and money to Michigan over the years. Additionally, Grand Rapids has tied, surpassed, or even been first runner-up to Asheville, North Carolina, for the title "Beer City, USA" for many years. If Michigan is looking to better its economy, then it seems that craft beer may be the way to go. But, water troubles in Flint and elsewhere in the United States will have to be corrected and monitored, since water is one of the four primary ingredients for beer; an appropriate water source can make good/great beer depending on the other ingredients used, but bad water makes bad beer . . . period! Michigan brewers should consider having their water source tested regularly in order to ensure quality and consistency of the brand.

In terms of the brand, labeling laws must be followed and differ slightly from New York and other states, but the standard government warning label must be included. However, there are some minor differences between New York and Michigan: "Alcoholic content on beer labels is not required in Michigan; however, labels may indicate alcohol as a percentage by volume" and "a Michigan 10 cent deposit is required," whereas New York has a five cent requirement for its bottles and cans. Now, what about growlers, crowlers, and growlets (aka howlers)?[22]

As of 2013, Michigan updated its growler laws to allow for growler fills at brewpubs, taverns, and taprooms (Michigan growler laws),[23] and unlike Massachusetts and New Jersey, they too can fill their own or others' which should increase sales. These changes to growler laws make sense, since Grand Rapids was classified and vies for the title of "Beer City, USA" each year.

If sales increase and expansion occurs, then taxes become important to the state for generating revenue. The current excise tax in Michigan is $6.30 per barrel, but brewers and microbrewers who brew under 50,000 barrels a year are eligible for a $2 tax credit per barrel up to the first 30,000 barrels: Taxes are collected biweekly, in some instances, but mostly monthly, with monthly reports to be submitted.[24] In Michigan, someone selling under 60,000 barrels per year is considered a microbrewer and may also provide free samples if licensed. Any establishment processing brew of any type must also have a food establishment license of some sort.[25] The good news for microbrewers that produce less than 1,000 barrels per year is that they may sell and deliver beer to a retailer as long as they comply with the state regulations.[26] For those who venture into the brewpub business, be sure to check the MLCC's licensing requirements too.[27] Consider your time wisely before deciding to self-distribute or use distributors and wholesalers.

Local

While most state laws supersede county laws, each county, city, or town has its own building codes and regulations, and some may have other vending laws in place that should not be overlooked. For example, in the city of Albany, New York, you may need an alcohol vending license beyond the state and federal laws and regulations, while health department permits may also be needed for food sold on premises.[28] Be sure to contact your local government agencies for clarity on laws and regulations in your area.

Now that you have some sense of the complexities of federal, state, and local laws, and you have met with a knowledgeable lawyer, you may be ready to open your business. But, just like the legalities included earlier, you will need to create an effective business plan, especially if you want to bring some investors into the fray. So, refill your beer and let's get down to business!

Creating a Business Plan

Before applying for licenses and permits, you should have a solid idea about certain aspects of your beer, such as names, labels, and locations firmed up. Then you should consider a more formal business plan, especially if you are seeking investors. Regardless of others involved, you must have a clear sense of what you will do and how you will do it, because if you hire employees, they need to be on the same page as you when it comes to *your* company. Here are some business plan basics to get you started, but there are plenty of resources online and at your local library to assist in the planning.

Business Plan Basics

It is wise to start by researching whether the name that you have in mind is available for use by Googling it and checking with the Secretary of State's website. You will need to complete this step in order to file for a specific business entity, usually an LLC (limited liability company), and then file a trademark for the name so you can protect your brand (beer names may also be trademarked as well).[29] Of course, in addition to these steps, choosing a good location is also essential, as is the contract agreement with the landlord. Not to get too specific here, but a "gross" lease mandates that the landlord pay all expenses associated with the property, including taxes, insurance, and maintenance, while a "triple net" agreement mandates some share of rent, taxes, insurance, and/or maintenance by both parties, with tax adjustments made at the end of the lease agreement; these types of leases vary, so be sure to research them further.[30] Also, be sure to secure insurance, licenses, permits, brewer's notice with TTB, employee agreements, and any other securities clearance for investors necessary for owning a business.

Phew! That's Just Part of the Business Plan

Now that some of the legalities are taken care of, let's get to other business basics, but be sure to visit the Small Business Administration website for samples and outlines.[31] Next are typical categories to be included in your business plan:

- *Executive Summary*—A brief overview of what brought you to this point, including company objectives. Think of this as your "elevator pitch" and include financials if recruiting investors.

Here is an opening paragraph sample for one microbrewery looking to expand its operation: "Martin Cove Brewing Company has been a successful microbrewery in southern Oregon for the past three years. Located in the city of Medford, the company has increased sales by 15 percent each year. The company's product lines are Martin Cove Pilsner and Red Ale. This year, Martin Cove Brewing Company, will gross $520,000 in sales. This was generated from an initial investment of $150,000."[32] Notice how this paragraph touts the brewery's success. When opening a brewery, you might try modeling your summary after Sedibeng Breweries, where they focus on what makes them experts in the field and what they want to accomplish, and provide a "pitch" to that end.[33]

- *Company Description*—Who are you? What is your brand? What makes you "different" but "necessary" in your market? Think of this as your extended elevator pitch, which includes more about the company. The Small Business Administration suggests you consider these items in your company description:[34]

  o Describe the nature of your business and list the marketplace needs you are trying to satisfy.

  o Explain how your products and services meet these needs.

  o List the specific consumers, organizations, or businesses that your company serves or will serve.

  o Explain the competitive advantages that you believe will make your business a success such as your location, expert personnel, efficient operations, or ability to bring value to your customers.

- *Organization and Management*—Whose who? And, who reports to you and others in the organization? What are the responsibilities assigned to each role? Here, you should provide an organizational chart that highlights different positions, including the CEO, brewmasters, accounting personnel, legal counsel, customer service representatives, and others for the brewery. The Finance Resource website provides a free plan with a sample chart to get your started.[35]

- *Service or Product*—What product are you selling? Beer. More specifically, your own brewed beer. How big is the brewing system? What type of ingredients will you use: regional, local, or homegrown? Are you organic? Here you want to describe your product in such a way that others *want* to buy and maybe sell your product. For example, one business plan "intends to develop a highly specialized microbrewery that will produce a number of seasonal and specialized beers such as stouts, pale ales, porters, lagers, and a number of specialized ales/lagers with proprietary formulas developed by the Company's brewmaster."[36]

- *Market Analysis*—Something as simple as knowing what is going on in the town, city, and state in which you expect to start your brewery. Knowing the competition and what niche your brewery fills or how it complements the local scene brewery scene are important. You might want to check with your local beer guild or association and visit your local chamber of commerce for details on similar businesses in your area and region. Establishing a foothold in the local scene is often harder than it seems. As a startup, you don't need major marketing research, but you do need to have a handle on what's happening in the local and regional brewing scene so you can uniquely identify how you stand against and with the competition. Check your state and local government small business sites for more assistance. If you are trying to expand your brewery and seek investments, then you probably want to hire a local marketing firm to secure your market analysis.

- *Promotion and Marketing Strategies and Tactics*—Based on your analysis of the environmental factors impacting your business, what steps will you take to promote and market your business to ensure customer relations and establish brand loyalty. Since we are currently embedded in a fast-paced interactive digital world, social media marketing and relationship development are as important as having a user-friendly website. Minimally, you should demonstrate consistency across all media platforms for logo usage, brand identification, and company mission. More about these strategies and tactics are discussed in the next chapter.

- *Financial Projections*—If you have investors then it is important you provide a clear sense of how you will grow the company;

increasing profits while decreasing expenditures or increasing profits while simultaneously increasing expenditures. Consider using a graph to show projected growth to your readers and potential investors. Seeking professional assistance for expanding your business is highly recommended. As a startup, what will it cost to get your business going: equipment, ingredients, space, and so on, and how much will you make from selling and/or distributing your product.

- *Appendix*—Supplemental items may include lease, licenses, permits, or anything else that will assist you in strengthening your case for business preparedness.

One way to further bolster your business plan and knowledge is by using some great resources that assist small business owners on multiple levels. Try the Small Business Administration,[37] the Internal Revenue Service,[38] the Service Corps of Retired Executives (SCORE),[39] the National Federation of Independent Business (NFIB),[40] and NOLO,[41] a company that offers legal advice, forms, and products.[42] Profitable Venture also offers free business templates for microbrewery proposals from executive summaries through marketing ideas and strategies.[43] Starting your business will not happen overnight; it takes perseverance, patience, and vision to be successful.

In this chapter we have provided a brief overview of laws and regulations and also provided many resources and samples to assist you in creating your plan. What you may have noticed is that operating a brewery, just like other businesses, requires planning and research on a continuing basis. The next chapter provides insight into marketing, public relations, and social media use for your brewery to drive consumers to buy your product or visit your establishment. For now, read the next "Talking from the Tap" interview . . . but fill your mug first! Cheers!

Talking from the Tap!

Interview with Billy Pyatt,[44] Co-owner, Catawba Brewing Co., Asheville, North Carolina

1. *When did you begin homebrewing?*

It was 1994, and I'm a hands-on guy, engineer. My wife gave me a five-gallon glass carboy for Christmas. I made it on the stovetop. She had to go to one of the few brew shops in Charlotte to get equipment and advice. I made the pale ale, dug in dumpsters for bottles, liked it, then kept tweaking and brewing. Then I wrote a computer program to tell us about the beer, bitterness, ab's, and more. I'm the only guy that still uses the program; Lotus Notes to Excel now. It helped me to understand the process and to repeat the beer quality and process. Then we switched to all-grain and built what we needed. My brother and I built a fifteen-gallon brewing system that we can wheel out and brew in our driveway.

Then late 1990s, we were making fifteen gallons and sharing with friends, but we had a few that we made often and liked. Revenuers Red is one. Still make it today with slight changes. I learned cell counting, history, styles, and more to appreciate things more in the beer industry. My brother and I went pro in a five-barrel system that we bought out in Colorado and then moved it here, but we outgrew that pretty quickly. We put it in the garage. Searched for a spot but kept my day job (Corning). Eventually we found a place in Glen Alpine, North Carolina. We made a batch of Indian Head Red (we bowed to political correctness, and call it something else now). Sold a keg or two, then kept making more and selling more. Basement of a mill, no glass, water, usable light, nothing. We renovated the space but were also paying $300 a month. We had to dig a pit in the floor to put twenty barrel fermentors in the building because the space was so small. Now we are in Morganton, North Carolina. But that experience allowed us to see that we could do this and become part of the industry. We had a bar for the first time there and that paid the rent. If we sell a keg we make about $100 with a distributor, about $200 if we self-distribute. And if we go retail, then we are looking at a $1,000 or so. We have grown incrementally. There's a balance point. For instance, one part of the floor was ripped out, but we didn't fix it and now about three weeks ago we did. I wish we would have done that earlier.

2. How important is the water for brewing?

We can figure out the water. Here it is a seven-barrel system. Yesterday we had Women's Brew Day. They worked with our Brewmaster. For each brew, we filter our water to make sure it is right. Once we got into the Morganton facility, I knew I wanted to do this full time. I didn't like sitting on the sideline and not see the growth I wanted. I left corporate and now I am doing this. I actually stayed a year longer than I wanted, but four years ago July, I had some money to invest in this. Bought a canning line, more manufacturing capacity, and opened a tasting room in Biltmore Village, then this one here in Asheville. Strategy was to make sure that we localized in western Carolina; we were born no too far from here and family history is here. We rebranded the whole company, used the new logo, so that upside down it is North and South Carolina, and our branding has been successful. We outsourced to a local graphic artist and have worked with him for four years. We have the opportunity to be here in Beer City, where people then go home and see us on the grocery shelf in their home towns in local states. Almost tripled sales with retail operations and bottling. We are opening in Charlotte too. It's where we started and so we have to be there. It's our second biggest market without even being there.

3. *Why did craft beer take off like it did?*

It's a craft economy. It's not just beer. People want to support the local craftsmen and have a relationship with them. Try to buy local when we can and we work with local charities to give back. It's symbiotic. This is why western North Carolina is a craft beer destination. People wanted something a little more different; they want something local so they can know the brewer and where the product is made. From a retail point of view, Sierra Nevada and New Belgium help bring in more people and they make us all better, Sierra Nevada says come use our labs, and Oskar Blues helped us with water issues; the packaging operator allowed us to investigate how to purge oxygen by taking apart the machines. Sierra Nevada has offered to sell ingredients to small brewers. We are 140 out of 4,200 and I'm proud of that. Those breweries bring us cachet and give back. I want to learn from them and try to make the industry better. If all goes well, we should be operating in Charlotte in August. We are using the ten-barrel system that we outgrew in Morganton. The thirty-barrel system there now, we get more than a barrel a square foot. The place is sized between 25 and 27, so we have an opportunity to grow and reap the benefits. The ten-barrel system was just sitting so we are now using that; it was meant for Charlotte. Highland Brew company, one we respect a lot, left the tanks in the ground in Asheville, so my brother and I retrieved the tanks. Tall, thin thirty-barrel tanks. We also got more equipment that was original from a Charlotte-based brew system and we also buy equipment posted on Craigslist.

4. *How would your employees describe Catawba?*

It relates to our mission statement. Our role is to educate. Make great beers year round and educate people, make our community better, and create jobs. Collaboration brews are low on our list because we have so much going on. Collaborations have been done with non-beer companies like a kayak company, Diamond Brand Outfitters, a hammock company, and others where we do one-off brews, support charities, and do cross-marketing to promote local ventures.

We tell a story, localize the beer, and share with others. We try to relate the message behind the beer as well, the identifiable label on the front and our story on the back. But it is nothing too eccentric. We aren't looking for edgy, weird, or different. It's not part of our brand.

5. Where do you see yourself in five years?

Our previous business plan was just surpassed, so I think we are back on the treadmill and can surpass the market. I want to see Charlotte open and take on more geography, like South Carolina, Georgia, and Tennessee. I think, philosophically, I just want us to stay relevant and be part of the North Carolina beer scene and continue to be a place to offer opportunities.

6. I heard you say you were expanding? How did you choose Alabama?

Our beers are getting known regionally and about a year ago a distributor asked us to allow them to sell our beers. The more I get to know them I think we can work together; they go to on- and off-premises accounts. They have the tools but not the product and we think we can get them the product and stand behind them.

7. Is that area growing?

Other states are playing catch up, especially with state alcohol laws. North Carolina has good laws and they make it easy to get into business: A bucket and a dream. South Carolina, Virginia, Tennessee, and Georgia are different. North Carolina allows us to make it and sell out. Alabama has made some law changes, but they are able to grow and a few cities are interesting, like Birmingham (cleaning up downtown); they are revitalizing the architecture and area. Huntsville, Mobile, Orange Beach, and Montgomery are going to be good for us; we are going statewide.

8. How do you distribute your beer?

North Carolina allows us to do up to 12,000 barrel self-distribution count. You can have in-state approval without federal approval. If I brew in the state, then I don't need the feds. You can negotiate self-distribution rights for big monies if you are up for it. It cuts down on other costs, like drivers, trucks, bottling, and more. Once you hit more than 5,000 barrels, self-distribution is hard. North Carolina State Brewers Guild works with the state. Craft Brewers are not always aligned with wine sellers in the ABC Commission.

9. *Do you require your employees to try all the beers?*
We don't have a lot of turnover, so that helps. But, our bartenders, sales, and others are well-trained so they can know the product.

10. *Do you have a favorite beer?*
It vacillates. Some of the session beers, like the session IPA made with the kayak flotation company; I like that a lot. But we have some Belgian beers I like a lot too.

11. *Finish this sentence: "I brew because . . ."*
"It gets to our mission statement. I want to create something that gives back, whether it's jobs, community building, or a unique opportunity in an industry that is so much fun. I want to tell our story."

HOW DO I MARKET AND PROMOTE MY BUSINESS?

It may appear easier for large breweries to garner publicity due to their multimillion-dollar budgets and ample resources focused on reaching their consumer base. What about small craft breweries, especially those that are just starting out? How do these organizations create a buzz around their products? This chapter is streamlined for busy brewers who aspire to hit the ground running with their public relations and marketing promotional efforts. Consider it a "Cliffs Notes" guide for craft brewers on how to best connect with consumers by increasing their visibility with public relations and marketing strategies that are smart and simple.

Next is a mini case study of a project conducted for Old Chicago Pizza and Taproom by Fish Consulting, a public relations firm.[1]

Old Chicago offers a unique selection of craft beer selections, and a World Beer Tour that rewards members for enjoying 110 of its best craft beers from across the globe. While popular among brand loyalists, Old Chicago Pizza & Taproom's craft beer selection and special offerings aren't widely known. Fish was tasked with promoting its Explorer Beer Series, which features one brewery and four to six beers for a two- to three-week period, nationally and in key U.S. markets.

Solution

Fish developed a national and local media relations campaign that focused on the unique aspects of Old Chicago's Explorer Beer Series and the brand's specific collaboration with Left Hand Brewery out of Longmont, Colo. The distinctive coffee pale ale, which World Beer Tour members helped create, was the centerpiece of the media relations campaign to drive consumer traffic that featured a national press release, customizable templates, breakthrough pitches and strategic taste tests for targeted food and beverage editors across the country. Fish specifically focused on target markets in Arizona, Colorado, Iowa, Illinois, Indiana, Kansas, Kentucky, Missouri, North Carolina, Oklahoma, Tennessee and Texas.

Results

As a result of our pitching efforts and tastings, Fish secured more than 30 stories resulting in more than 72 million impressions. Craftworks saw a spike in same store sales numbers during Fish's engagement on the project. The client also attributed a surge in Explorer Beer Series tastings to Fish's efforts during that same time frame. The level of detail provided, uniqueness of the offering and the wide net Fish cast resulted in considerable media coverage from local newspapers to national websites and television; which all helped drive traffic into the restaurants and interest in the brand.

The Communications Plan

Effective promotional strategies begin with the creation of a communications plan comprised of both marketing and public relations. Communications plans identify the goals, messaging, strategy, and tactics of any business. However, before you can sit down and create a plan, you must conduct some research. Research, when executed properly, can eliminate bias and give a realistic picture of how various stakeholders of the public perceive your company.[4] Consider this: If you were to rely solely on your own biased opinions of how the public views your beer, then you might risk not knowing how

---

Difference between Public Relations and Marketing

Public Relations: Public relations is a strategic communication process that builds mutually beneficial relationships between organizations and their publics.[2]

Marketing: Marketing is the activity, set of institutions, and processes for creating, communicating, delivering, and exchanging offerings that have value for customers, clients, partners, and society at large.[3]

to appropriately connect with your audience or what they want from your small brewery. The findings from your research will allow you to formulate marketing solutions for any identified challenges and weaknesses that were revealed. Additionally, based on your findings, you can also identify various opportunities for the company to grow and build brand awareness. Through the utilization of sound strategies and tactics, an overarching communication plan can effectively meet core organizational objectives.

Writing the Communications Plan

The following planning model provides a simple template that helps to create a comprehensive public relations and marketing plan by aligning the outcomes directly with important organizational goals. The idea of incorporating social media within a business strategy is something that requires a large investment in planning, support, and execution. The written communication plan, which should include both public relations and marketing strategies, becomes a tangible driver for new leads and provides a platform for customers to participate in important conversations related to the brands that are important to them.[5]

Following the ROSTIR model—*R*esearch, *O*bjectives, *S*trategies, *T*actics, *I*mplementation, and *R*eporting[6]—readers are provided a guide to support the creation of a full communications plan of their own.

Research

The first phase of any public relations and marketing planning process involves identifying and learning about three key elements:

1. The client—for whom the program is being prepared

2. The opportunity or the problem—why the client needs the program at this moment

3. The audiences—who are targeted for communication in the PR program

Within this first phase, it is necessary to state why you have developed a communications strategy and what you hope to achieve with it. For example:

"This communications strategy shows how effective public relations and marketing can:

- help us achieve our overall objectives;
- engage effectively with patrons;
- ensure people understand the quality of our products."[7]

Briefly outline some interesting points about your brewery, types of beer brewed, where you are located, and where people might find your beer.

Part of the research process is to perform a SWOT analysis on your company, which involves listing your organization's strengths, weaknesses, opportunities, and threats. Think about what this means in terms of your communications priorities. How can threats be turned into opportunities, and how can you play on your strengths through effective communications? Another useful tool when assessing your current situation is to look at what your competitors are doing (competitive analysis). This can be a relatively simple exercise where you identify your main competitors and rank them against certain criteria.

Objectives and Goals

In this section you should understand your organization's overall vision and tie that to your core objectives. Objectives should be written in quantifiable, measurable terms that allow the result to be easily compared against the goals set forth. Professionals use the "SMART" method when developing objectives:[8]

S—specific, significant, stretching
M—measurable, meaningful, motivational
A—agreed-upon, attainable, achievable, acceptable, action-oriented
R—realistic, relevant, reasonable, rewarding, results-oriented
T—time-based, time-bound, timely, tangible, trackable

For example, a set of goals and objectives for a small brewery may look like this:

Goals:

1. To raise awareness of our craft beer offerings across targeted publics and influencers within the craft beer industry.

2. To develop effective media relationships within our region.

3. To develop and implement a strategic way to communicate with audiences through planned internal and external events.

Objectives:

1. To increase to the extent of public awareness of the brewery's core flavors by 75 percent through Q3 (Quarter three).

2. To produce monthly events to create a favorable attitude among more than 50 percent of potential craft beer consumers of the news, events, and activities within X brewery over one year.

3. Garner five media placements over a six-month time frame to provide the public with in-depth information about our craft beer products.

Strategies and Tactics

Strategies and tactics work together, but have different purposes. Strategies identify what you can do to fulfill an objective, and include the channel(s) through which messages will be sent to motivate a particular action. Strategies are the big-picture choices made to utilize specific channels. The strategy focuses on achieving the objectives. Describe how and why various campaign components will accomplish the overall goals. Multiple strategies may be required to ensure you reach your overarching business objectives.[9] Tactics, on the other hand, are the tangible elements used to execute the objectives and strategies. Some tactics include media placement through media relations, videos, social media, special events, blogs, websites, and infographics. The following options serve as a sampling of some of the easier-to-implement tactics commonly adopted by small businesses.

Media Relations

Media relations is not a one-size-fits-all strategy; targeted media outreach needs to be adapted specifically to your goals and objectives. Your media relations strategy will depend on what you want to accomplish.[10] Are you launching a new line of flavors for fall? How about sharing the news of a brand new location opening? Or maybe you've just won the Best Craft Beer Award? In each of these examples the strategies would be much different.

When looking to achieve media placements, the most common tool used is a press release. This is a type of communication is directed at the media to announce a new product, partnership, event, or other newsworthy item. Oftentimes editors, reporters, journalists, and bloggers depend on press releases to alert them to new and interesting products, trends, and changes in a community's business landscape.

Here are a few achievements that are considered newsworthy:[11]

- Grand opening for businesses just starting out;

- New product offering—new flavors, seasonal flavors, pairings with food;

- New website;

- Launching a blog;

- Joint venture with another brewer, restaurant, or community partner;

- Events such as food pairings, festivals, or sponsorships;

- Corporate philanthropy—volunteer work or donations to community partners; or

- Brewery Milestones—customers served and years in business.

When a press release is properly used, it is an excellent way to promote your business. Whenever something newsworthy happens, make sure the local news outlets receive the announcement. In addition to sending your release to local media, use online communities to your advantage. Businesses live in an online, 24/7 world. Ensure that you post all of your press releases to your website because this will increase the likelihood of users finding your news and site when searching for the type of product you provide.

Community Events and Sponsorships

Craft beer brands are one conversation at a time. That is why a critical component of any public relations and marketing plan should include community events and sponsorships. Participating in community events or sponsoring an event should be used to achieve a specific public relations purpose. Community events and sponsorships give companies a platform from which they can increase sales and achieve higher corporate visibility. These types of external relations can improve the bottom line of the brand by allowing the consumer's mind to form a link between the event they are attending and those sponsoring the event. Beer festivals, on-site promotions, off-premises hand-sells, and social media are all opportunities to engage in conversations. Plus, community events and sponsorships can also be featured on your website for potential customers to read.

Social Media

Use of social media is an incredibly powerful tactic to employ because it allows small breweries to discuss core messages that you tell in person at your brewpub, beer dinners, and beer festivals with thousands of people daily.[12] Here are three easy to implement social media strategies from Gerry Moran:[13]

1. Use a hashtag to promote your craft beer bar. Your craft beer bar needs to use the language your social media–using beer drinkers are using. Hashtags unify conversations on Twitter and Instagram. Use them to share information, but also to communicate with your audience.

2. Pictures say a thousand words. Establish an Instagram account and get your customers to take pictures, and post Instagram photos to evangelize your craft beer bar.

3. Post your daily tap list on Facebook. Customers want to know what you have for sale. People want to visit your business if you have what they want. Craft beer drinkers always want to know what your current tap list and on-deck list looks like. A great craft beer marketing idea is to post your daily tap list to help increase customers coming through your door, spending more, and then getting them to return quicker than planned.

If beer brands hope to engage consumers, they have to adopt a social media strategy that ensures they'll stand out. Just look at the ingenuity of Great Lakes Brewing Company as they conceived and executed a brand refresh, using social media as the go-to tool to promote its new look. "Regionally—and especially locally—this is a beloved cult brand with a really loyal following. Branding is a sensitive area, and using videos on social media allowed us to walk fans through the changes in a fun and approachable way and let them know we respect the brand's story."[14] Brokaw, an independent, strategic-creative-media-digital agency, worked with Favorite Brother to produce a series of social videos that explained the company's origins and the evolution of the brand's labeling, which were posted on Vimeo and Facebook. Using an unpaid approach with the videos and sharing them with their followers as a fun complement to a larger digital campaign, the effort successfully increased site traffic and increased social engagement. For Great Lakes Brewing, Facebook and Instagram are the social sites with the most value, the former for its targeting capabilities and the latter to visually communicate brand imagery to consumers. Twitter is used to gather "valuable feedback on flavor and quality." As social media is handled both by the brand and its agency, with regional sales people also posting on the brand's behalf, Brokaw developed a social media playbook for use by all. Beyond staying consistent, the lesson for beer brands is this: Social media content must be exclusive, distinctive, and have substance. In this industry, there's no room for bad form.

Online Event Calendars

Take advantage of online event calendars. Not only can they disseminate your event to a wide audience, they are typically free. For example, if you are taking part in a local summer festival, post the details on calendars in the local newspaper, radio, TV, chamber of commerce, and other community websites. This is a great opportunity for free exposure, wider visibility, and a potential for increased attendance at the event.

Contributed Articles

Contributed articles speak about a particular subject, and are generally written by someone in your organization. They tend to not be product specific, and as the author of the piece, you will gain credibility as an expert in your industry. For example, you may pen an article about how your brewery is experimenting with nitrogenated beer techniques and submit it to a relevant trade publication. To determine if a particular publication accepts contributed articles, review its media kit or contact an editor to find out.

Award Opportunities

National and local award opportunities are an excellent way to gain and sustain credibility within your field. Whether the award is company based, such as a best place to work, or product based, such as the best craft beer in the world given by World Beer Award, this is a great news announcement and also an opportunity to establish you as a leader in the industry. Award achievements are newsworthy so be sure to share this news with local media, customers, and associates, as well as featuring it on your website.

Implementation

Now that the plan is in place and goals, objectives, strategies, and tactics have been appropriately aligned, it is time to create a realistic timeline to implement the plan. Work with others on your team to assign deliverable dates to the tactics. Creating a timeline for the brewery's public relations campaign(s) and marketing plan allows you to determine when each stage of the campaign will be completed and how long each stage should take you to complete.[15]

Reporting

Finally, think about how you will know if you've executed on your plan successfully. Reporting, also referred to as evaluation, connects directly to the stated objectives. In this phase you want to examine whether or not there were certain metrics you achieved; media outlets you were featured in; or increases in sales within a certain number of months after the campaign. By understanding what success means to your brewery, reporting and evaluating the overarching campaign will be much easier.

The Importance of Public Relations and Marketing

Public relations and marketing are ongoing processes. They are not something you can do once and forget about. To be successful, you must keep on top of what's going on in your business and continue to build long-lasting relationships that establish your craft brewery while also getting your message out.

Now that you have gotten some of the promotional aspects under your belt, refill your beer and read this "Talking from the Tap" from one communications specialist in the industry. Cheers!

Talking from the Tap!

Susanne Hackett,[16] Community and Media Relations Specialist,
New Belgium Brewery, Asheville, North Carolina

1. *How did you get into the business?*

I am a consultant with community-minded businesses and collaborations here in Asheville, so New Belgium sought me out. I like that workers and visitors can bike and walk to us, and we are built along the water on eighteen acres. The location makes it look big. While I don't have a background in beer, I am quite interested in businesses that want to connect with the community and the world.

I was hired full time in 2014 after being part time for about a year. There is also some "make your own job" here; if you do something that benefits the business, New Belgium may open new positions. Community and Media Relations started as a challenge for me. People were concerned about trucks on the roadways and a connection to the place (Asheville) and its history, so we have become a repository for the history and place via videos where we honor this place. We also have a leaders roundtable where we meet with business leaders and the community to find solutions. For example, we were able to lease shorter trucks to keep them off of Main Street and that was appreciated. New Belgium is a place; it's not just a property. It has created a lot of opportunities to face-to-face with community to host conversation and build community partners—it takes a village!

2. *Where do you get grains, equipment, and more?*

We work with suppliers through Fort Collins, but we definitely consider environmental footprint as much as possible, such as local hops for smaller batch brews. A sustainability team works with local suppliers. But where it concerns needed quantity small farms can't handle the load. We built a Western North Carolina Communities nonprofit. The nonprofit created the brewer's grain alliance to sell at a reduced cost.

3. *Why did New Belgium see an Asheville expansion?*

The capacity in Fort Collins was becoming a problem, so we were going to build in California, but carbon footprint and opportunities for employees and the company were a concern, like the water source and finding a place where employees can live, work, and play. Asheville won out.

4. *Do you do collaborations with local brewers?*

Some. We started an initiative with Highland Brewery here to focus on greenways and improvements and then we opened it to others. We will work with The Wedge (brewery) next, across the way. We also work with Ben and Jerry's on a larger scale and seek collaborations around nonprofits. New Belgium also ensures that workers receive at least a living wage, profit sharing, and benefits. There is a lot of giving in the brewing community.

We lean on each other to grow the industry. We have only about 15 percent of the share in beer. Quality is a necessity, and sharing what we learn with others; we help smaller breweries in our lab or our brewmaster helps other breweries in the area. But the industry is competitive too.

Initially, members of the Asheville Brewers Alliance were concerned because of Oskar Blues, Sierra Nevada, and us moving into the region. But we work with breweries to align with how we are giving and who we are giving to. Our focus is really: How can we do the best for our community?

We have needed a bit more than entry-level positions to get started here, but we have a lot of people from the area working here, about one hundred right now; we also hope to have interns from local college programs here, as we do in Fort Collins.

5. *What has been your biggest challenge in the industry?*

Learning; brewing is a lot of chemistry and there are nuances of brewing. How do you keep from messing it up? I've been part of panels too and that has helped.

6. *What is the panel you refer to here?*

Expert taste panels where we assess whether the beer is acceptable to the brand. We work with the process from the maturation vessel through packaging.

7. *What advice can you give to others who will be working in positions similar to yours?*

Be clear on message: "Who are you?" and "What are your values?" are so important. Find a fun way to share them. Recognize that beer is a connector and you can do good things when you bring people together. Make sure you know what you do well! Be authentic. Make sure you know the people you are talking to; they aren't dumb so don't dumb it down. People are smart and interested.

8. *Where do you think women are in the industry?*

Strong female leaders and founders here at New Belgium, but a balance of masculine and feminine characteristics is needed to be a good leader. But women have better palettes and a different thinking process. The craft brewing industry has to improve its diversity on many levels.

9. *Where do you see yourself in five to ten years?*

This is a family friendly company. I'm excited for the next twenty-five years. I think we will have to consider new ways to communicate and innovate in the industry. We must broaden our reach, but also try to maintain the family local feel; not all industries or breweries have that feel. Our leadership creates that environment and work hard to do that too.

10. *Do you anticipate any changes in this region in the next two months?*

We feel like we are part of the community, not the new guy. People are learning how we can really help and not just hitting us up for everything. Just when we think Asheville has its last brewery to open, another one opens. But, saturation may lead to some breweries closing due to educated consumers seeking quality. New Belgium is a neighborhood hangout and people don't often come to get drunk or tipsy. Many more people come to enjoy the beer and atmosphere, with their families, children included.

11. *Finish this sentence for us: "I enjoy the brewing industry because . . ."*

". . . there is never a dull moment. You can talk about saving prairie dogs on the land one day, trucks the next day, a new beer another, and more. Innovation drives this experience. And, craft brewing is becoming cross-generational. I can drink a six pack of New Belgium Fat Tire with my dad and we can both enjoy it."

I THINK I'M A PEOPLE PERSON
How Do I Manage a Small Business?

> The future of craft beer depends on educated and enthusiastic advocates.
>
> —The Brewers Association's Guide to American Craft Beer

The Art of Small Business Management

Most small business owners will agree that the secret to success is assembling a good team that fully embraces the company philosophy, culture, and values. The individuals that work for you and represent your brewery and brand are paramount to the success you will achieve. This chapter focuses on sound principles for building a strong team, developing your brewery's culture and philosophy, and managing crisis situations.

People First

Businesses need employees, so hiring the right talent and coaching them to do their best pays off. It is not possible do everything by yourself. Finding and selecting the best people should be a priority for any small business owner; especially valuable are those who care as much about what they are doing and are willing to work toward common goals. "It's not just good beer and food that makes a brewpub a successful one; it's the people who work there, too. They are an integral piece of the puzzle when it comes to creating an experience for a customer. The beer may sell itself, but somebody's got to serve it—and serve it well."[1] And, this is true for all parts of the beer industry. Look for passion in potential employees. Find out what they truly *care* about and what *motivates* them. Skills can be taught, but attitude, initiative, a good work ethic, and personality are innate. When it comes to finding the right candidate, attitude is oftentimes a better gauge than the right set of skills.[2] Someone who is enthusiastic about your brand will do whatever it takes to ensure that your brewery and brand become a success.

Why, you ask? Because a brand is something that gets you noticed in the local, regional, national, and even, international markets. Effective branding can help build your reputation, make you stand out from your competition, and project your values to both your employees and customers.[3] Engaged employees help build strong brands. Building a strong brand requires that employees feel connected to the company culture and understand their role in embodying that culture and sharing with others. One survey firm defines "Employee Engagement" as "a measurable degree of an employee's positive or negative emotional attachment to their job, colleagues and organization that profoundly influences their willingness to learn and perform at work."[4] When employees feel valued they will work harder, personify the company culture, and share that with others.

When you are known as an employer of choice in your industry, it will be much easier to not only find qualified candidates, but to attract good talent.[5] Devon Hamilton,[6] of Paradox Brewery in the Adirondacks, chatted up his current employer while cleaning tanks and doing other lower-level jobs for another local brewer. When Paradox needed a brewer, Devon was courted for the position, and neither party has regrets. People are drawn to companies that take care of their employees. Having a competitive compensation package with benefits, flexible schedule to support a good work-life balance, and available training opportunities are some of the initial steps businesses can take to attract and retain good employees. For example, Susanne Hackett[7] of New Belgium Brewing noted that when her company was seeking employees for their East Coast establishment in Asheville, North Carolina, it emphasized the importance of a living wage for its employees, and she found that the company feels like family; whether in North Carolina or Colorado, the company's mission and employee focus are primary. There are many other factors that go into being an employer whose reputation precedes it. Employees want:[8]

- To work in a positive atmosphere. Positivity and passion for the product and the company should be exuded at all levels and from all employees, including waitstaff, fermentation tank maintenance workers, and owners; everyone must stand behind the product and the company for its quality and consistency.

- To serve and represent beer and food of high caliber. No one wants to pay for a poor product or a good product in a negative atmosphere, no matter the price. From visiting food trucks that sustain breweries to the full-blown bar and restaurant, food and drink must maintain quality measures; even if chips or pretzels are available for taprooms or tasting rooms, make sure they aren't stale. Also, ensure that the staff learn the art and craft of a good pour!

- To feel motivated and be part of a skilled service staff. Years ago, bartenders and waitstaff may not have been as well-trained in the beer industry to serve others. A too-foamy topper or a beer without carbonation served by an uninformed novice can harm the brand, especially where craft beers are concerned. From selecting the most appropriate serving glass, presenting the beer to a customer, and even filling growlers, the people who serve the beer must know all of this and more, especially when it comes to knowing about the history and origins of the brew. Arranging tastings for those servers who are of legal drinking age and conducting more formal training for waitstaff in beer and food pairing can further establish the integrity of the brand. You aren't hiring a part-time worker; rather, you are hiring an impassioned and informed member of your company.

- To be part of a happy, energetic, cohesive overall company team. Most of the brewers with whom we spoke agreed that developing a solid team is imperative. Everyone needs to know that no matter what position they hold, what matters is their service to the company and its brand. When people feel connected to a company (feeling more like a family), they are more willing to assist in maintaining the brand and creating that positive work atmosphere; they become stakeholders. There are certainly management approaches that could establish this early on with new employees and sustaining it with current employees.

- A grounded, structured, consistent, and considerate management approach. No matter the approach, consistency with a clear purpose makes a real difference to these stakeholders. Knowing that their voices are valued at weekly employee meetings may be a simple and appropriate start, but they also need to see progress if ideas are valued. Some breweries are simply too big to hold weekly meetings, but there are other ways to connect with these stakeholders. For example, you could create an online company forum where internal stakeholders can make suggestions and comments in an open way. It may also be beneficial to ask stakeholders for suggestions on new recipes in order to further establish open communication among employees.

- Employers' willingness to provide staff members with new skills (otherwise known as continuing education or personal career development). Offering training for those who want to learn more about the brewing business, whether working in the office with the media relations staff or shadowing a head brewer to learn the brewing process, can lead to innovation. Those who feel empowered and want to grow with the company and the industry need to be involved and nurtured to help sustain or grow your brand.

Once you have established a reputation for providing a quality work environment, it will be considerably easier to attract worthwhile candidates for open positions. They might even seek you out for employment!

Robust Job Descriptions

Job descriptions are also an essential part of hiring and managing any employee. These written summaries ensure applicants and employees understand their roles and what they need to do to be successful if hired by your organization. A job description should accurately reflect your needs. Begin with an overview of your company, then include individual tasks involved, the methods used to complete the tasks, the purpose and responsibilities of the job, the relationship of the job to other jobs, and the qualifications needed for the job. Job descriptions typically include:[9]

- Job title

- Job objective or overall purpose statement

- Summary of the general nature and level of the job

- Description of the broad function and scope of the position

- List of duties or tasks performed critical to success

- Key functional and relational responsibilities in order of significance

Description of the relationships and roles within the company, including supervisory positions, subordinating roles, and other working relationships should be somewhat flexible. Jobs change over time as do people. A less rigid job description encourages employees to grow within their position and contribute over time to your overall business objectives.[10] There needs to be clarity in the communication of expectations and responsibilities. As much as we might think things are obvious, they never are. Everyone has different thought processes, and we are all influenced by our own experiences and perceptions. Clear communication alleviates employees' stress when they understand your expectations. Job descriptions help communicate clear expectations from the start.

Through the job description you can also give a glimpse into the culture of your company. The Wild Wolf Brewing Company out of Nellysford, Virginia, included this line in a job description they were hiring for "The right person loves the craft beer industry and will be excited to become a part of a young and growing company,"[11] while Drake's Brewing Company from San Leandro, California wrote, "Do you spend all your free time talking about or thinking about beer? One of the Bay Area's established breweries is looking for an energetic and enthusiastic craft beer lover to join our marketing team and help us to foster engaging experiences. This role is on the front lines of our brand, helping to coordinate and execute our participation in hundreds of community events every year. From working with nonprofit community organizers to setting up festival booths, the Local Events Coordinator should have a tireless enthusiasm for getting customers excited about our brewery one-by-one."[12] The company culture is essentially the DNA of your brewery. It is the glue that binds an organization together and it is the hardest thing for competitors to copy.[13]

Company Culture and Philosophy

You probably already have a company culture, but you may not have it down on paper. If you don't, then take time to put into words the makeup of your brewery. Founders Brewing Company's culture is stated this way, "We don't brew beer for the masses. Instead, our beers are crafted for a chosen few, a small cadre of renegades and rebels who enjoy a beer that pushes the limits of what is commonly accepted as taste. In short, we make beer for people like us."[14] Wiseacre Brewing Co. out of Memphis, Tennessee, personifies a certain company culture and philosophy throughout their website. From the corporate bios—such as, "Andy McQuary: Our resident lollygagger and expert on redneck dentistry is descendent of Scottish sheep thieves"—to lighthearted photos, one can easily get a feel for the type of brewery they are.[15] Understanding and articulating company culture can help ensure a consistently positive working environment.

Winning company cultures are comprised of two connected and supporting elements. First, every high-performing company has a unique identity that includes distinctive characteristics that set it apart from other organizations.[16] These characteristics give employees a sense of meaning just from being part of the company and also create passion for what the company does.

Second, the best-performing companies display a set of attributes that align with the company's strategy and reinforce the right employee behaviors. Some of the most common attributes include being honest, collaborative, innovative, adaptive, accountable, focused, and having drive.[17]

The company culture and philosophy of Catawba Brewing Co. from Glen Alpine, North Carolina, is clearly articulated on their website:

From the sale of our first 5-barrel batch in 1999 to the christening of our new, 30-barrel brew house in 2016, our mission has remained the same:

- Produce drinkable flagship beers of the highest quality.
- Create unique, small-batch beers inspired by our communities, folklore, and lifestyle.
- Service our distributor partner with availability of product and support.
- Educate anyone interested in craft brewing and craft beer.
- Grow a solid business that creates jobs, withstands the inevitable ups and downs of our industry, and actively gives-back to our communities.[18]

Developing a company culture and philosophy can help build a cohesive and productive business that is equipped to handle whatever challenges that may lie ahead.[19] Company culture is not something that can be seen. It is the sense of purpose employees feel, the leadership style that emanates from managers, and the people that make up the brewery—it comprises the most important elements of creating and designing the employee experience.[20]

Training and Support

Proper training and support is essential. Tony Simmons from Pagosa Brewing and Grill says, "server education is crucial for success in brewpubs, breweries, and taprooms. As brewers, we spend countless hours honing recipes, carefully brewing, and cellaring beers to craft that perfect pint. Yet a single inexperienced server or careless dishwasher can ruin that experience for your customer, possibly forever."[21]

In general, most people want to be successful within their profession and they want to do a good job for their employer. Being a respectable coach and mentor to your staff will make them more proficient, confident, and happier. For example, filling a growler may seem easy, but there is a technique one must follow. If an inexperienced staffer doesn't know to start with a chilled growler when necessary, then there may be a loss of product. An experienced staffer knows that as the beer approaches the neck of the growler, it will start to foam and speed up, so it is time to stop the flow and remove the growler. Customers always feel special when they have the opportunity to meet and talk with brewers and owners, yet they are not always available. Bartenders and servers are the face of the company in their communication and interaction with customers and your brand depends on them. Your staff needs the tools, information, and education to be strong advocates for your product, whether in a taproom or tasting room. To address that need, offer server training programs and extra education. Some of the more important areas of server training should include:[22]

- Beer Style Education
- Beer and Food Pairings
- Glassware Cleaning and Draught Pouring

Once the basics are mastered, make work more challenging so employees have the opportunity to stretch and grow.[23] Empowering people to make decisions and take on more responsibility gives them a sense of pride. Your trust in their abilities will help them develop and rise to the occasion. The

Brewers Association offers a free training guide and reference manual that covers everything from hiring, training, and retaining great people.[24]

Say Thank You!

Your staff wants to know that they are appreciated. You can never thank them enough for a job well done.[25] When employees feel a sense of ownership in the business and are treated like partners rather than simply hourly employees, they are motivated to take pride in their work and go the extra mile. Thank-yous can take many forms including, but not limited to, a full growler of beer for those of legal drinking age to a gift certificate for a retail establishment or coffee shop, or even a bonus when one isn't expected. Most of all, uttering the words, "Thank you for your hard work and commitment" to someone within the company at any level can certainly go a long way for maintaining them, and your brand!

Crisis 101 for Small Businesses

One thing we know for certain is that crises arise when least expected and can't be anticipated. Crises can be large (a bad batch of beer was distributed) or an employee may have been involved in some legal offense. Even a bad review of your beer on social media can lead to a crisis. No matter the scenario, all businesses, large or small, must have a crisis communications strategy that all employees are aware of and can implement, *immediately*.

According to Daniel Cherrin, president and managing partner of North Coast Strategies, businesses need a blueprint during a crisis.[26] Particularly for small business, a full crisis plan is not always necessary, but developing a blueprint with the stakeholders to reach out to and the tools and resources available for reaching them is something to consider.

Crisis Management Blueprint

This four-step process to responding to a crisis can help navigate anything from an upset customer to a building fire, or even worse, a gasket failure causing you to lose thousands of gallons of beer. Think it can't happen to you? Think again. Jack's Abby brewing lost thirteen hundred cases of beer after one of their tanks sprung a leak overnight.[27] Imagine coming in to work and literally watching a batch of beer go down the drain. Rather than prepare a plan to anticipate risk and help respond to crisis, it is better to have a blueprint as a guide should a crisis occur.[28]

1. Readiness—Anticipate areas where you are vulnerable

   a. Listen to your constituents and don't be quick to dismiss the agitators.

   b. Leverage social media as a resource to anticipate problems.

   c. If you find an issue, then work diligently to avoid having the issue become a wicked problem.

2. Response—Respond to a crisis. Don't React!

   a. Take control of the situation by responding first, communicating often, remaining empathetic, and sticking to the facts.

      i. Prepare an FAQ to gather your thoughts and watch for key messages to emerge.

      ii. Assure the public that you are doing everything possible to resolve issue.

      iii. Express concern for victims and their families.

      iv. Leverage your website and social media channels for news, information, and sympathy.

   b. Talk only about what you know: Tell the truth and stick to the facts. Correct mistakes or misinformation being reported.

   c. The Value of an Apology: Saying I'm sorry or I was wrong is never an easy thing to do. But in preserving your reputation it can mean everything. We know that no one is perfect. In fact, it is even okay to screw up every now and then. If you do, just admit that you did and are working to restore trust and making positive changes as a result of the experience.

3. Reassurance—Reassure the public that their needs are being adequately addressed by communicating all of the pertinent details.

   a. Address the issues head on:

      i. Focus on the positives.

      ii. Don't be defensive. Don't speculate. Don't share your opinion.

    b. Give frequent updates with new information.

        i. Use the website and social media to provide updates.

        ii. Leave investigative details to the police, attorney general, FBI, or others.

        iii. Focus on safety as your utmost priority.

    c. When a crisis affects people's lives—forget politics.

4. Recovery—Ongoing communication regarding company-wide changes is an important part of demonstrating your organization's responsiveness and continued commitment to making things right.

When managing a crisis, it is important for owners and managers to be confident in their business, employees, and company culture.[29] Create the crisis management blueprint when everything is running smoothly and when you can think clearly. Advance planning allows you to take the time to seriously think about the ideal circumstances to manage various types of crises. Discussions about crises may make you tense, so now is the time to breathe and relax. Fill your glass and enjoy your beer while reading the next "Talking from the Tap." Cheers!

Talking from the Tap!

Interview with Ingrid Alvarez Cherney,[30]
Owner of the High Dive Bar in San Diego, California

1. *What time do you arrive at the bar?*
    Around 8:00 a.m.

2. *What do you have to do?*
    They open at 9:00 a.m. So I deal with issues like servers who call out, conduct inventory, prepare the beer order, set up the bar, and more.

3. *How did you get interested in beer?*
    It's a funny thing. I was a historian, and one of the things I did was to put together a panel and I had to work with a graphic designer whose grandmother owned a bar in San Diego. So we discussed going to dive bars and how there really wasn't a dive bar in San Diego, so we decided to pool resources to open

one. We were an Anheuser-Busch bar to the point where they bought our lines and we had three or four of their handles. We sell their beer for two years for their assistance with the bar. This gentleman came in and told me he had Yellow Tail and that you could get it down the street. So I met the people from Ballast Point and got interested in craft beer. And I learned how influential beer was in society, so I started in beer the opposite way: reading then tasting. I read everything I could about beer and beer history; who was making it and why. Everyone was extremely receptive, and I really wanted to bring craft beer to my bar, but my partners at that time didn't see it as a very lucrative venture. So I broke the beer into ounces and the cost savings with local kegs. They agreed to a six-month trial of all craft beers, and now I own the bar by myself.

4. *So how did you decide on the beers to use at the bar?*
Well, beer is not just beer. If you think about it, when you ask people "What was your first craft beer or what made you want to go into craft beer?" It's more than the beer; it's who you were with at the time. And then I tried many different beers with brewers; it's the environment you're drinking it in. It's like when people talk about the best wine. Well, where was it? At the beach, with friends? So I choose based on taste and stick with friends' beers from the relationships I formed with the sales representative or the brewer; it is not about their "liquid in a box" it should be about the relationships around it.

5. *Is there a camaraderie?*
Some of that is going away as competition grows. Collaboration beers have been going on forever but nobody was talking about it. Now they do. Two types: longtime people are willing to learn from those who have been around, and then there are those who say, "Nope, forget it, I'm doing it my own way." Part of that is sad because there is so much tradition worldwide and that is ignored.

6. *The connection of beer and people is fascinating. How fast is this segment growing and why?*
People want to latch onto something to get away from their daily lives and I think that is what craft beer allows for; people can latch onto it and be part of something. They don't have to be aficionados, but they can belong to a movement. It's a farm-to-table movement, and people are staunch about their breweries. And many times it's not about the beer, it's about their experience with the beer or the brewery and its environment.

Beer has given them a hobby or something to look forward to. But in Austria, which is where I'm from, beer was water. Now it's not about all-day consumption it's about more than that. And, as a bar owner, reps (representatives) come to me to "sell" their beer.

7. What is "Chicks for Beer"?

It was hard for women to get into the business. It was hard to break into a brewery because of the heavy-lifting and other things that many people thought women couldn't handle. But so many women have been so successful and bucked the system. They need a way to work together and support each other; fight the "good ole boys" theme. In my experience, I had a good camaraderie with local folks in the industry. Biggest thing is that Pink Boots Society is for women who are doing anything in the industry, from serving it to brewing it. The frontline women have contact with the audience and promote the beer. Women tend to be more emotional, so we are more likely to tell a story as to why we like a beer. I didn't know the extent to which Pink Boots Society helped all women in the industry until recently, but now I know.

Chicks for Beer was mainly because serving women at my bar I noticed that women didn't want to try the beer. They would come in with their boyfriends or friends and they didn't want to be intimidated if they didn't like it. So I wanted to create a forum to make them feel as comfortable as possible: all women, not impressing anyone, have fun, listen to brewer and more. I wanted to bring craft brews to women so I saw this as an opportunity to introduce them to new experiences. For example, at one food pairing, I started with a lemon bar by having them put a piece in their mouths and swirl it around to get more of the flavor of the bar. This is how I introduced them to beer. Forty-five women attend, it sells out, and brewers share their stories with them. The brewers don't talk so much about the IBUs or hops, but instead focus on the stories because that's what people want to know. Those stories they remember when they see that beer in the future; they can partake in the experience though the emotional connection. People are now doing beer dinners around the country to build similar experiences.

8. Finish this sentence: I like being part of the brewing industry because . . .

"I know the feeling of camaraderie, the friends, the experiences. . . . I like being part of the industry because of the amazing friends I have made! Without beer, I would have never met my husband and others. I like being part of somebody's moment."

Part IV

IMMERSING YOURSELF IN CRAFT BEER CULTURE: IT'S TIME FOR SOME FUN . . . AND BEER!

This is all thousands of years old. It's the same the world over. Anyone who has ever walked upright has loved beer, celebrated over it, told talks over it, hatched plots over it, courted over it. It's what we do as a species. It's what makes us human. We brew.

—Alan Eames

CHAPTER TEN

GETTING FAMILIAR WITH OTHERS IN THE INDUSTRY
More about Learning and Drinking

So far, you've learned about the history and culture of brewing; beer basics; advanced beer basics and science; plus legal, marketing, public relations, and management topics relating to the complex world of craft beer. But, if you think all of this sounds like "too much work," you may simply want to just experience beer as it was meant to be experienced—drinking it!

To help you along, this chapter highlights some local, regional, and national beer events and festivals that may be "just the ticket" you are looking for. Afterward, we provide a sampling of resources and links to some of the best associations, suppliers, breweries, and the like to contact if you want to move beyond only drinking the product. We also highly recommend reading the materials included in the bibliography and visiting as many breweries as possible.

Partaking in the Product and Networking in the Industry

Next is a brief sampling of craft beer and brewing resources and events available to anyone that is interested.

National Beer Festival

The most widely known and popular national festival is the *Great American Beer Festival*[1] held each year in Colorado. Why Colorado? Well, beer has been a staple of this state for decades and it is home to many brewers, breweries, and festivals. Each year, come October, upward of fifty thousand people make the trek to enjoy great beer, good company, and lively music. With over six hundred breweries and thousands of beers to sample, get your tickets early as this event tends to sell out quickly. October 2016 celebrated the thirty-seventh annual festival, and there will be many more to follow. With seminars, entertainment, food pairings, and more, it is a week full of splendid events for the novice, expert, and everyone in between. In addition to this festival, there are also many regional and local beer festivals.

Regional beer festivals include:

- Arizona's Premiere Canned Craft Beer Fest[2]
- Beer City Festival[3]
- Beer City Spring Fest[4]
- California Festival of Beers[5]
- Great Beer Expo[6]
- Oregon Brewers Festival[7]
- Quad State Beer Festival[8]
- San Diego International Beer Fest[9]
- Six One Pour[10]
- Southern Brewers Festival[11]
- TAP-NY Craft Beer and Food Festival[12]
- Vermont Brewers Festival[13]
- Yellowstone Beer Fest[14]

Local beer festivals across the nation:

- Boulder Craft Beer Festival[15]
- Capital Region Craft Trail Event, "Drink Albany"—Albany, New York, October 2016[16]
- Mid-Valley Brew Fest[17]

- Mountain True Winter Warmer Beer Fest[18]

- Palm Beach Winter Beer Fest[19]

- River Bend Brew Fest[20]

- San Diego Winter Brew Fest[21]

- Saratoga Beer Week[22]

- Winter Beer Festival[23]

If you are interested in more than a sample in a celebratory environment, consider trying one of the following beer conferences or events, many sponsored by a variety of professional beer associations, or pick up a newspaper or magazine, listen to a podcast, watch a DVD, or use some Internet sites, listservs, or social media apps.

Beer Conferences and Events

From local food pairings to national discussions of industry trends, there are many beer events that you can attend to learn more; and drinking beer doesn't have to be a priority. One example is the National Homebrewer's Conference[24] held in June each year (it also showcases homebrews in its Homebrew Competition[25]). Here, novice and experienced homebrewers gather to discuss topics such as the basics for building your own Kegerator or Keezer, understanding malt, and countless other learning opportunities.

Another example is Homebrew Day[26] which occurs simultaneously across the nation and encourages beer drinkers to create and sample their own homebrew creations. Mark your calendars for early May to participate in this event. Google can also surprise you with other simultaneous events and celebrations across the nation and around the world.

Want another specific option that happens to fall in May as well? Try American Craft Beer Week,[27] where craft beer drinkers are encouraged to imbibe craft beers from their local scenes and then partake in a toast on Thursday evening where everyone raises a glass to celebrate the growth and possibilities for the industry.

Prefer April? Try the Craft Brewers Conference[28] and Brew Expo America.[29] Each year the Brewers Association holds this conference in a different location. In 2016, Philadelphia was the host city for the conference; "let freedom ring" resonated for those interested in all things homebrewing![30]

In addition to these events and conferences, there are plenty of opportunities for digital networking, print outreach, and in-person gatherings focused on education in more social settings. Associations, newspapers, magazines, podcasts, and more allow us to take our learning on-the-go.

Associations

- American Homebrewers Association[31] (about two thousand clubs in the United States)
- Beer Judge Certification Program[32]
- Brewers Association[33]
- Master Brewers Association[34]
- New York Beer Association[35] (see individual states [at Brew-Wiki[36]])
- Pink Boots Society[37]

Newspapers and Magazines—Top 10 subscriptions as reported by Cision[38]

1. *DRAFT Magazine*[39]—167,571
2. *Ale Street News*[40]—85,000
3. *Northwest Brewing News*[41]—60,000
4. *The Celebrator Beer News*[42]—55,000
5. *Great Lakes Brewing News*[43]—50,000
6. *Yankee Brew News*[44]—50,000
7. *Brew Your Own*[45]—50,000
8. *BeerAdvocate*[46]—45,000
9. *Beer West Magazine*[47]—40,000
10. *Rocky Mountain Brewing News*[48]—40,000

Podcasts/CD-ROMs/Videos/Websites

- Sam Calagione's *Brewmasters* DVD[49]
- "7 Beer Podcasts for Hibernating"[50]

- Basic Brewing Radio[51]
- Craft Beer Radio[52]
- "Experimental Brewing"[53]
- "Good Beer Hunting"[54]—podcast
- "The Beer Hunter" by Michael Jackson[55]
- "The Best Beer Podcasts in iTunes"[56]
- The Brewing Network[57]

Related Websites and Listservs

- Beer Advocate[58]
- Brewer's Friend[59]
- Chicago Beer Society[60]—CBS-HB (listserv)
- craftbrewenvirolistserv-subscribe@yahoogroups.com[61]
- Home Brew Digest[62]—e-mail listserv
- HOPS Listserv[63]
- Realbeer[64]
- RateBeer[65]

If you are overstimulated by the sheer number of beer media and networking opportunities, then perhaps you should research the cost of your own brew setup. Try these resources for assistance:

Online Suppliers

- American Beer Equipment[66]
- Brewmasters Warehouse[67]
- Midwest Supplies[68]
- MoreBeer![69]
- Northern Brewer Supply Company[70]

- Rebel Brewer Home Brewing[71]

- Williams Brewing[72]

Okay, you've really had enough research and learning for now. Why not take a break with a favorite local beer at home or better yet, visit a local brewery. Perhaps a new one-off beer or collaboration brew is on tap, or may be available in growlers, growlets, crowlers, cans, or bottles. Here are some breweries we have visited over the past year, some more than once, so begin your beer adventure today.

Breweries

With over four thousand breweries in the mix in the United States alone, here are a few that we visited: Adirondack Brewing (NY), C.H. Evans Brewing Company (NY), Canton Brewing (MI), Catawba Brewing Company (NC), Davidson Brothers Brewing (NY), Founders Brewing Company (MI), Helderberg Mountain Brewing Company (NY), Honey Hollow Brewing (NY), Hudson Brewing Company (NY), New Belgium Brewing (NC), Old Claverack Brewery (NY), Paradox Brewery (NY), Rareform Brewery (NY), Sierra Nevada (NC), Treehouse Brewing (MA), and Wolf Hollow Brewing (NY). Additionally, we interviewed a number of brewers for this book but couldn't visit them all. Breweries included, but were not limited to, Left Hand Brewing (CA), Stone Brewing (CA) and Ballast Point (CA); and, those we want to visit in the future, such as Brooklyn Brewery (NY), Rogue Ales and Spirits (OR), Lawsons (VT), and many others across the nation. To remind us of all the places we have been and the beers we may have been drinking, we use social media platforms and apps to network and record our journeys.

So, while you are out pursuing new breweries and beers, use your smartphone to broaden your beer travel experience. The following is a brief list of some popular apps for beer lovers and learners.

Smartphone Apps

- Any Beer ABV[73]

- Beer?![74]

- Beer Menu[75]

- BJCP (Beer Judge Certification Program)[76]
- Brew Guru[77]
- Brewery Maps[78]
- iBrewmaster[79]
- My Beer Nation[80]
- Next Glass[81]
- Pintley[82]
- SipSnapp[83]
- Untappd[84]

Now that you have been visiting breweries and researching beer-related interests, including hop growing to starting your own brewery, perhaps you would like to enhance your knowledge base in a more formal "educational" environment. If so, then before diving in too deep, limit the monetary risks by engaging in a bit more beer tourism and consider experiencing weekend getaways, beer camps, earned college certificates, and more.

"Hangin' with Those in the Know"

Beer Tourism

- "10 Best Craft Beer Destinations"[85]
- "America's 20 Best Cities for Beer"[86]
- America's Best Beercations[87]
- "Beer Tourism"[88]
- Craft Beer Trails (check the Brewers Association[89] for details in your state).
- Google "Beer Tourism in _____" for tours and more.
- The Duluth Experience[90]

Weekend Getaways

- Bed & Brew with Brewery Ommegang[91]
- New England Inns and Resorts[92]
- Vermont Bed & Brew[93]

Beer Camps, Courses, and Programs

- American Brewer's Guild[94]
- Craft Brewer's Apprenticeship[95]
- Siebel Institute[96]
- Sierra Nevada Beer Camp[97]
- University of Vermont—Apprenticeships[98]
- UC-Davis's 10-Week Apprenticeship with the Brewers Guild[99]

University Affiliated Brewing Programs in the United States as of October 2016:[100]

- Appalachian State University: Brewing Short Course, Boone, NC[101]

- Auburn University Graduate Certificate: Brewing Science & Operations, Auburn, AL[102]

- California State Polytechnic University Pomona: Brewer's Certificate, Pomona, CA;[103] E-mail: ceuinfo@cpp.edu

- Central Michigan University: Certificate of Fermentation Science, Mount Pleasant, MI;[104] E-mail: cst@cmich.edu

- Central New Mexico Community College: Brewing and Beverage Management, Albuquerque, NM;[105] E-mail: ttorres57@cnm.edu

- Central Washington University: Craft Brewing Certificate, Ellensburg, WA;[106] E-mail: KuntzM@cwu.edu

- Colorado State University: BS in Fermentation Science and Technology, Fort Collins, CO;[107] E-mail: jeffrey.callaway@colo state.edu

- Craft Beverage Institute of the Southeast at Asheville-Buncombe Technical Community College: Brewing, Distillation, and Fermentation A.A.S. Degree Asheville, NC;[108] E-mail: jef freymirvin@abtech.edu

- Eastern Michigan University: Fermentation Science, Ypsilanti, MI;[109] E-mail: cemal@emich.edu

- Kalamazoo Valley Community College: Sustainable Brewing, Kalamazoo, MI;[110] E-mail: phogg@kvcc.edu

- Metropolitan State University of Denver: Bachelor of Science in Brewery or Brewpub Operations, Denver, CO;[111] E-mail: skerk man@msudenver.edu

- Oregon State University: Four Year Program in Fermentation Science, Corvallis, OR;[112] E-mail: linda.dunn@oregonstate.edu

- Regis University: Certificate in Applied Craft Brewing, Denver, CO;[113] E-mail: ruadmissions@regis.edu

- Schoolcraft College: Brewing and Distillation Technology, Livonia, MI;[114] E-mail: sfrader@schoolcraft.edu

- South College: Certificate in Professional Brewing Science (North Carolina), Asheville, NC;[115] E-mail: dwalsh@southcollegenc.edu

- South College: Certificate in Professional Brewing Science (Tennessee), Knoxville, TN;[116] E-mail: twhite@southcollegetn.edu

- Southern Illinois University: Fermentation Science, Carbondale, IL;[117] E-mail: mmccarroll@siu.edu

- UC Davis Extension Davis, CA; website: Extension.UCDavis. edu/brew; E-mail: extension@ucdavis.edu

- UC Davis: Department of Food Science and Technology Davis, CA; website: Faculty.bftv.ucdavis.edu/fst/Bamforth; E-mail: cwbamforth@ucdavis.edu

- UC San Diego Extension: Professional Certificate in Brewing, La Jolla, CA;[118] E-mail: brewing@ucsd.edu

- University of the Sciences: Brewing Science Certificate, Philadelphia, PA;[119] E-mail: m.farber@usciences.edu

- University of Wisconsin Stevens Point: Microbiology for Brewers, Stevens Point, WI;[120] E-mail: spech@uwsp.edu

- Western Kentucky University: Undergraduate and Graduate Certificate in Brewing and Distilling Arts and Sciences, Bowling Green, KY;[121] E-mail: andrew.mcmichael@wku.edu

Since 2015, the following New York–based programs have been developed at the college/university level. Keep an eye out for new opportunities in your neck of the woods:

- Cornell University[122]

- Culinary Institute of America, Hyde Park (CIA)[123]

- Draft Beer Quality Certification Program[124]

- Erie Community College in Buffalo, New York[125]

- Paul Smith's College[126]

- Schenectady County Community College[127]

Auxiliary Programs—Food Pairing

- Beer and Food Course, Brewers Association[128]

- "Chicks for Beer" (Ingrid Alvarez Cherney, owner of High Dive Bar, San Diego).[129]

- Craft Beer and Food Course[130]

As you can tell, there are countless opportunities to learn, develop, and drink in the craft beer industry. We hope that the information provided in this book will assist you in getting involved in the craft beer culture in some way. So, refill your beer and then try brewing one of the recipes included in our last chapter! But first, read the next "Talking from the Tap" with a social media guru. Cheers!

Talking from the Tap!

Erin Peters,[131] @TheBeer Goddess (Twitter), Beer Blogger, and Digital Marketing Specialist

1. *What's your background with beer?*

I was interested in cooking and culinary arts in high school in Thousand Oaks and then went to SDSU in 1992, where I took classes in public relations and marketing. Then Stone Brewing popped up like 1996 or so. I was drawn to it on the marketing side and then beer side with all the breweries around I got interested in Arrogant Bastard and others. Then I moved to Redondo Beach and came back to Simi Valley and LA then started the blog. I was doing a lot of driving and interviewing at breweries and with beer masters, and now I am settled in Palm Springs. My ex-boyfriend encouraged me to start writing about beer and then I researched blogging, and beer blogging was my focus. Throughout the years I have made a lot of great contacts and they are all humble and kind, so that is why I love the history and people help each other out.

2. *How did you get your title of "Beer Goddess"?*

I felt like I had to grow into that. A couple of friends used that moniker with me then I researched its availability and bought the domain. Then I expanded into festivals and breweries in person and on other social media.

3. *How do you drive traffic to your blog?*

Well, I moved around a lot, I haven't focused solely on one area, which is good and bad. The "brew local" moniker is great. When I moved to Palm Springs there was only one brewery here. Then, two more popped up within eight months in Coachella Valley. It's not always quantity over quality. I'll drive to Thousand Oaks and Ventura to meet family and get involved in the Southern California area. Put out new and interesting things, not just evaluating a beer on the blog. Google is about quality content, so the more engaging the content the more traffic you get.

4. *What is your perception of women in the beer industry?*

Comparatively, it's male-dominated and will be for a while but there are some amazing women, like Tree Weavers in Englewood, California. While the industry is largely male dominated, many more women are opening their own breweries and becoming brewmasters. Completely female owned, award winning, and I have had the pleasure of meeting so many women who I look up to. While it is becoming more common to have women involved, some beer companies are now trying to market to women, who also love beer, but they do so in ways that may not always be about the quality of that beer. It can be disappointing when they market beer to women rather than marketing good beer to everyone. It leads to good discussion about making good beer; not all women like light beer.

5. *Is there a craft beer culture?*

For me it boils down to the people in the industry—brewers, beer drinkers, and other workers; it helps our economy and is very collaborative. Breweries are collaborative since the industry is changing and evolving. Always a new innovative, fun, collaborative culture where people work with both sides of the brain—creative and scientific. It's a revolution of sorts.

6. *Why did craft brewing take off these past few years?*

It was a revolution with economy and politics; voting for the little guy, keeping local, making something with your hand, crafting something from nothing, fighting bigger beer companies and their control of the market share. I like helping the local economy and people need help making it. It's also about the experience and the quality. In the 1990s I was just sipping and trying but with more research, you learn that people are just so amazing. It makes me teary-eyed.

7. *Do you have a favorite brew?*

There are so many. It depends on my mood, time of year, what I'm eating, and the weather. When I lived in Big Bear, I created Stout Day because it was snowing outside and I wanted a heavier beer. In the hot weather I drink more IPAs, fruit beers, and sours.

8. *What learning opportunities exist for those who want to know more about craft beer or brewing?*

San Diego State University (SDSU) and University of California-Davis are two well-known places to hone your skills and knowledge. Boot camps are available too. So, those who want to learn more about the industry can seek programs in their state, go to festivals, and read beer books and beer blogs to keep up to date and make contacts; collaboration is key to learning more.

9. *Finish this sentence: "I like the craft beer industry because . . ."*

"[t]hese are the kind of people I want to hang out with for the rest of my life!"

READY, SET, BREW!
Enough Networking, Let's Get Down to Brewing: Six Recipes

W hile there are many wonderful recipes available to you, we have chosen six to get you started. We hope that you enjoy these, others, and especially, your own, in the years to come!

Helderberg Mountain Brewing Company (Original: ESB)—Mike Wenzel,[1] Head Brewer

I have a simple recipe that we always used to brew over the years. It is an English Special Bitter (ESB). This beer is an easy drinking ESB that highlights the English hop varieties Willamette and East Kent Goldings. It also uses Maris Otter malt for a little more of that bready or toasty flavor that comes through as well. The beer finishes around at around 5 percent ABV. The beer won first place in the New Jersey State Fair Homebrew Competition in the English Pale Ale category in 2007 and 2013.[2] The challenging aspect of brewing this beer is that there is nothing there to hide any flaws in it, unlike a dark beer. This was one of our go-to brews enjoyed all year round. When brewing this five-gallon batch of beer, we would use one package of the Wyeast Activator pack, which contains approximately a hundred billion cells and is sized for the five-gallon batch of beer. White Labs also has small vials of yeast that contain the same amount of cells. As far as the brewing of the beer goes, it is pretty much the same steps the professional's employ but on a smaller scale. The only difference that I had was that instead of fly sparging or continuous sparging (the rinsing of the sugars from grains after the mash), I would use a technique called batch sparging.

Turnpike ESB

Ingredients
Wyeast 1968 London Extra Special Bitter—Yeast
90% Maris Otter Pale Malt
10% British Crystal 50/60 Malt
Willamette 44 IBU @ 60 minutes
East Kent Goldings 5.5 IBU @ 15 minutes
East Kent Goldings 3.3 IBU @ 5 minutes

or for a five-gallon batch:

9 lbs Maris Otter Pale Malt
1 lb British Crystal 50/60 Malt
2 oz Willamette pellets 5% AA @ 60 minutes
1 oz East Kent Goldings pellets 4.1% AA @ 15 minutes
1 oz East Kent Goldings pellets 4.1% AA @ 5 minutes

Founders All Day IPA Clone[3]
(Recipe by Amahl Turczyn)

Ingredients for 5.5 US gallons (20.82 L)
6.75 lbs (3.06 kg) pale two-row malt (77.1%)
0.5 lb (227 g) 60°L crystal malt (5.7%)
0.5 lb (227 g) 20°L Munich malt (5.7%)
0.5 lb (227 g) 9°L dark wheat malt (5.7%)
0.25 lb (113 g) flaked maize (2.9%)
0.25 lb (113 g) flaked oats (2.9%)
0.5 oz (14 g) Simcoe, 13% a.a. (60 min)
0.5 oz (14 g) Amarillo Gold, 8% a.a. (15 min)
0.5 oz (14 g) Simcoe, 13% a.a. (15 min)
1.0 oz (28 g) Amarillo Gold, 8% a.a. (whirlpool 10 min)
1.0 oz (28 g) Crystal, 3.5% a.a. (whirlpool 10 min)
1.0 oz (28 g) Amarillo Gold (dry hop 3 days)
1.0 oz (28 g) Simcoe (dry hop 3 days)
White Labs WLP001 California ale yeast

Specifications
- Boil Time: 60 min
- Brewhouse Efficiency: 75%

- Estimated Original Gravity: 1.043 SG

- Estimated Final Gravity: 1.007 SG

- Bitterness: 46 IBU

- Estimated Alcohol by Volume: 4.7%

Directions
Mash at 148°F (64°C) for 60 minutes.
Ferment at 67°F (19°C) for 7 days.
Steep dry hops for three days, then remove and package.

Extract Version
Substitute 4.5 lb (2.04 kg) pale malt extract syrup for 6 lb (2.72 kg) of the pale malt. Mash remaining 12 oz (340 g) pale malt with wheat, crystal, and Munich malts, along with the adjunct grains at 155 degrees F (68°C) for one hour. Rinse, dissolve extract completely and proceed with boil. *Expect a slightly higher finishing gravity with the extract recipe.*

Sweet Milk Stout[4]

Malt Extract Recipe
This recipe was inspired by the Milk Stout made by Left Hand Brewing Co. in Longmont, Colorado. The ingredients list is found on www. lefthandbrewing.com.

Ingredients for 5.25 U.S. Gallons (20 Liters)
2 cans (6.6 lb or 3 kg) Coopers Light Malt Extract
0.5 lb (227 g) Coopers Light Dry Malt Extract
1.0 lb (454 g) Milk Sugar
0.25 lb (113 g) Chocolate Malt (350°L)
0.5 lb (227 g) Crystal Malt (105°L)
0.75 lb (340 g) Roasted Barley (450°L)
0.25 lb (113g) Flaked Barley
0.25 lb (113g) Flaked Oats
1.0 oz (28 g) *U.S. Golding pellet hops, 4.75% a.a. (14 IBU) (60 min)
0.25 oz (7 g) *Magnum pellet hops, 14% a.a. (10 IBU) (60 min)

2 packages Wyeast 1099 Whitbread Ale Yeast, or 2 vials White Labs WLP006
Bedford British Ale Yeast, or 10 g Ferments Safale S-04 Coopers Brewery Carbonation Drops for bottling.

(* Use a similar hop, if listed hops are unavailable.)

Specifications
- Original Gravity: 1.060
- Final Gravity: 1.017–1.022
- IBU: 24
- ABV: 5.5–6%

Directions
Steep grains in 2.3 gallons (8.7 liters) of cool water, heat to 170°F (77°C), strain and sparge with 2/3 gallon (2.5 liters) hot water. Stir in liquid and dry malt extract, and bring to a boil. Add the battering hops at the beginning of the boil and boil for 60 minutes. Add the milk sugar at the end of the boil. Shut off heat, and cool the wort. Pour the wort into a clean and sanitized fermentor with enough cold water (~2.25 gallons, 8.5 liters) to make 5.25 gallons (20 liters). Aerate and pitch yeast when temperature drops to 65°F (18°C). Ferment at 67°F (19°C) from now to two weeks or until fermentation is complete. Prime with Coopers Brewery carbonation drops at bottling (at room temperature); aim for a low carbonation level.

Classic American Pilsner[5]

All-Grain Version
(5 gallons/19 L, all-grain)

Specifications
- Original Gravity = 1.060 (14.7°P)
- Final Gravity = 1.014 (3.6°P)
- IBU = 35 SRM = 4 ABV = 6%

Ingredients

4.4 lb (2 kg) Great Western domestic two-row malt (2°L)

4.4 lb (2 kg) Best Malz continental Pilsner malt (2°L)

3.3 lb (1.5 kg) Briess flaked corn (1°L)

6.5 AAU Czech Saaz hops

(1.87 oz/53 g at 3.5% alpha acids) (60 min.)

3.5 AAU Czech Saaz hops

(1 oz/28 g of 3.5% alpha acids) (15 min.)

3.5 AAU Czech Saaz hops

(1 oz/28 g of 3.5% alpha acids) (0 min.)

White Labs WLP800 (Pilsner Lager) or Wyeast 2001 (Urquell) yeast

Step by Step

Mill the grains and dough-in targeting a mash of around 1.5 quarts of water to 1 pound of grain (a liquor-to-grist ratio of about 3:1 by weight) and a temperature of 149°F (65°C). Hold the mash at 149°F (65°C) until enzymatic conversion is complete. You might want to extend your mash time, due to the lower mash temperature and the need to convert the corn. Infuse the mash with near boiling water while stirring or with a recirculating mash system raise the temperature to mash out at 168°F (76°C). Sparge slowly with 170°F (77°C) water, collecting wort until the pre-boil kettle volume is around 6.5 gallons (24.4 L) and the gravity is 1.046 (11.5°P).

The total boil time will be 90 minutes. Add the bittering hops 30 minutes after the wort starts boiling. Add Irish moss or other kettle finings and the second hop addition with 15 minutes left in the boil. Add the last hop addition just before shutting off the burner. Chill the wort rapidly to 50°F (10°C), let the break material settle, rack to the fermentor, pitch the yeast, and aerate thoroughly.

You will need to pitch 4 packages of fresh yeast or make a large starter to have enough yeast to best ferment this beer. You might consider first brewing a small batch of lower gravity Munich Helles or something similar to grow up the yeast you need. Once you have pitched enough clean, healthy yeast, ferment at 50°F (10°C).

When fermentation is finished, carbonate the beer to approximately 2.5 volumes.

CHAPTER ELEVEN

Classic American Pilsner

Extract Version
(5 gallons/19 L, extract only)

Specifications
- Original Gravity = 1.060 (14.7°P)
- Final Gravity = 1.014 (3.6°P)
- IBU = 35 SRM = 4 ABV = 6%

Ingredients
6 lb (2.7 kg) Pilsner liquid malt extract (2°L)
2.2 lb (1 kg) high maltose corn or rice syrup (0°L)
6.5 AAU Czech Saaz hops
(1.87 oz/53 g at 3.5% alpha acids) (60 min)
3.5 AAU Czech Saaz hops
(1 oz/28 g of 3.5% alpha acids) (15 min)
3.5 AAU Czech Saaz hops
(1 oz/28 g of 3.5% alpha acids) (0 min)
White Labs WLP800 (Pilsner Lager) or Wyeast 2001 (Urquell) yeast

Step by Step
I have used a number of Pilsner-type extracts, all with success. Always choose the freshest extract that fits the beer style. If you cannot get fresh liquid malt extract, use an appropriate amount of dried extract instead. Using fresh extract is very important to this style. Finding high maltose rice or corn syrups can be difficult in smaller quantities, but some homebrew shops do carry them. Alternatively, you could use dextrose in place of the syrup. Ideally, you would do a partial mash with corn or leave this style to all-grain.

Add enough water to the malt extract to make a pre-boil volume of 5.9 gallons (22.3 liters) and the gravity is 1.051 (12.6°P). Stir the wort thoroughly to help dissolve the extract and bring to a boil.

Once the wort is boiling, add the bittering hops. The total wort boil time is 1 hour after adding the first hops. Add Irish moss or other kettle finings and the second hop addition with 15 minutes left in the boil. Add the last hop addition just before shutting off the burner. Chill the wort rapidly to 50°F (10°C), let the break material settle, rack to the fermentor, pitch the yeast and aerate thoroughly.

You will need to pitch four packages of fresh yeast or make a large starter to have enough yeast to best ferment this beer. You might consider first brewing a small batch of lower-gravity Munich Helles or something similar to grow up the yeast you need. Once you have pitched enough clean, healthy yeast, ferment at 50°F (10°C). When fermentation is finished, carbonate the beer to approximately 2.5 volumes.

Get Ready for the Fall and Winter Holidays!

Milk Stout with Pumpkin, Coffee, and Vanilla Specialty Beer[6]

Tapping into the pumpkin beer phenomenon that dominates the fall months, Sean Gallagher, from Orange County, California, created this beer recipe that pays homage to all those who fall head over heels for everything pumpkin. After researching and sourcing information to create the recipe, he tweaked it a couple of times to get it where it is now. Sean has been homebrewing for about three years and still considers himself rather new to the hobby. He made the switch to all-grain at the beginning of 2015. This pumpkin beer recipe is the first recipe he crafted entirely on his own, having previously only made other people's recipes with minor tweaks. The vanilla and pumpkin spices complement each other really well, and the coffee helps balance the beer and bring everything together in one delicious sip. Brew it now and have it ready for the holidays!

Ingredients for Five Gallons (19 L)
12.5 lbs (5.7 kg) 2-Row malt
2.0 lbs (0.9 kg) Flaked Barley
1.5 lbs (0.7 kg) Pale Chocolate malt
0.5 lb (227 g) Roasted Barley
0.5 lb (227 g) Midnight Wheat malt
0.8 oz (23 g) Magnum pellets (60 min)
1.0 oz (28 g) Golding pellets (30 min)
1.0 lb (454 g) Lactose (10 min)
2 tsp Pumpkin Spice (1 min)
2 Fresh Madagascar Vanilla Beans, whole (7 days)
0.5 lb (227 g) Medium-roast coffee beans (cold brew, add at bottling)
White Labs San Diego Super Yeast (WLP090)

Specifications

- Original Gravity: 1.091

- Final Gravity: 1.019

- ABV: 9.45%

- IBU: 38

- SRM: 46

Directions

To brew this milk stout pumpkin beer recipe, mash at 153°F (67°C) for 60 minutes. Batch sparge. Boil for 60 minutes, following boil schedule. Chop vanilla beans and scrape out the inside. Stuff the collection in to a small jar with enough vodka to cover the beans. Let this sit for about a week. Toss into primary fermentation. Anywhere from 12 to 24 hours before packaging, make a cold brew coffee using 8 oz (454 g) of your favorite medium roast coffee. Add this to your bottling bucket or keg to taste, and carbonate up to 2.4 vol.

With all of the development, innovation, and resources available to novice, advanced, and expert brewers in the United States, it makes sense that this chapter brings us to an end. We knew we couldn't capture all of the details related to each topic of focus, but we did our best to highlight key areas and information from the industry as a whole into one book. We hope you continue to learn and share with each other for years to come. As Benjamin Franklin once said, "Beer is proof that God loves us and want to be happy."[7] So, let's not let God or anyone else down. Instead, let's enjoy beer, and each other. Next is our final "Talking from the Tap" interview. We hope you enjoy it, and your final beer while reading. Cheers!

Talking from the Tap!

Interview with Laura Ulrich,[8] Small-Batch Brewer and President of the Pink Boots Society, Stone Brewing

1. *How did you get interested in brewing?*

I was never a homebrewer but I grew up in St. Louis and then moved to Fort Collins, Colorado, after college and worked in a bar and saw the beer come through and found that interesting. I wasn't a drinker until then. Then I moved to O'Dell Brewing and was packaging [a bottle line] for a year and a half; it was tough, but I was determined. I was learning how to package beer and clean beer lines at other bars. After that I wanted something else, so I moved to Southern California, I ended up in San Diego at Stone Brewing after an interview and worked up the ranks. I didn't want to take a brewing position until I knew other aspects of the brewing process. They kept asking if I wanted to do more, and I did. Within a short period of time, I took over brewing when one brewer left. I am grateful to have learned all the aspects of brewing.

2. Can you explain what it means to be a small-batch brewer?

I am part of a team that does development from malt, new recipes, hops innovation in our system, recipes from brewers, and more in a seven-barrel system. Anything with barreling is also part of what I do. We have an off-shoot warehouse that has about fourteen hundred barrels and a barreling line; filtering to packaging and brewing. I work with other brewers one time a year to create a collaboration brew. Last year I went to Odell Brewing and worked on their pilot system.

3. What has been your largest obstacle to overcome?

Me. I put up roadblocks and took leaps of faith. I was self-critical. I didn't apply for open jobs because I thought I needed to know more.

4. How important is the Pinks Boots Society to you?

Super important, because meeting other women in the industry is important. Working with and talking with other females leads to conversations about experiences, successes, and struggles. Women may be a bit more emotional at times and think differently about our experiences in the industry than men, which spotlights bonding over personal stories and goals. This is an organization for women who take part in the beer industry to learn more about the craft beer culture, networking, talking to neighbors, asking questions, and sharing ideas together. We showcase star women who want to share with others and get the time and attention they need to keep going creatively. Anyone making a profit from beer can join. More organizations are popping up, such as women's collaboration brew day. There are opportunities for interested homebrewers to reach out to us.

5. *Do you see a craft brew culture around you?*

In San Diego, yes. It's networking, going to your neighbors for advice, idea creation, questions and more. All the breweries here seem to be open to conversation. They are passionate about beer and want to share, despite competition.

6. *Why do you think craft beer has taken off so much in the past few years?*

People are tired of the same old thing; they wanted something different and craft beer was it. It was about their local bars and breweries having something different from the regular options. There wasn't much variety, so now people want more choices and they want local. We want what we want and we want it now.

7. *What are some of the trends you notice in the craft beer industry?*

Fruit-flavored beers, sours, nitro IPAs, and more. We are trying an IPA on nitro here but I don't think about that as much.

8. *How much do you need to know about science and chemistry to do this job?*

A fair amount, depending on where you are at. Fermentation understanding is valuable. If you shadow somebody, you can learn from people around you. They educate you on what's happening in the process.

9. *How do you decide on recipes?*

A lot come from conversations you hear and take part in. Hops we are getting in also influence our recipes. We want to draw out the taste and other qualities; we trial it and move on from there.

10. *Do you have a go-to beer style?*

IPA; for the hoppyness mostly.

11. *Any advice for novice brewers?*

Ask for assistance, be patient, and mostly, surround yourself with good people.

12. *Finish this sentence: "I brew because . . ."*

"I love craft beer."

ACKNOWLEDGMENTS

Karen McGrath would like to thank Rowman & Littlefield for their belief in this project. She would also like to thank her coauthors (Regina, Todd, and Sean) for working so diligently on this project over the past year; her family (Mom Betty, Dad Robert, brothers Bobby and Tim, extended family and friends, and Miss Luna) for their continued support; and Kim and Mike Young for the many road trips for beer tastings and discussion. Special thank-you messages to Mike Wenzel (wordsmith) for providing insight, writing our foreword, and brewing great beer!; Joe Rissacher, graduate assistant and recent MBA graduate from the College of Saint Rose, for his work on this project and taking on a new challenge—the *Chicago Style Manual*; Paola Ely, graphic designer; and Dr. James T. Como for lighting a fire under me as an undergraduate student and preparing me for bigger and better things. Mostly, however, a big shout-out and thank-you goes to Sean McGrath, my life partner, comedic sidekick, and "common sewer" (aka "connoisseur") of beer, without whose patience and support nothing ever gets done . . . without beer!

Regina Luttrell would like to acknowledge her family for always supporting her research and writing endeavors. Especially my daughters, whom I admire for the smart young women you are becoming. One day you will both surpass me. Most importantly, my husband, Todd. We've shared many adventures, but writing this book together has been quite special. Thank you for encouraging me, supporting me, and never saying no. I love you . . . more. My mom, Catherine Franco, for helping to make sure lunches are made and that everyone is picked up from the bus stop. Whatever would we do without you? No writing endeavor is ever complete without my fur baby, Coco-Bean. My writing process wouldn't be the same if it were not for her snuggling in all those hours on my lap. To my very special friend Karen, for leading and shepherding this project to the end. Your passion, direction, and vision are what inspired us all. You are simply amazing. Sean, thank you for jumping on board and being our chief brewing expert. A gracious thank-you to all those who gave their time to talk about the craft beer industry. This book would not have been possible without your keen insights. Finally, to Rowman & Littlefield and Suzanne Staszak-Silva, I want to thank you for believing in all of us and our project.

Todd Luttrell would like to extend a sincere thank-you to our publisher, Rowman & Littlefield, and editor, Suzanne Staszak-Silva, for their support of this project and to our coauthors Karen and Sean for their creativity, passion, and undying interest in the awesome world of beer. Cheers! To my wife, Gina, for believing that I had something interesting to contribute to such an amazing publication and for encouraging me to taste test "as often of humanly possible" throughout the project; being on the front end is considerably different than serving behind the scenes! Thank you, from the bottom of my heart. To the little ladies of my life, thanks for keeping me honest and pointing out my countless writing errors and correcting my subpar chemical structures. The world is a far better place with you on the lookout. You both make me a better person! Finally, to all of our contributors, thank you for your insights, passion, and willingness to share your expertise with the greater audience.

Sean McGrath would like to thank Rowman & Littlefield for their belief in this project, Sonia McGrath for her continued love and support, Kim and Mike Young for their willingness to attend many tastings and share great craft beers, and Mike Wenzel of Helderberg Mountain Brewing Company for encouraging me to pursue my brewing passion and allowing me to learn the trade through our many weekend brew sessions. A special thank-you to Gina and Todd Luttrell for inviting me in on this project and working so hard to create a strong end product. And, last, but not least, I want to thank my wife, coauthor, and soul mate, Karen McGrath, for believing in this project and in everything I do by persevering through all of my procrastination. I love you more than anything . . . even beer!

All of the authors would like to thank over two dozen industry folk from across the country who have participated in this project, including Emily Armstrong and Jeff Joslin (Left Hand Brewing), Brian Bales, PhD (General Electric), Barry and Cara Boggs (Canton Brew Works), Lilly Calderwood, PhD (Cornell Cooperative Extension), Dave Carpenter (*Zymurgy* and American Homebrewers Association), Ingrid Alvarez Cherney (High Dive Bar and Chicks for Beer), Gwen Conley (Lost Abbey/Port Brewing), Mike Dixon and Scott Bickham (BJCP.com), Fish Consulting (especially Amanda Bortzfield [DelPrete]), Susanne Hackett (New Belgium Brewing—Asheville), Devon Hamilton (Paradox Brewing), Old Chicago Pizza & Taproom, Erin Peters (@TheBeerGoddess), Billy Pyatt (Catawba Brewing Company), Brad Ring (*Brew Your Own*), Lauren Salazar (New Belgium, Colorado), Mike Stevens (Founders), Luke Trautwein (Brewers Association), Laura Ulrich (Stone Brewing), Bart Watson (Brewers Association), Mike Wenzel (Helderberg Mountain Brewing Company), Dave Wills (Freshops.com), and Lauren Zeidler (Ballast Point Brewing). Their willingness to share their experiences with us and others has contributed to the success of this book. Mostly, however, it is their spirit of collaboration that makes the craft beer industry such a success. A beer or two in their honor is necessary. Cheers to you all!

NOTES

Preface

1. Erin Peters, personal interview, May 2016.
2. Mike Wenzel, personal conversation, June, 2016
3. "GrainToGlass," Dogfish Head Craft Brewed Ales, June 9, 2016, http://www.dogfish .com/brews-spirits/the-brews/brewpub-exclusives/graintoglass.htm.
4. Billy Pyatt, personal interview, June 2016.

Chapter 1: Craft Beer History and Culture: "What Can Knowledge Do for You?"

1. Jen Christensen, "5000-Year-Old Brewery Discovered in China," CNN, May 31, 2016, updated June 6, 2016, http://www.cnn.com/2016/05/31/health/5000-year-old-beer-found -china/index.html.
2. Gregg Smith, *Beer: A History of Suds and Civilization from Mesopotamia to Microbreweries* (New York: Avon Books, 1995), 5.
3. Ibid., 19.
4. Ibid., 24.
5. Tara Nurin, "How Women Brewsters Saved the World," *Craft Beer & Brewing*, April 21, 2016, accessed June 6, 2016, https://beerandbrewing.com/VNN4oCYAAGdLRZ-1/ article/how-women-brewsters-saved-the-world.
6. "The Growler: Beer-to-Go," *Beer Advocate*, July 31, 2002, accessed July 28, 2016, https://www.beeradvocate.com/articles/384/.
7. Martin Stack, "A Concise History of America's Brewing Industry," in *EH.Net Encyclopedia*, ed. Robert Whaples, July 4, 2003, accessed August 9, 2016, http://eh.net/ encyclopedia/a-concise-history-of-americas-brewing-industry/.
8. Mike Snider, "Women to Get Their Own Beer; Will They Want It?" *USA Today*, May 28, 2016, accessed June 6, 2016, http://www.usatoday.com/story/money/2016/05/21/ women-get-but-want-their-own-beer/83857942/.

NOTES

9. Christensen, "5000-Year-Old Brewery."

10. Keith Gribbins, "Are You a Woman Looking to Work in Craft Beer? We Ask Female Leaders to Share Their Stories and Advice." *Craft Brewing Business*, April 12, 2016, https://www.craftbrewingbusiness.com/featured/woman-looking-work-craft-beer-ask-female-leaders-share-stories-advice/.

11. Julia Herz, "Women, Craft Beer, and Centerfolds," *CraftBeer*, August 19, 2010, accessed June 6, 2016, http://www.craftbeer.com/craft-beer-muses/women-crft-beer-and-centerfolds.

12. Gwen Conley, personal interview, May 2016.

13. "Modern History," *Beer History*, accessed December 12, 2016, http://www.beerhistory.com/library/holdings/raley_timetable.shtml.

14. Andy Skelton, "Women Shaping the Brewing of Beer," *CraftBeer*, updated July 15, 2016, https://www.craftbeer.com/craft-beer-muses/women-shaping-brewing-beer.

15. Snider, "Women to Get Their Own Beer."

16. Kimberly Bellstrom, "Do Women Need a Beer Named after a Stiletto?" *Fortune*, May 28, 2016, accessed August 11, 2016, http://fortune.com/2016/05/28/high-heel-womens-beer/.

17. Ellen Barclay, "Are Women Better Beer Tasters Than Men?" *NPR: The Salt*, August 31, 2013, http://www.npr.org/sections/thesalt/2015/08/31/427735692/are-women-better-tasters-than-men.

18. Heather Vandenengel, "The Reality of Being a Woman in the Beer Industry," *All about Beer Magazine*, February 9, 2016, accessed June 6, 2016, http://allaboutbeer.com/article/women-in-beer/.

19. Pink Boots Society, http://pinkbootssociety.org/.

20. Alastair Bland, "Why Aren't There More People of Color in Craft Brewing?" *NPR: The Salt*, September 11, 2013, accessed August 12, 2016, http://www.npr.org/sections/thesalt/2013/09/06/219721800/why-aren-t-there-more-people-of-color-in-craft-brewing; Dave Infante, "There Are Almost No Black People Brewing Craft Beer. Here's Why," *Thrillist*, January 18, 2016, accessed August 12, 2016, https://www.thrillist.com/drink/nation/there-are-almost-no-black-people-brewing-craft-beer-heres-why.

21. Stack, "A Concise History of America's Brewing Industry."

22. Dylan Roach, "These 5 Beer Makers Own More Than Half of the World's Beer," *Business Insider*, February 9, 2016, http://www.businessinsider.com/biggest-beer-companies-in-the-world-2016-1.

23. "State Craft Beer Sales and Production Statistics, 2015," Brewers Association, accessed July 2, 2016, http://www.brewersassociation.org/statistics/by-state/.

24. "Craft Brewer Defined," Brewers Association, accessed July 11, 2016, http://brewersassociation.org/statistics/craft-brewer-defined/.

25. Jason Alstrom and Todd Alstrom, "Craft Beer and Brewer, Defined." *Beer Smack* 17 (June 2008), https://www.beeradvocate.com/mag/2212/craft-beer-and-brewer-defined/.

26. Steve Hindy, *The Craft Beer Revolution: How a Band of Microbreweries Is Transforming the World's Favorite Drink* (New York: Palgrave Macmillan, 2015), prologue.

27. Jess Baker, "Join Us for the Renaissance: An Invitation from CraftBeer.com Editor in Chief, Jess Baker." *Craftbeer*, July 14, 2016, https://www.craftbeer.com/brewers_banter/craftbeer-renaissance-letter-from-editor.

28. Martin Slagter, "Three-Hearted Ales: Friends Share Unique Bond Over Beer, Open Heart Surgery," *MLive.com*, May 11, 2016, http://www.mlive.com/news/ann-arbor/index .ssf/2016/05/three_hearted_ales_friends_sha.html.

29. "American Craft Beer Week, " *CraftBeer.com*, accessed, June 9, 2016, https://www .craftbeer.com/news/american-craft-beer-week.

30. Suzanne Hackett, personal interview, June 2016.

31. Lauren Salazar, personal interview, June 2016.

32. Gwen Conley, personal interview, May 2016.

33. Billy Pyatt, personal interview, June 2016.

34. Mike Stevens, personal interview, April 2016.

35. Ibid.

Chapter 2: Beer Basics: What Do I Need to Know?

1. "World's Strongest Beer, 'Snake Venom,' Clocks in at 67.5 percent ABV," *Huffington Post: Taste*, October 29, 2013, http://www.huffingtonpost.com/2013/10/24/worlds -strongest-beer-snake-venom_n_4157580.html.

2. Dave Carpenter, "What Is the Difference between Ale and Lager?" *Craft Beer and Brewing Magazine*, December 16, 2015, https://beerandbrewing.com/VmsqtyQAADM 1mZHK/article/what-is-the-difference-between-ale-and-lager.

3. http://beeracademy.com; http://beeradvocate.org.

4. "BJCP Color Guide," Beer Judge Certificate Program, http://www.bjcp.org/color guide.php.

5. Brian Handwerk, "Celebrating 500 years of Germany's Beer Purity Laws," *Smithsonian Magazine*, April 22, 2016, http://www.smithsonianmag.com/history/celebrating -500-years-germans-beer-purity-law-180958878/.

6. "Hops Alpha Acid Table," *Brewer's Friend*, Sept. 14, 2008, http://www.brewersfriend .com/2008/09/14/hops-alpha-acid-table/.

7. http://www.byo.com.

8. Reprinted with permission from *Brew Your Own* magazine, http://www.byo.com.

9. Lauren Zeidler, personal interview, July 2016.

10. Devon Hamilton, personal interview, July 2016.

11. "Farm Brewery," New York State Brewers Association, http://newyorkcraftbeer.com/ farm-brewery; "Farm Brewery License," Alcoholic Beverage Control, Article 51-a, public .leginfo.state.ny.us/lawssrch.cgi?NVLWO.

12. John Holl, "Nano-Breweries: Talk of the Craft Beer Nation," *CraftBeer*, http://www .craftbeer.com/craft-beer-muses/nano-breweriesmdash-tlk-of-the-craft-beer-nation.

13. "Craft Beer Industry Market Segments," Brewers Association, http://brewersassocia tion.org/statistics/market-segments/.

14. Joshua Mason and John Remakel, "Brew Pub vs. Taproom: Which Business Model is Right for You?" Monroe, Moxness, Berg, August 18, 2015, http://mmblawfirm.com/brew -pub-v-taproom-which-business-model-is-right-for-you/.

15. Deena Prichep, "Wine Has Sommeliers; Now Beer Has Cicerones," *NPR: Weekend Edition*, August 24, 2013, http://www.npr.org/sections/thesalt/2013/08/24/214582851/wine-has-sommeliers-now-beer-has-cicerones.

16. Zeidler, July 2016.

Chapter 3: Brewin' Up Some Beer: Barely Gettin' Started

1. See preface for a "Talking from the Tap" with coauthor, Sean McGrath. Helpful hints for brewing are included.

2. Marty Nachel, *Homebrewing for Dummies* (Hoboken, NJ: Wiley, 1997), 18–23.

3. John J. Palmer, *How to Brew: Everything You Need to Know to Brew Beer Right the First Time* (Boulder, CO: Brewers Publications, 2006), 7.

4. Ibid., 23.

5. Ibid., 37–38.

6. Ibid., 54–56.

7. Ibid., 29

8. Ibid., 30.

9. Ibid., 81–82.

10. Nachel, *Homebrewing for Dummies*, 53.

11. "How to Take an Accurate Hydrometer Reading," Homebrew Association, https://www.homebrewersassociation.org/how-to-brew/how-to-take-an-accurate-hydrometer-reading/.

12. "Home Brew Bottling Calculator," Brewer's Friend, http://www.brewersfriend.com/bottling-calculator/.

13. American Homebrewers Association, *Introduction to Homebrewing*, https://www.home brewersassociation.org/how-to-brew/beginner/videos/; "Learning to Homebrew, Lesson 9," American Homebrewers Association, https://www.youtube.com/watch?v=_tqYGHqI9bs.

14. Michael Young, personal e-mail exchange, November 2016.

15. Devon Hamilton, personal interview, July 2016.

Chapter 4: More about Primary Beer Ingredients

1. "Supporting New York State Agriculture," Cornell University, http://cce.cornell.edu/sites/default/files/connecting_campus_and_communities_2015_annual_report_3.pdf.

2. Cole Mellino, "Climate Change Poses Threat to Key Ingredient in Beer, NOAA Warns," *EcoWatch*, http://www.ecowatch.com/climate-change-poses-threat-to-key-ingredient-in-beer-noaa-warns-1882168560.html.

3. "Governor Cuomo Hosts Third Wine, Beer, Spirits, and Cider Summit," October 7, 2015, https://www.governor.ny.gov/news/governor-cuomo-hosts-third-wine-beer-spirits-and-cider-summit.

4. David H. Gent, James D. Barbour, Amy J. Dreves, David G. James, Robert Parker, and Douglas B. Walsh, tech eds., *Field Guide for Integrated Pest Management in Hops*, A Cooperative Publication Produced by Oregon State University, University of Idaho, U.S. Department

of Agriculture—Agricultural Research Service, and Washington State University, 2009, https://ipm.wsu.edu/field/pdf/hophandbook2009.pdf.

5. Laura Ten Eyck and Dietrich Gehring, *The Hop Grower's Handbook: The Essential Guide for Sustainable, Small-Scale Production for Home and Market* (White River Junction, VT: Chelsea Green Publishing, 2015), 149–61.

6. Cornell Store, https://store.cornell.edu/c-873-cornell-coop-ext.aspx.

7. "Introduction to Hop Diseases and Pests," *Fresh Hops*. December 27, 2016, http://freshops.com/hop-diseases-pests/.

8. Ethan Johnston, "Hop Rhizomes: How, What, and When," *Fifth Season Gardening Company*. March 27, 2015, http://fifthseasongardening.com/hop-rhizomes-what-how-and-when.

9. Bryce Eddings, "Growing and Harvesting Hops for Homebrewing," *Beer.About .Com*. March 2, 2016, http://beer.about.com/od/commercialbeers/a/growinghop.htm; "Hop Gender Identification," *Great Lakes Hops*, http://greatlakeshops.com/hops-blog/hop-iden tification; "Hop Gardening," Freshops, http://freshops.com/hop-gardening; Ten Eyck and Dietrich, "Female Hops Plants."

10. Ten Eyck and Gehring, *The Hop Grower's Handbook*.

11. Steve Miller, Cornell Cooperative Extension, http://madisoncountycce.org/agricul ture/hops-program/frequently-asked-questions.

12. Miller, "Frequently Asked Questions."

13. Ten Eyck and Gehring, *The Hop Grower's Handbook*, 196.

14. Ibid., 197.

15. John Moorhead, "How to Harvest, Prepare, and Store Homegrown Hops: Hops Drying Methods," American Brewers Association, https://www.homebrewersassociation.org/how-to-brew/how-to-harvest-prepare-and-store-homegrown-hops/.

16. USA Hops Organization, http://www.usahops.org/index.cfm?fuseaction=hop_ farming&pageID=4.

17. Nick Carr, "Pellet Hops vs. Whole Hops: Comparing the Pros and Cons," *Kegerator*, November 12, 2014, accessed October 24, 2016, http://learn.kegerator.com/author/nick/.

18. "Hops Types Pellet Plug Leaf," *Brewer's Friend*, March 21, 2010, http://www.brew ersdfriend.com/2010/03/21/hops-types-pellet-plug-leaf/.

19. "What Is the Difference between Hop Pellets, Hop Plugs, Whole Leaf, and Extract?" Midwest Homebrewing & Winemaking Supplies, https://www.midwestsupplies.com/media/ pdf-printouts/different_hops_1.pdf.

20. Ibid.

21. Nick Carr, "Pellet Hops vs. Whole Hops."

22. Ibid.

23. "Dry vs. Wet-hopped—What's the Difference?" *Drewsbrewsreviews*, October 12, 2015, https://drewsbrewsreviews.com/2015/01/28/dry-vs-wet-hopped-whats-the-difference.

24. Ibid.

25. "You've Heard about IBUs in Beer Before . . . But What Is an IBU?" *The Brew Enthusiast*, http://www.thebrewenthusiast.com/ibus/.

26. "International Bittering Units." *Homebrewing*, http://www.homebrewing.org/Interna tional-Bittering-Units_ep_49-1.html.

27. Brian Patrick, "The Science behind Hops Part 1—Alpha and Beta Acids," *Craft Beer Academy*, http://craftbeeracademy.com/the-science-behind-hops-part-1-alpha-and-beta-acids/.

28. Ibid.

29. Stan Hieronymus, *For the Love of Hops*. Boulder, CO: Brewers Publications, 2012.

30. Joshua A. Bernstein, "How the 10 Most Important Grains in Beer Affect Flavor," *Bonappetit*, September 17, 2013, http://www.bonappetit.com/drinks/beer/article/how -the-1o-most-important-grains-in-beer-affect-flavor.

31. "Grains and Adjuncts Chart," *Brew Your Own*, https://byo.com/resources/grains ?view=grains.

32. Bernstein, "How the 10 Most Important Grains in Beer Affect Flavor."

33. Greg Kitsock, "Craft Beer: Corn Gets a New Look from Brewers, and Not as a Mere Filler," *Washington Post*, August 5, 2014, https://www.washingtonpost.com/lifestyle/ food/craft-beer-corn-gets-a-new-look-from-brewers-and-not-as-a-mere-filler/2014/08/04/ f5a27d4a-199b-11e4-9349-84d4a85be981_story.html; Bryce Eddings, "Why Do Some Brewers Use Rice or Corn in Their Beer?" *About Food*, September 26, 2016, http://beer .about.com/od/homebrewingextract/f/Why-Do-Some-Brewers-Use-Rice-Or-Corn-In -Their-Beer.htm.

34. Bernstein, "How the 10 Most Important Grains in Beer Affect Flavor."

35. Allan Wolfe, "Oats, Wheat and Rye: What Adjunct Grains Add to Your Beer," *Craftbeer*, http://www.craftbeer.com/craft-beer-muses/oats-wheat-rye-adjunct-grains-add-beer.

36. Bernstein, "How the 10 Most Important Grains in Beer Affect Flavor."

37. Wolfe, "Oats, Wheat & Rye"; Bernstein, "How the 10 Most Important Grains in Beer Affect Flavor."

38. Eric Reinsvold, "Brewing with Mushrooms," *Beer & Brewing*, April 1, 2016, https:// beerandbrewing.com/Vv2KjScAALouiXmi/article/brewing-with-mushrooms.

39. Emma Janzen, "Mushrooms Have Entered the Craft Beer Game," *Food Republic*, January 21, 2015, http://www.foodrepublic.com/2015/01/21/mushrooms-have-entered-the -craft-beer-game/.

40. Andrew Gill, "What Is Mushroom Beer, and How (and Why) Do You Brew It?" *AV Club*, September 22, 2016, http://www.avclub.com/article/what-mushroom-beer-and-how -and-why-do-you-brew-it-242544.

41. Joshua A. Bernstein, "11 Beers Made with Breakfast Foods Like Bacon, Oats, and Coffee," January 24, 2014, *Bonappetit*, http://www.bonappetit.com/drinks/beer/slidewhow/ liquid-breakfast-eleven-great-morning-inspired-beers-drink-noon; Joshua Ocampo and Alex Delany, "We Tried the Weirdest Beers Out There—and We Mean Weird," *Bonappetit*, April 14, 2016, http://www.bonappetit.com/beer/article/weird-beer-flavors; Chris Guest, "Strange Brews—the 10 Weirdest Beer Ingredients," *Beerconnoisseur*, November 27, 2015, http://www .beerconnoissuer.com/articles/strange-brews-10-weirdest-beer-ingredients.

42. Bret Stetka, "8 Unusual Beer Styles You Need to Know," *Firstwefeast*, November 12, 2012, http://firstwefeast.com/drink/2012/11/8-unusual-beer-styles-you-need-to-know/ 15922.

43. Brad Smith, "Why Oxygen Is Bad in Your Home Brewed Beer," *BeerSmith Home Brewing Blog*, June 18, 2015, http://beersmith.com/blog/2015/06/18/why-oxygen-is-bad-in -your-home-brewed-beer/.

44. Roger Barth, "Sugars and Starches," *Wiley Online Library*, March 1, 2014, http:// onlinelibrary.wiley.com/doi/10.1002/9781118733745.ch6/summary.

45. "Attenuation," Northern Brewer Homebrew Supply, https://www.northernbrewer .com/connect/2011/08/attenuation/.

46. Christopher White, "Flocculation Basics," http://www.whitelabs.com/sites/default/ files/Flocculation_help.pdf.

47. "Homebrew Yeast Strains Chart," https://byo.com/resources/yeast.

48. "Yeast Pitching Rates," *Northern Brewer*, https://www.northernbrewer.com/documen tation/YeastPitchingRates.pdf.

49. "Yeast Pitch Rate and Starter Calculator," *Brewer's Friend*, http://www.brewersfriend .com/yeast-pitch-rate-and-starter-calculator/.

50. Lily Calderwood, PhD, personal interview, July 2016.

Chapter 5: You Don't Have to Be Einstein: The Science behind a Good Brew

1. David G. Miller, *Brewing the World's Great Beers: A Step-by-Step Guide* (Pownal, VT: Storey Communications, 1992).

2. Roger Barth, *The Chemistry of Beer: The Science in the Suds* (Hoboken, NJ: John Wiley & Sons, 2013).

3. Marty Nachel and Steve Ettlinger, *Beer for Dummies* (Foster City, CA: IDG Books Worldwide, 1996).

4. Barth, *The Chemistry of Beer*.

5. "What Are Carbohydrates?" *LiveScience*, accessed December 3, 2016, http://www .livescience.com/51976-carbohydrates.html.

6. Barth, *The Chemistry of Beer*.

7. "Brewing Process," *The Beer Temple*, accessed December 3, 2016, http://craftbeer temple.com/videoblog/brewing-process/.

8. Paul Held, "Enzymatic Digestion of Polysaccharides (Part II)," February 27, 2012, accessed December 3, 2016, http://www.biotek.com/resources/articles/enzymatic-digestion -of-polysaccharides-2.html.

9. "What Are Carbohydrates?" *LiveScience*, accessed December 3, 2016, http://www .livescience.com/51976-carbohydrates.html.

10. Dave Carpenter, "Lautering and Sparging," *Craft Beer & Brewing Magazine*, February 9, 2016, accessed December 3, 2016, https://beerandbrewing.com/VJnL-CsAACgA34Pq/ article/lautering-and-sparging.

11. Miller, *Brewing the World's Great Beers*.

12. Barth, *The Chemistry of Beer*.

13. "Yeast Guide," *Beer Advocate*, accessed December 3, 2016, https://www.beeradvocate .com/beer/101/yeast/.

14. Held, "Enzymatic Digestion of Polysaccharides (Part II)."

15. Ibid.

16. Denis DeKeukeleire, Arne Heyerick, Kevin Huvaere, Leif Skibsted, and Mogens Andersen, "Beer Lighstruck Flavor: The Full Story." *Beer Sensory Science*, Cerevisia 33, no. 3 (2008): 133–44.

17. David Williamson, "UNC Chemists Figure Out What Causes 'Skunky Beer'" *EurekAlert!* UNC News Services, October 17, 2001.

18. Barth, *The Chemistry of Beer*.

19. John Palmer, "Brewing Water," *Craft Beer and Brewing Magazine*, January 29, 2016.

20. Miller, *Brewing the World's Great Beers*.

21. Jeff Flowers, "Comparing Different Types of Water for Homebrewing," Kegerator. com, February 28, 2014 accessed December 8, 2016, http://learn.kegerator.com/types-of -water-for-homebrewing/.

22. Barth, *The Chemistry of Beer*.

23. Gwen Conley, personal interview, May 2016.

Chapter 6: From Extract to Grains: Brewing Bigger!

1. William Herkewitz and Andrew Han, "How to Build Your Own Home-Brewing Mash Tun," *Popular Mechanics*, July 29, 2014, http://www.popularmechanics.com/home/ how-to/g1580/how-to-build-your-own-home-brewing-mash-tun/.

2. John Palmer, "Building the Manifold," *How to Brew*, http://howtobrew.com/book/ appendices/appendix-d/building-the-manifold; "Copper Manifold for a 50 qt Rubbermaid Cooler," https://www.youtube.com/watch?v=r7W_SSrIdeQ.

3. "Hot Liquor Tank," The Electric Brewery, http://www.theelectricbrewery.com/hot -liquor-tank.

4. Chugger and March are the two most common brands.

5. "Weldless Ball Valve Installation," https://www.youtube.com/watch?v=7pvuhg6sEiY.

6. While a heat source is necessary, some brewers like an electric startup versus a propane one.

7. Blichmann Engineering, http://www.blichmannengineering.com/products/fermenator.

8. "Edelmetall-Bru Kettle," Midwest Supplies, https://www.midwestsupplies.com/edel metall-bru-kettle?gclid=CN_EpciA99ACFZlMDQodz0IFNQ.

9. Northern Brewer, http://www.northernbrewer.com/brewing/brewing-equipment/all -grain-equipment.

10. More Beer, "Kegging Homebrew," https://www.morebeer.com/content/kegging -homebrew.

11. Northern Brewer, "How to Build a Keezer," https://www.youtube.com/watch?v= zHWy_Vlw3J4.

12. "Mash and Sparge Water Calculation," *Brew365*, January 2, 2017, http://www .brew365.com/mash_sparge_water_calculator.php.

13. Billy Pierce, "Calculating Water Usage: Advanced Brewing," *Brew Your Own*, posted November 2006, https://byo.com/bock/item/410-calculating-water-usage-advanced-brewing.

14. For clear distinctions on the types of sparging, see American Homebrewers Association, "Fly Sparging vs. Batch Sparging," https://www.homebrewersassociation.org/how-to -brew/fly-sparing-vs-batch-sparging/.

15. Emily Armstrong with Jeff Joslin, personal interview, Left Hand Brewing, July 2016.

Chapter 7: "How Do I Get My Business Approved?" The Ever-Changing Landscape of the Beer Industry

1. "Economic Impact," Brewers Association, https://www.brewersassociation.org/statis tics/economic-impact-data/.

2. Danielle Teagarden, "Can I Sell Homebrew? Can I Make Pro Brew at Home?," *Brewery Law.* http://brewerylaw.com/2016/06/can-i-sell-homebrew-can-i-make-pro-brew -at-home.

3. "Beer Industry," Alcohol and Tobacco Tax and Trade Bureau, https://www.ttb.gov/ beer/index.shtml.

4. Candace L. Moon, Craft Beer Attorney, http://craftbeerattorney.com.

5. Lehrman Beverage Law, http://www.bevlaw.com.

6. "Eighteenth and Twenty-first Amendments," *History*, http://www.history.com/ topics/18th-and-21st-amendments.

7. "Beer for Personal or Family Use," Electronic Code of Federal Regulations, http://www .ecfr.gov/cgi-bin/text-idx?c=ecfr;sid=33fc0c0194b58b6fe95208945b5c637a;rgn=div5;view =text;node=27%3a1.0.1.1.20;idno=27;cc=ecfr#sg27.1.25_1203.sg20.

8. "Labeling and Formulation Regulations," Alcohol and Tobacco Trade Bureau. August 1, 2016. http://www.ecfr.gov/cgi-bin/text-idx?c=ecfr&sid=fd8b0ad16b93584273ae fb7460a98eb4&tpl=/ecfrbrowse/Title27/27cfr16_main_02.tpl; Electronic Code of Federal Regulations,

9. "SLA Announces 'One Stop' Contact for Craft Beverage Questions," New York State Liquor Authority, July 28, 2016, https://www.sla.ny.gov.

10. "Governor Cuomo Signs Legislation to Strengthen and Support New York's Craft Breweries," New York State, https://www.governor.ny.gov/news/governor-cuomo-signs -legislation-strengthen-and-support-new-yorks-craft-breweries.

11. "Governor Cuomo Hosts Third Wine, Beer, Spirits, and Cider Summit," New York State, https://www.governor.ny.gov/news/governor-cuomo-hosts-third-wine-beer-spirits -and-cider-summit.

12. "Small Business Is Big Business in New York State: Information and Resources for Small Businesses," Empire State Development, 2016, nyfirst.ny.gov, https://cdn.esd.ny.gov/ smallbusiness/data/smallbizbrochure.pdf.

13. "Growlers 101: Why Every Beer Geek Should Own One," *Kegerator*, July 28, 2016, http://learn.kegerator.com/growlers/.

14. "How Do New York's Beer Laws Compare to Other States?," *Brew York*, October 6, 2015, http://brewyorknewyork.com/post/130646485898/how-do-new-yorks-beer-laws -compare-to-other.

15. Aaron Goldfarb, "Don't Tread on My Growler," *Esquire*, September 19, 2013, accessed July 28, 2016, http://www.esquire.com/food-drink/drinks/a24773/growler-state-laws-0913/.

16. "TTB'S 'Growler' Policy," Brewers Association, accessed July 28, 2016, https://www.brewersassociation.org/government-affairs/laws/growler-laws/ttbs-growler-policy/.

17. Loren Green, "Cans and Growlers Meet in the Crowler," *Growler Magazine*, March 13, 2015, accessed July 28, 2016, http://growlermag.com/cans-and-growlers-meet-in-the-crowler/.

18. "Wyoming: Alcohol Excise Taxes," Sales Tax Handbook, https://www.salestaxhandbook.com/wyoming/alcohol.

19. "Self-Distribution," Brewers Association, accessed July 29, 2016, https://www.brewersassociation.org/government-affairs/laws/self-distribution-laws/.

20. "Brand Labeling," New York State Liquor Authority, accessed July 11, 2016, https://www.sla.ny.gov/brand-labeling-1.

21. "Enrolled Senate Bill No. 27," Michigan Legislature, http://www.legislature.mi.gov/(S(tq1bctzqdn11a2oqoepxlq34))/mileg.aspx?page=GetObject&objectName=2015-SB-0027.

22. "Beer, Wine and Mixed Spirit Drink Label Registration," States of Michigan, accessed August 1, 2016, https://www.michigan.gov/documents/CIS_LCC_labelreg_32064_7.pdf.

23. "Filling and Selling Growlers of Beer," Senate Bill 27, Senate Fiscal Agency, https://www.legislature.mi.gov/documents/2013-2014/billanalysis/senate/pdf/2013-SFA-0027-E.pdf.

24. "Michigan Brewer and Microbrewer Requirements and General Information," Michigan Liquor Control Commission (MLCC), accessed August 1, 2016, https://www.michigan.gov/documents/cis/Brewer-_Micro_Brewer_211769_7.pdf.

25. Ibid.

26. Ibid.

27. "Brewpub Licensing Requirements and General Information," Michigan Department of Licensing and Regulatory Affairs Michigan Liquor Control Commission (MLCC), accessed August 1, 2016, http://www.michigan.gov/lara/0,4601,7-154-10570---,00.html.

28. City of Albany website, http://www.albanyny.org/Home.aspx.

29. Gregory B. Perleberg and Jeffrey C. O'Brien, "Ten Legal Steps You Need to Start Your Own Brewery," *Growler Magazine*, http://growler.mag.com/so-you-want-to-start-your-own-brewery/.

30. Letty M. Bierschenk, Kurt R. Bierschenk, and William C. Bierschenk, "Singling Out Triple Net Leases," CCIM Institute, March/April 1999, http://www.ccim.com/cire-magazine/articles/singling-out-triple-net-leases/?gmSsoPc=1.

31. http://www.sba.gov.

32. "Microbrewery Business Plans: Executive Summary," *BPlans*, http://www.bplans.com/microbrewery_business_plan/executive_summary_fc.php.

33. "Brewery Business Plan: Sedibeng Brewery," http://www.bplans.com/brewery_business_plan/executive_summary_fc.php.

34. "Starting and Managing," Small Business Association, https://www.sba.gov/starting-business/write-your-business-plan/company-description.

35. "Free Microbrewery Business Plan," The Finance Resource, http://www.thefinanceresource.com/free_business_plans/free_microbrewery_business_plan.aspx; Free Sample Busi-

ness Plans," *BPlans*, http://www.bplans.com/microbrewery_business_plan/executive_sum mary_fc.php.

36. "Free Microbrewery Business Plan."

37. sba.gov.

38. http://irs.com.

39. http://www.score.org.

40. http://www.nfib.org.

41. http://www.nolo.org.

42. Paul Tiffany and Steven D. Peterson, *Business Plans for Dummies*, 2nd ed. (Hoboken, NJ: Wiley, 2005).

43. http://www.profitableventure.com/business-plans/.

44. Billy Pyatt, personal interview, June 2016.

Chapter 8: How Do I Market and Promote My Business?

1. "Consumer Marketing: Old Chicago Pizza and Taproom Explorer Beer Series," Fish Consulting, accessed December 12, 2016, http://fish-consulting.com/case-study/national -consumer-event-old-chicago-pizza-taproom/.

2. "Public Relations Defined," Public Relations Society of America, accessed October 28, 2016, https://www.prsa.org/aboutprsa/publicrelationsdefined/#.WDxGjPkrLIU.

3. "Definition of Marketing," American Marketing Association, accessed October 28, 2016, https://www.ama.org/AboutAMA/Pages/Definition-of-Marketing.aspx.

4. Steven Symes, "How Is Research Important to Strategic Public Relations Plans?," *Chron.com*, accessed October 28, 2016, http://smallbusiness.chron.com/research-important -strategic-public-relations-plans-15586.html.

5. Regina Luttrell, *Social Media: How to Engage, Share, and Connect*, 2nd ed. (Lanham, MD: Rowman & Littlefield, 2016).

6. Regina Luttrell and Luke Capizzo, *Public Relations Campaigns: An Integrated Campaigns Approach* (Thousand Oaks, CA: Sage, Forthcoming).

7. Caroline Oubridge, "Developing a Communications Strategy," DHA Communications, February 12, 2014, accessed November 28, 2016, https://knowhownonprofit.org/ campaigns/communications/communications-strategy.

8. Kim Harrison, *How to Create a Top Public Relations Plan* (Perth, WA: Century Consulting Group, n.d.), e-book, available at http://www.cuttingedgepr.com/ebooks/prplan.asp.

9. Laurie J. Wilson and Joseph D. Ogden, *Strategic Communications: Planning for Public Relations and Marketing* (Dubuque, IA: Kendall/Hunt, 2015).

10. Eliza Bianco, "Elements of a Successful Media Relations Strategy," *Overit* (blog), February 16, 2015, accessed December 12, 2016, http://overit.com/blog/media-relations-strategy.

11. "How Small Business Owners Can Use PR to Attract Coverage," SmallBizContent, June 14, 2014, accessed December 12, 2016, https://smallbizcontent.wordpress.com/tag/ pr-plan/.

12. Derek Bullard, "The Ultimate Guide to Craft Beer Social Media Marketing," PortableBarCompany, 2014, accessed December 12, 2016, https://theportablebarcompany.com/ craft-beer-social-media-marketing/.

13. Gerry Moran, "How to Use Social Media for Craft Beer Marketing," *Marketing Think*, accessed December 12, 2016, https://marketingthink.com/craft-beer-marketing-how-to-use-social-media-to-promote-your-craft-beer-bar/.

14. Tessa Weger, "3 Beer Brands Brewing Great Social Media Campaigns," *The Content Strategist*, June 7, 2016, accessed December 12, 2016, https://contently.com/strategist/2016/06/06/3-beer-brands-brewing-great-social-media-campaigns/.

15. Monica Rosenfeld, "Developing an Effective Public Relations Campaign and Marketing Plan in 6 Easy Steps!," *WordStorm* (blog), December 29, 2015, Accessed December 12, 2016, http://wordstormpr.com.au/blog/developing-effective-public-relations-campaign-marketing-plan-6-easy-steps/.

16. Suzanne Hackett, personal interview, June 2016.

Chapter 9: I Think I'm a People Person: How Do I Manage a Small Business?

1. Ginger Tin, "Ramping Up Server Training," *Brewers Association*, April 28, 2014, accessed December 20, 2016, https://www.brewersassociation.org/articles/ramping-up-server-training/.

2. Leonie Barnett, "5 Secrets to Hiring the Right People," *RecruitLoop Blog*, July 12, 2016, accessed December 19, 2016, http://recruitloop.com/blog/5-secrets-hiring-right-people/.

3. Debra Murphy, "Benefits of a Strong Brand Identity," *Small Business Marketing Blog*, May 15, 2015, accessed December 21, 2016, https://masterful-marketing.com/benefits-of-a-strong-brand-identity/.

4. William Arruda, "Three Steps for Transforming Employees into Brand Ambassadors," *Forbes*, October 8, 2013, accessed December 21, 2016, http://www.forbes.com/sites/williamarruda/2013/10/08/three-steps-for-transforming-employees-into-brand-ambassadors/#7229796c3a53.

5. Barnett, "5 Secrets to Hiring the Right People."

6. Devon Hamilton, personal interview, July 2016.

7. Susanne Hackett, personal interview, June 2016.

8. Brewers Association, *A Manual for Hiring, Training and Retaining Great People*, https://www.brewersassociation.org/wp-content/uploads/2015/04/Beer-Server-Training-For-Brewpubs.pdf.

9. "Writing Effective Job Descriptions," U.S. Small Business Administration, accessed December 19, 2016, https://www.sba.gov/starting-business/hire-retain-employees/writing-effective-job-descriptions.

10. Ibid.

11. "Dining Guest from Lynchburg, VA," Wild Wolf Brewing Company, 2011, accessed December 19, 2016, https://www.wildwolfbeer.com/google5b62b2b66732bd5b.html/our-story/.

12. "People," Drake's Brewing, accessed December 19, 2016, http://drinkdrakes.com/the-brewery/the-people/.

13. Michael C. Mankins, "The Defining Elements of a Winning Culture," *Harvard Business Review*, December 19, 2013, accessed December 19, 2016, https://hbr.org/2013/12/the-definitive-elements-of-a-winning-culture.

14. "History," Founders Brewing Co., accessed December 19, 2016, https://foundersbrewing.com/history/.

15. "Meet the Team," Wiseacre Brewing, accessed December 21, 2016, http://wiseacrebrew.com/culture/meet-the-team/.

16. Mankins, "The Defining Elements of a Winning Culture."

17. Ibid.

18. "History," Catawba Brewing Co., accessed December 19, 2016, http://catawbabrewing.com/about-us.

19. Adele Burney, "The Importance of Business Philosophy," *Houston Chronicle*, Chron.com, accessed December 19, 2016, http://smallbusiness.chron.com/importance-business-philosophy-37798.html.

20. Jacob Morgan, "How Corporate Culture Impacts the Employee Experience," *Forbes* (December 10, 2015), http://www.forbes.com/sites/jacobmorgan/2015/12/10/how-corporate-culture-impacts-the-employee-experience/#3cd2677466fa.

21. Brewers Association, *A Manual for Hiring, Training and Retaining Great People*.

22. "Server Education for Brewpubs+Taprooms," Brewers Association, July 3, 2012, accessed December 19, 2016, https://www.brewersassociation.org/articles/brewpubs-server-education/.

23. Bonnie Harry, "8 Keys to Managing Employees as a Small Business Owner," *Great Harvest* (blog), November 4, 2013, accessed December 20, 2016, https://blog.greatharvest.com/the-bread-business-blog/small-business-employee-management.

24. Brewers Association, *A Manual for Hiring, Training and Retaining Great People*.

25. Harry, "8 Keys to Managing Employees as a Small Business Owner."

26. Daniel Cherrin, Regina Luttrell, and Jamie Ward, "Climate of Denial: #Flint Water Crisis," presented at *Public Relations Society of America 2017 International Conference*, Boston, October 25, 2017, http://www.prsa.org/conferences/internationalconference/program/data/display/7172/climate_of_denial_flint_water_crisis.

27. "Jack Abbey Brewery Wasted 3,000 Gallon of Beer after Gasket Fails," YouTube, December 12, 2013, accessed December 21, 2016, https://www.youtube.com/watch?v=AFAuqOSzQIQ.

28. Cherrin et al., "Climate of Denial."

29. "Crisis Management for Small Business," Bernstein Crisis Management Blog, 2012, accessed December 21, 2016, http://www.bernsteincrisismanagement.com/crisis-management-for-small-business/.

30. Ingrid Alvarez Cherney, personal interview, June 2016.

Chapter 10: Getting Familiar with Others in the Industry: More about Learning and Drinking

1. https://www.greatamericancanbeerfestival.com.

2. http://cannedcraftbeerfest.com.

NOTES

3. http://www.beercityfestival.com.
4. https://www.facebook.com/BeerCitySpringFest.
5. http://www.californiafestivalofbeers.com.
6. http://www.greatbeerexpo.com/philly/.
7. http://www.oregonbrewfest.com.
8. http://www.quadstatebeerfest.com.
9. https://sandiegobeerfestival.com.
10. http://www.columbusbeerweek.com/sixonepour/.
11. http://www.southernbrewersfestival.com/#home.
12. http://www.tap-ny.com.
13. http://www.vtbrewfest.com.
14. http://www.oregonbrewfest.com.
15. https://www.boulderdowntown.com/events/boulder-craft-beer-festival.
16. https://www.facebook.com/events/1761425807441667/.
17. http://midvalleybrewfest.com.
18. http://www.ashevillebeerfest.com.
19. http://www.x1023.com/event/palm-beach-winter-beer-fest/.
20. http://visitingmontgomery.com/calendar/event/riverbend-brewfest.
21. http://www.sandiegobrewfest.com.
22. http://saratogabeerweek.com.
23. http://www.mibeer.com/winter-festival.
24. http://www.homebrewcon.org.
25. https://www.homebrewersassociation.org/competitions/aha-bjcp-sanctioned
-competition/?gclid=COWii9jR-dACFYIWDQodPFwFxQ.
26. https://www.homebrewersassociation.org/aha-events/national-homebrew-day/.
27. https://www.craftbeer.com/category/acbw-news.
28. https://www.craftbrewersconference.com.
29. http://www.craftbrewersconference.com/trade-show/about-brewexpo-america.
30. http://www.craftbrewersconference.com/news/2016-philadelphia-convention-center.
31. https://www.homebrewersassociation.org.
32. http://www.bjcp.org.
33. https://www.brewersassociation.org.
34. http://www.mbaa.com/Pages/default.aspx.
35. http://newyorkcraftbeer.com.
36. http://brewwiki.com.
37. https://www.pinkbootssociety.org.
38. http://www.cision.com/us/2012/05/top-10-beer-magazines/.
39. http://draftmag.com.
40. https://alestreetnews.com.
41. http://www.brewingnews.com/northwest/.
42. http://celebrator.com.
43. http://www.brewingnews.com/greatlakes/.
44. http://www.brewingnews.com/yankeebrew/.

45. http://www.byo.com.
46. https://www.beeradvocate.com/mag/.
47. http://www.beerwestmag.com.
48. http://www.brewingnews.com/rockymountain/.
49. https://www.amazon.com/Brew-Masters-Sam-Calagione/dp/B007HZEBW4.
50. http://draftmag.com/7-beer-podcasts-hibernating/.
51. http://www.basicbrewing.com/index.php?page=radio.
52. https://itunes.apple.com/us/podcast/craft-beer-radio-podcast/id73802691?mt=2.
53. https://www.experimentalbrew.com/podcast.
54. http://goodbeerhunting.com/gbh-podcast/.
55. http://allaboutbeer.com/the-beer-hunter-tv-show-25-years-on/.
56. http://microbrewr.com/best-craft-beer-podcasts/.
57. http://www.thebrewingnetwork.com/shows/.
58. https://www.beeradvocate.com.
59. http://www.brewersfriend.com.
60. http://chibeer.org/about/.
61. http://pprc.org/index.php/2016/pprc/resources-for-craft-breweries/.
62. http://hbd.org.
63. https://southcenters.osu.edu.
64. http://www.realbeer.com.
65. http://www.ratebeer.com.
66. http://www.americanbeerequipment.com.
67. http://www.brewmasterswarehouse.com/.
68. http://www.midwestsupplies.com.
69. http://www.morebeer.com.
70. http://www.northernbrewer.com.
71. http://www.rebelbrewer.com/shoppingcart/.
72. https://www.williamsbrewing.com.
73. https://itunes.apple.com/us/app/any-beer-abv/id596562309?mt=8.
74. http://beerapp.co.
75. https://itunes.apple.com/us/app/beermenus-find-great-beer/id917882057?mt=8.
76. https://itunes.apple.com/us/app/bjcp-styles/id293788663?mt=8.
77. https://www.homebrewersassociation.org/brew-guru/.
78. http://www.brewerymap.com.
79. https://itunes.apple.com/us/app/ibrewmaster/id315820829?mt=8.
80. https://itunes.apple.com/us/app/mybeernation-beer-journal/id471229531?mt=8.
81. https://www.thrillist.com/drink/nation/beer-recommendations-next-glass-beer-and
-wine-recommendation-app.
82. http://www.pintley.com/about/mobile-apps/.
83. https://itunes.apple.com/us/app/sipsnapp/id905494677?mt=8.
84. https://untappd.com.
85. https://www.thestreet.com/story/11134042/1/10-best-craft-beer-vacation-destina
tions.html.

86. http://www.travelandleisure.com/slideshows/americas-best-beer-cities.

87. https://www.thrillist.com/travel/nation/americas-seven-best-beercations-combining-the-best-in-beers-and-vacations.

88. http://beerbloggersconference.org/2015/09/beer-tourism/.

89. http://brewersassociation.org.

90. http://www.theduluthexperience.com.

91. http://www.innatcooperstown.com/package/bed-brew-package-with-brewery-ommegang.

92. http://www.newenglandinnsandresorts.com/specials-packages/whats-brewinn/.

93. http://www.madrivervalley.com/beer.

94. http://www.abgbrew.com.

95. http://www.abgbrew.com/index.php/programs/cba#.WAD2FjKZPVo.

96. https://www.siebelinstitute.com.

97. http://www.sierranevada.com/beer/specialty/beer-camp-across-america.

98. https://learn.uvm.edu/program/business-of-craft-beer/apprenticeship-partners/.

99. https://extension.ucdavis.edu/areas-study/brewing.

100. https://www.brewersassociation.org/resources/schools-organizations/.

101. http://www.appstate.edu.

102. http://humsci.auburn.edu.

103. ceu.cpp.edu/courses.

104. cmich.edu/colleges/cst.

105. cnm.edu.

106. cwu.edu/sciences/craft-brewing.

107. fshn.chhs.colostate.edu.

108. abtech.edu.

109. emich.edu.

110. kvcc.edu/programs/human/brew.

111. msudenver.edu/beer.

112. oregonstate.edu/foodsci.

113. regis.edu.

114. schoolcraft.edu.

115. southcollegenc.edu.

116. southcollegetn.edu.

117. fermentation.siu.edu.

118. Extension.UCSD.edu/brewing.

119. usciences.edu/brewingscience.

120. wsp.edu.

121. wku.edu/bdas.

122. http://blogs.cornell.edu/brewing/training/workshop/.

123. https://www.ciachef.edu/student-brewed-beer-available/.

124. http://www.twcnews.com/nys/capital-region/news/2016/01/21/nys-brewers-association-launches-new-quality-certification-program.html.

125. https://www.ecc.edu/brewing/.

126. http://www.paulsmiths.edu/registrar/files/2016/04/CRAFT-BEER-STUDIES-AND-MANAGEMENT-2cokgll.pdf.

127. http://sunysccc.edu/Academics/School-of-Hotel-Culinary-Arts-and-Tourism/-Academic-Programs/Craft-Beer-Brewing-AAS.

128. http://members.brewersassociation.org/store/detail.aspx?id=564.

129. https://www.facebook.com/chicksforbeer.

130. http://www.craftbeer.com/wp-content/uploads/CB_Food_Course/BeerAndFood Course_LR.pdf.

131. Erin Peters, personal interview, June 2016.

Chapter 11: Ready, Set, Brew! Enough Networking, Let's Get Down to Brewing: Six Recipes

1. Permission granted from Mike Wenzel to print this recipe.

2. http://scubabrewclub.com/index.php/13-nj-state-fair-competition.

3. Reprinted from *Zymurgy* with permission of the Brewers Association.

4. Reprinted from *Zymurgy* with permission of the Brewers Association.

5. Reprinted with Permission from *Brew Your Own*.

6. Reprinted with Permission from the American Homebrewers Association.

7. Ben Franklin may have been taking poetic liberty here in paraphrasing a famous wine quote. Fred Shapiro, "Quotes Uncovered: Beer or Wine as Proof?," *Freakonomics*, http://freakonomics.com/2011/03/24/quotes-uncovered-beer-or-wine-as-proof/

8. Laura Ulrich, personal interview, June 2016.

BIBLIOGRAPHY

"4 Home-Brewing Mistakes Most Beginners Make." *Popular Mechanics*. http://www
.popularmechanicscom/home/how-to/a9560/4-home-brewing-mistakes-most-beginners
-make-16039544/.

"10 Gallon Igloo Cooler HLT." *Adventures in Homebrewing*. http://www.homebrewing
.org/10-Gallon-Igloo-Cooler-HLT-_p_2733.html.

"11 Mistakes Every New Homebrewer Makes." *The Mad Fermentationist*. February 21, 2012.
http://www.themadfermentationist.com/2012/02/11-mistakes-every-new-homebrewer
-makes.html.

"18th and 21st Amendments." *History*. 2010. http://www.history.com/topics/18th-and-21st
-amendments.

"2016–2017 Beer Festivals." *Cooking Classes Directory*. http://www.cookingclassesdirectory
.com/2016-2017-beer-festivals/.

"A Brief History of Beer." *Beer Academy*, July 14, 2016. http://www.beeracademy.co.uk/beer
-info/history-of-beer/.

Acitelli, Tom. *The Audacity of Hops: The History of America's Craft Beer Revolution*. Chicago:
Chicago Review Press, 2013.

"Act No. 101." Public Acts of 2013. State of Michigan. July 2, 2013. Accessed August 1,
2016.

"Advisory #2014-11." State of New York Liquor Authority. April 10, 2014. https://www.sla
.ny.gov/system/files/Advisory_2014-11_-_Growlers.pdf.

"Alcohol Beverage Authorities in United States, Canada, and Puerto Rico." https://www.ttb
.gov/wine/state-ABC.shtml#US.

Ale Street News 25, no. 1, February 3, 2016. http://editions.us.com/alestreet_main_0216/files/
assets/basic-html/page-1.html#.

Ale Trails of America. "Field Guide to Breweries in and Around Asheville, NC." *Asheville
AleTrail.com*, Spring/Summer edition.

"All-Grain Brewing." *Brew Your Own*. https://byo.com/newbrew/all-grain.

"All Grain Homebrewing." *Adventures in Brewing*. http://www.homebrewing.org/All-Grain -Homebrewing_ep_47-1.html.

Alstrom, Jason, and Todd Alstrom. "Craft Beer and Brewer, Defined." *Beer Smack*, no. 17, June 2008. https://www.beeradvocate.com/mag/2212/craft-beer-and-brewer-defined/.

Amazon Review, *For the Love of Hops*. December 2012. https://www.amazon.co.uk/LOVE -HOPS-Brewing-Elements/dp/1938469011.

"American Craft Beer Week." About. *CraftBeer.com*, June 9, 2016.

Armstrong, Emily. Phone interview, with Jeff Joslin. Longmont, CO: Left Hand Brewing.

"Attenuation." Northern Brewer Homebrew Supply. https://www.northernbrewer.com/con nect/2011/08/attenuation/.

Baker, Jess. "Join Us for the Renaissance: An Invitation from CraftBeer.com Editor in Chief, Jess Baker." *Craftbeer*. https://www.craftbeer.com/editors-picks/craftbeer-renaissance-let ter-from-editor.

Barber, Tyler. "Adventure in Homebrewing: International Bitterness Units." *homebrewers.org*. http://www.homebrewing.org/International-Bittering-Units_ep_49-1.html.

Barclay, Ellen. "Are Women Better Beer Tasters Than Men?" *NPR: The Salt*, August 31, 2013. Accessed August 11, 2016. http://www.npr.org/sections/thesalt/2015/08/31/427735692/ are-women-better-tasters-than-men.

Barnett, Leonie. "5 Secrets to Hiring the Right People." *RecruitLoop Blog*, July 12, 2016. Accessed December 19, 2016. http://recruitloop.com/blog/5-secrets-hiring-right-people/.

Barth, Roger. *The Chemistry of Beer: The Science in the Suds*. Hoboken, NJ: Wiley , 2013.

———. "Sugars and Starches." *Wiley Online Library*. March 1, 2014. http://online library.wiley.com/doi/10.1002/9781118733745.ch6/summary.

"Basic All Grain Homebrewing Instructions." *The Brewer's Apprentice*. http://www.brewapp .com/pages/basic-all-grain-homebrewing-instructions.

"Beer FAQs." *Brewing Industry*. July 11, 2016. TTB.gov/beer/beer-faqs.shtml.

"Beer Industry." Alcohol, Tax, and Trade Bureau. December 2016. https://www.ttb.gov/ beer/index.shtml.

"Beer Judge Certification Program 2015 Guidelines." Beer Judge Certification Program. http://www.bjcp.org/docs/2015_Guidelines_Beer.pdf.

"Beer Smarts: Tap Your Knowledge." *BeerSmarts Card Game*. 2015. www.smartsco.com.

"Beer Styles." *Beer Academy*, July 14, 2016 (third class—specialty beers). http://www.beer academy.co.uk/beer-info/beer-styles/.

"Beer Styles." *Beer Advocate*, June 10, 2016. http://www.beeradvocate.com/beer/style/.

"Beer Styles Guide." *BeerTutor*, June 10, 2016. http://www.beertutor.com/styles/beer_styles .shtml.

"Beer, Wine and Mixed Spirit Drink Label Registration." State of Michigan. August 1, 2016. https://www.michigan.gov/documents/CIS_LCC_labelreg_32064_7.pdf.

Bellstrom, Kimberly. "Do Women Need a Beer Named after a Stiletto?" *Fortune*, May 28, 2016. http://fortune.com/2016/05/28/high-heel-womens-beer/.

Bernstein, Joshua A. "How the 10 Most Important Grains in Beer Affect Flavor." *Bonappetit*, September 17, 2013. http://www.bonappetit.com/drinks/beer/article/how-the-10-most -important-grains-in-beer-affect-flavor.

Bernstein, Joshua A. "11 Beers Made with Breakfast Foods Like Bacon, Oats, and Coffee." *Bonappetit*, January 24, 2014. http://www.bonappetit.com/drinks/beer/slidewhow/liquid-breakfast-eleven-great-morning-inspired-beers-drink-noon.

"The Best Beer Kits Money Can Buy." Northern Brewer Homebrew Supply. Summer 2016. Roseville, MN. norrthernbrewer.com.

Bianco, Eliza. "Elements of a Successful Media Relations Strategy." *Overit*, February 16, 2015. http://overit.com/blog/media-relations-strategy.

Bierschenk, Letty, M. Kurt R. Bierschenk, and William C. Bierschenk, "Singling Out Triple Net Leases." CCIM Institute. Mar/Apr 1999. http://www.ccim.com/cire-magazine/articles/singling-out-triple-net-leases/?gmSsoPc=1.

"Black Root Rot." *Freshops*. http://freshops.com/hop-diseases-pests/.

Bland, Alastair. "Why Aren't There More People of Color in Craft Brewing?" *NPR: The Salt*, September 11, 2013. http://www.npr.org/sections/thesalt/2013/09/06/219721800/why-aren-t-there-more-people-of-color-in-craft-brewing.

Boggs, Barry, and Cara Boggs. Personal interview. Canton, MI: Canton Brew Works.

"Bottling Calculator." *Brewer's Friend*, August 9, 2016. http://www.brewersfriend.com/bottling-calculator/.

"Brand Labeling." New York State Liquor Authority. https://www.sla.ny.gov/brand-labeling-1. Accessed July 11, 2016.

"Breakdown of Types of Craft Breweries." *Women Enjoying Beer*, June 14, 2016. http://www.womenenjoyingbeer.com/craft-beer/breakdown-of-types-of-craft-breweries/.

"Brewers Association Marketing and Advertising Code." Brewers Association. http://www.brewersassociation.org/. Accessed July 11, 2016.

"Brewpub Licensing Requirements and General Information." Michigan Department of Licensing and Regulatory Affairs Liquor Control Commission (MLCC). http://www.michigan.gov/lara/0,4601,7-154-10570---,00.html. Accessed August 1, 2016.

Brew Your Own: The How-To Homebrew Beer Magazine 22, no. 4 (July/August). www.byo.com

Brown, Pete. *Man Walks into a Pub: A Sociable History of Beer*. London: Pan Books, 2010.

"Building a Keggle: A Keg Conversion Project." *HomeBrewing.com*. http://www.homebrewing.com/articles/keggle/.

"Building a Mash Tun Has Never Been So Easy." American Homebrewers Association. https://www.homebrewersassociation.org/pimp-my-system/building-a-mash-tun-has-never-been-so-easy/.

Bullard, Derek. "The Ultimate Guide to Craft Beer Social Media Marketing—PortableBar-Company." PortableBarCompany. 2014. https://theportablebarcompany.com/craft-beer-social-media-marketing/.

"Business and Professions Code." California Code of Regulations. TTB.gov. Accessed July 11, 2016.

"Business, Vendor, and Event Forms. City of Albany." http://www.albanyny.org/Government/Departments/CityClerk/. Accessed July 11, 2016.

Calagione, Sam. *Brewing Up a Business: Adventures in Beer from the Founder of Dogfish Head Craft Brewery*. Revised and updated. Hoboken, NJ: Wiley , 2011.

Calderwood, Lily, PhD. Personal interview. July 19, 2016 , Troy, New York.

Carolina Brew Scene, no. 1, Summer 2016. carolinabrewscene.com.

BIBLIOGRAPHY

Carpenter, Dave. "Lautering and Sparging." *Craft Beer & Brewing Magazine*, February 9, 2016. https://beerandbrewing.com/VJnL-CsAACgA34Pq/article/lautering-and-sparging.

———. "What Is the Difference Between Ale and Lager?" *Craft Beer and Brewing Magazine*, December 16, 2015. https://beerandbrewing.com/VmsqtyQAADM1mZHK/article/what-is-the-difference-between-ale-and-lager.

Carr, Nick. "Pellet Hops vs. Whole Hops: Comparing the Pros and Cons." Kegerator, November 12, 2014. http://learn.kegerator.com/author/nick/.

"CBC 2016: Philadelphia Convention Center." Craft Brewers Conference. http://www.craft brewersconference.com/news/2016-philadelphia-convention-center.

"Certification/Exemption of Label/Bottle Approval (COLA)." https://ttb.gov/alfd/alfd_cola_exemption.shtml. Accessed May 17, 2017.

Chaney, Eric. "Wild Pints: Fascination with Foraged Beer." *Craft Beer*, August 23, 2016. http://www.craftbeer.com/craft-beer-muses/wild-pints-fascination-foraged-beers ?src=81116_FB1.

Cherney, Ingrid Alvarez. Personal interview. San Diego, CA: High Dive Bar.

Cherrin, Daniel, Regina Luttrell, and Jamie Ward. "Climate of Denial: #Flint Water Crisis." Presented at Public Relations Society of America 2017 International Conference, Boston, October 25, 2017. http://www.prsa.org/conferences/internationalconference/program/data/display/7172/climate_of_denial_flint_water_crisis.

Christensen, Emma. "Beer Guide: What Are Hops? *Kitchn*, April 8, 2009. http://www.the kitchn.com/beer-guide-what=are-hops-81267. Accessed May 17, 2017.

Christensen, Jen. "5000-Year-Old Brewery Discovered in China." *CNN*. http://www.cnn .com/2016/05/31/health/5000-year-old-beer-found-china/index.html. Accessed June 6, 2016.

"Colorado Beer Code." Colorado Code of Regulations. TTB.gov. Accessed May 17, 2017.

"Company Description." Small Business Administration. https://www.sba.gov/starting -business/write-your-business-plan/company-description. Accessed May 17, 2017.

Conley, Gwen. Personal phone interview. San Marcos, CA: Port Brewing/Lost Abbey.

"Consumer Marketing: Old Chicago Pizza and Taproom Explorer Beer Series." Fish Consulting. http://fish-consulting.com/case-study/national-consumer-event-old-chicago -pizza-taproom/.

Cornell Cooperative Extension. *2016 Cornell Integrated Hops Production Guide*. Ithaca, NY: Cornell University, 2016.

"Craft Beer Industry Market Segments." Brewers Association. http://brewersassociation.org/statistics/market-segments/. Accessed May 17, 2017.

"Craft Brewer Defined." Brewers Association. http://brewersassociation.org/statistics/craft -brewer-defined/. Accessed May 17, 2017.

Craft Beer and Brewing Magazine, June–July 2016. https://beerandbrewing.com.

DeKeukeleire, Denis, Arne Heyerick, Kevin Huvaere, Leif Skibsted, and Mogens Andersen. "Beer Lighstruck Flavor: The Full Story." *Beer Sensory Science*, March 17, 2011. https://www.researchgate.net/publication/285025989_Beer_lightstruck_flavor_The_full_story.

"Dry vs Wet-Hopped—What's the Difference?" *Drewsbrewsreviews*, October 12, 2015. https://drewsbrewsreviews.com/2015/01/28/dry-vs-wet-hopped-whats-the-difference.

"Dining Guest from Lynchburg, VA." Wild Wolf Brewing Company. 2011. https://www
.wildwolfbeer.com/google5b62b2b66732bd5b.html/our-story/.

Eames, Alan D. *The Secret Life of Beer! Exposed: Legends, Lore, and Little-Known Facts.* North
Adams, MA: Storey Publishing, 2004.

"Economic Impact." Brewers Association. http://brewersassociaiton.org/statistics/economic
-impact-data/. Accessed May 17, 2017.

Eddings, Bryce. "Growing and Harvesting Hops for Homebrewing." *Beer.About.Com*, March
2, 2016. http://beer.about.com/od/commercialbeers/a/growinghop.htm.

———. "Why Do Some Brewers Use Rice or Corn in Their Beer?" *About Food*, September
26, 2016. http://beer.about.com/od/homebrewingextract/f/Why-Do-Some-Brewers-Use
-Rice-Or-Corn-In-Their-Beer.htm.

"Education for Working or Would-Be Brewers Who Can't Get Away!" American Brewers
Guild. http://abgbrew.com/. Accessed May 17, 2017.

Electronic Code of Federal Regulations. http://www.ecfr.gov/cgi-bin/text-idx?c=ecfr;sid=33
fc0c0194b58b6fe95208945b5c637a;rgn=div5;view=text;node=27%3a1.0.1.1.20;idno=27;cc
=ecfr. Accessed May 17, 2017.

Empire State Development. 2016. "Small Business Is Big Business in New York State: Information and Resources for Small Businesses." nyfirst.ny.gov. Brochure.

"Enrolled Senate Bill No. 27," Michigan Legislature, http://www.legislature.mi.gov/
(S(tq1bctzqdn11a2oqoepxlq34))/mileg.aspx?page=GetObject&objectName=2015
-SB-0027. Accessed December 20, 2016.

"Farm Brewery." New York State Brewers Association. http://newyorkcraftbeer.com/farm
-brewery. Accessed May 17, 2017.

"Farm Brewery License." Alcoholic Beverage Control. Article 51-a. public.leginfo.state
.ny.us/lawssrch.cgi?NVLWO. Accessed May 17, 2017.

Fisher, Joe, and Dennis Fisher. *The Homebrewer's Garden: How to Grow, Prepare and Use Your
Own Hops, Malts and Brewing Herbs.* 2nd ed. North Adams, MA: Storey Press, 2016.

Flowers, Jeff. "Comparing Different Types of Water for Homebrewing." Kegerator, February
28, 2014. http://learn.kegerator.com/types-of-water-for-homebrewing/.

"Free Microbrewery Business Plan." *The Financial Resource.* http://www.thefinanceresource
.com/free_business_plans/free_microbrewery_business_plan.aspx.

"Free Sample Business Plans." *BPlans.* http://www.bplans.com/microbrewery_business_plan/
executive_summary_fc.php. Accessed May 17, 2017.

"Frequently Asked Questions." Empire State Development. http://esd.ny.gov/nysbeverage
biz/faq.html. Accessed May 17, 2017.

"Founders All Day IPA Clone." *Zymurgy*, July/August 2014, p. 32.

"GABF Week Events." *Great American Beer Festival.* https://www.greatamericanbeerfestival
.com/travel/week-events/.

Garofalo, Peter. "How to Judge Beer." Beer Judge Certification Program. http://www.bjcp
.org/docs/How_to_Judge_Beer.pdf. Accessed May 17, 2017.

Gent, David H., James D. Barbour, Amy J. Dreves, David G. James, Robert Parker, and
Douglas B. Walsh, Technical Editors. *Field Guide for Integrated Pest Management in Hops.*
A Cooperative Publication Produced by Oregon State University, University of Idaho,

U.S. Department of Agriculture—Agricultural Research Service, and Washington State University, 2009. https://ipm.wsu.edu/field/pdf/hophandbook2009.pdf.

"Getting Started in a TTB-related Industry." https://ttb.gov/industry-startup/industry-startup.shtml. Accessed May 17, 2017.

Gill, Andrew. "What Is Mushroom Beer, and How (and Why) Do You Brew It?" *AV Club*, September 22, 2016. http://www.avclub.com/article/what-mushroom-beer-and-how-and-why-do-you-brew-it-242544.

Glenn, Anne Fritten. *Asheville Beer: An Intoxicating History of Mountain Brewing*. Charleston, SC: American Palate, History Press, 2012.

Godard, Thierry. "The Economics of Craft Beer." *SmartAsset.com*. https://smartasset.com/insights/the-economics-of-craft-beer. Accessed May 17, 2017.

Goldfarb, Aaron. "Don't Tread on My Growler." *Esquire*, September 19, 2013. http://www.esquire.com/food-drink/drinks/a24773/growler-state-laws-0913/.

"Governor Cuomo Hosts Third Wine, Beer, Spirits, and Cider Summit," October 7, 2015. https://www.governor.ny.gov/news/governor-cuomo-hosts-third-wine-beer-spirits-and-cider-summit.

"Governor Cuomo Signs Legislation to Strengthen and Support New York's Craft Breweries," July 18, 2012. https://www.governor.ny.gov/news/governor-cuomo-signs-legislation-strengthen-and-support-new-yorks-craft-breweries.

Governor's Program Bill: 2012. http://www.governor.ny.gov/sites/governor.ny.gov/files/archive/assets/documents/GPB-42-BEER-PRODUCTION-TAX-CREDIT-MEMO.pdf.

Governor's Program Bill: June 20, 2013. https://www.governor.ny.gov/news/governor-cuomo-and-legislative-leaders-announce-agreement-bills-allow-licenses-ny-cideries-and. Accessed July 27, 2016.

"GrainToGlass." *Dogfish Head Craft Brewed Ales*. http://www.dogfish.com/brews-spirits/the-brews/brewpub-exclusives/graintoglass.htm. Accessed May 17, 2017.

"Great American Beer Festival Winner 2016." Great American Beer Festival. https://www.greatamericanbeerfestival.com/wp-content/uploads/2016/10/16_GABF_winners.pdf.

Green, Loren. "Cans and Growlers Meet in the Crowler." *Growler Magazine*, March 13, 2015. http://growlermag.com/cans-and-growlers-meet-in-the-crowler/. Accessed July 28, 2016.

Gribbins, Keith. "Are You a Woman Looking to Work in Craft Beer? We Ask Female Leaders to Share Their Stories and Advice." *Craft Brewing Business*, April 12, 2016. http://www.craftbrewingbusiness.com/featured/woman-looking-work-craft-beer-ask-female-leaders-share-stpries-advice/2/.

Guest, Chris. "Strange Brews—the 10 Weirdest Beer Ingredients." *Beerconnoisseur*, November 27, 2015. http://www.beerconnoissuer.com/articles/strange-brews-10-weirdest-beer-ingredients.

"The Growler: Beer-to-Go." *Beer Advocate*, July 31, 2002. https://www.beeradvocate.com/articles/384/. Accessed July 28, 2016.

"Growlers 101: Why Every Beer Geek Should Own One." Kegerator. http://learn.kegerator.com/growlers/.

Hackett, Suzanne. Personal interview. June 20, 2016. Asheville, NC: New Belgium Brewery.

Hamilton, Devon. Personal interview. Schroon Lake, NY: Paradox Brewery.

Han, Andrew, and William Herkewitz. "How to Build Your Own Home-Brewing Mash Tun." *Popular Mechanics*, July 29, 2014. http://www.popularmechanics.com/home/how-to/g1580/how-to-build-your-own-home-brewing-mash-tun/.

Handwerk, Brian. "Celebrating 500 Years of Germany's Beer Purity Laws." *Smithsonian Magazine*, April 22, 2016, http://www.smithsonianmag.com/history/celebrating-500-years-germans-beer-purity-law-180958878/. Accessed December 12, 2016.

Harrison, Kim. *How to Create a Top Public Relations Plan*. Perth, WA: Cutting Edge PR. http://www.cuttingedgepr.com/ebooks/prplan.asp. Accessed May 17, 2017.

HarryBrew69. "Easy All-Grain Brewing for Beginners, Part 4 Fermentation." YouTube, August 21, 2012. http://www.youtube.com/watch?v=2D-eu3Ujo0A.

"Harvest." *USA Hops*. http://www.usahops.org/index.cfm?fuseaction=hop_farming&pageID=4.

Held, Paul. "Enzymatic Digestion of Polysaccharides (Part II)." February 27, 2012. http://www.biotek.com/resources/articles/enzymatic-digestion-of-polysaccharides-2.html.

Herz, Julia. "Dissecting Craft Brewer Data." Brewers Association, January 13, 2016. https://www.brewersassociation.org/communicating-craft/dissecting-craft-brewer-data/.

———. "Women, Craft Beer, and Centerfolds." *CraftBeer*, August 19, 2010. http://www.craftbeer.com/craft-beer-muses/women-crft-beer-and-centerfolds. Accessed June 6, 2016.

Hg2. "Craft Beer in New York: The Modern Growler." *The Hedonist*, August 6, 2013. http://hg2.com/magazine/craft-beer-in-new-york-the-modern-growler/. Accessed May 17, 2017.

Hieronymus, Stan. *Brewing Local: American Grown Beer*. Boulder, CO: Brewers Publications, 2016.

———. *For the Love of Hops: The Practical Guide to Aroma, Bitterness and the Culture of Hops*. Boulder, CO: Brewers Publications, 2012.

Hindy, Steve. *The Craft Beer Revolution: How a Band of Microbreweries Is Transforming the World's Favorite Drink*. New York: Palgrave Macmillan, 2015.

Holl, John. "Nano-Breweries: Talk of the Craft Beer Nation." *CraftBeer*. http://www.craftbeer.com/craft-beer-muses/nano-breweriesmdash-tlk-of-the-craft-beer-nation.

"Home Brew Yeast Strains Chart." *Brew Your Own*. https://byo.com/resources/yeast.

"Home Manufacture of Alcoholic Beverages State Statutes." National Conference of State Legislatures, July 9, 2013. http://www.ncls.org/research/financial-services-and-commerce/home-manufacture-of-alcohol-state-statutes.aspx.

"Homebrewing Stats." Brewers Association. http://www.brewersassociation.org/membership/homebrewing-stats/.

"Hop Gardening." *Freshops*. http://freshops.com/hop-gardening.

"Hop Gender Identification." *Great Lakes Hops*. http://greatlakeshops.com/hops-blog/hop-identification.

"Hop Grower Codes." Brewers Association, May 23, 2014. http://www.brewersassociation.org/best-practices/hops/hop-grower-codes/.

"Hop Variety Descriptions." *Freshhops*. http://www.freshhops.com/hop-variety-descriptions/. Accessed July 2, 2016.

"Hops Alpha Acid Table." *Brewer's Friend*, September 14, 2008. http://www.brewersfriend.com/2008/09/14/hops-alpha-acid-table/.

"Hops Types Pellet Plug Leaf." *Brewers Friend*, March 21, 2010. http://www.brewersdfriend.com/2010/03/21/hops-types-pellet-plug-leaf/.

"Hot Liquor Tank for All Grain Brewing." *Brewer's Friend*, February 13, 2011. http://www .brewersfriend.com/2011/02/13/hot-liquor-tank-for-all-grain-brewing/.

"How Do New York's Beer Laws Compare to Other States?" *Brew York*, October 6, 2015. http://brewyorknewyork.com/post/130646485898/how-do-new-yorks-beer-laws-com pare-to-other.

"How Small Business Owners Can Use PR to Attract Coverage." *SmallBizContent*, June 14, 2014. https://smallbizcontent.wordpress.com/tag/pr-plan/.

"How to Build a Keezer Style Kegerator." *Homebrew Academy*. http://homebrewacademy .com/how-to-build-a-keezer/.

"How to Take an Accurate Hydrometer Reading." American Homebrewers Association. https://www.homebrewersassociation.org/how-to-brew/how-to-take-an-accurate-hydro meter-reading/.

Infante, Dave. "There Are Almost No Black People Brewing Craft Beer. Here's Why." *Thril- list*. January 18, 2016. https://www.thrillist.com/drink/nation/there-are-almost-no-black -people-brewing-craft-beer-heres-why.

"International Bittering Units." *Homebrewing*. http://www.homebrewing.org/International -Bittering-Units_ep_49-1.html.

"Introduction to Hop Diseases and Pests." *Fresh Hops*. http://freshops.com/hop-diseases-pests/.

Janzen, Emma. "Deciphering Craft Beer Terminology: Farmhouse vs. Farm Brewing." *Food Republic*, March 3, 2015. http://www.foodrepyblic.com/2015/03/03/deciphering-craft -beer-terminology-farmhouses-vs-farm-brewing/.

———. "Mushrooms Have Entered the Craft Beer Game." *Food Republic*, January 21, 2015. http://www.foodrepublic.com/2015/01/21/mushrooms-have-entered-the-craft-beer-game/.

Johnston, Ethan. "Hop Rhizomes: How, What, and When." *Fifth Season Gardening Company*, March 27, 2015. http://fifthseasongardening.com/hop-rhizomes-what-how-and-when.

Kitsock, Greg. "Craft Beer: Corn Gets a New Look from Brewers, and Not as a Mere Filler." *Washington Post*, August 5, 2014. https://www.washingtonpost.com/lifestyle/food/ craft-beer-corn-gets-a-new-look-from-brewers-and-not-as-a-mere-filler/2014/08/04/ f5a27d4a-199b-11e4-9349-84d4a85be981_story.html.

Koenig, Steve. "10 Tips for Beginning Homebrewers." *Craft Beer and Brewing*. http://beer andbrewing.com/.

"Labeling and Formulation Regulations." Alcohol and Tobacco Trade Bureau. http://www .ecfr.gov/cgi-bin/text-idx?c=ecfr&sid=fd8b0ad16b93584273aefb7460a98eb4&tpl=/ecfr browse/Title27/27cfr16_main_02.tpl. Accessed August 1, 2016.

"Legal To Do List for Starting a Brewery in New York." New York State Brewers Asso- ciation, November 24, 2015. http://newyorkcraftbeer.com/2015/11/legal-to-do-list-for -starting-a-brewery-in-new-york/.

"Legislation." *New York Craft Beer*. http://newyorkcraftbeer.com/about/legislation/.

Luttrell, Regina. *Social Media: How to Engage, Share, and Connect*. 2nd ed. Lanham, MD: Rowman & Littlefield, 2016.

Luttrell, Regina, and Luke Capizzo. *Public Relations Campaigns: An Integrated Campaigns Approach*. Thousand Oaks, CA: Sage, forthcoming.

"Mandatory Labeling Information." Electronic Code of Federal Regulations. http://www .ecfr.gov/cgi-bin/text-idx c=ecfr;sid=983bd180567866ce0fe74b0e936816ea;rgn=div5;view =text;node=27%3A1.0.1.1.12;idno=27;cc=ecfr#se27.1.16_121.

A Manual for Hiring, Training and Retaining Great People, Brewers Association. https:// www.brewersassociation.org/wp-content/uploads/2015/04/Beer-Server-Training-For -Brewpubs.pdf.

Mason, Joshua, and John Remakel. "Brew Pub vs. Taproom: Which Business Model Is Right for You?" Monroe, Moxness, Berg, August 18, 2015. http://mmblawfirm.com/brew-pub -v-taproom-which-business-model-is-right-for-you/.

Mellino, Cole. "Climate Change Poses Threat to Key Ingredient in Beer NOAA Warns." *EcoWatch*, February 7, 2016. http://www.ecowatch.com/climate-change-poses-threat-to -key-ingredient-in-beer-noaa-warns-1882168560.html.

"Michigan Brewer & Microbrewer Requirements and General Information." https://www .michigan.gov/documents/cis/Brewer-_Micro_Brewer_211769_7.pdf.

"Microbrewery Business Plan." *Profitable Venture*. http://www.profitableventure.com/micro brewery-business-plan/.

"Milk Stout with Pumpkin, Coffee, and Vanilla." American Homebrewers Association. https://www.homebrewersassociation.org/homebrew-recipe/milk-stout-pumpkin-beer -recipe-with-coffee-vanilla/.

Miller, David G. *Brewing the World's Great Beers: A Step-by-Step Guide*. Pownal, VT: Storey Communications, 1992.

Miller, Steve. "Frequently Asked Questions." Cornell Cooperative Extension, Madison County. http://madisoncountycce.org/agriculture/hops-program/frequently-asked-questions.

"Modern History." *Beer History*. http://www.beerhistory.com/library/holdings/raley_time table.shtml.

Mondalek, Alexandra. "Patagonia Is Releasing a Beer That Will Give You an Eco-Friendly Buzz." *Money*, October 3, 2016. http://time.com/money/4516648/patagonia-craft-beer -long-root-ale/.

Moorhead, John. "How to Harvest, Prepare, and Store Homegrown Hops: Hops Drying Methods." American Brewers Association. https://www.homebrewersassociation.org/ how-to-brew/how-to-harvest-prepare-and-store-homegrown-hops/.

Moran, Gerry. "How to Use Social Media for Craft Beer Marketing." *Marketing Think*. https://marketingthink.com/craft-beer-marketing-how-to-use-social-media-to-promote -your-craft-beer-bar/.

Murphy, Debra. "Benefits of a Strong Brand Identity." *Small Business Marketing Blog*, May 15, 2015. Accessed December 21, 2016. https://masterful-marketing.com/benefits-of-a -strong-brand-identity/.

Nachel, Marty. *Homebrewing for Dummies*. Hoboken, NJ: Wiley Publishing, 1997.

Nachel, Marty, and Steve Ettlinger. *Beer for Dummies*. Foster City, CA: IDG Books World-wide, 1996.

"National Beer Sales and Production Data." Brewers Association. http://brewersassociation .org/statistics/national-beer-sales-production-data/.

NorthernBrewerTV. "All-Grain Brewing with John Palmer." YouTube. Last modified August 24, 2012. https://www.youtube.com/watch?v=h5J8S5nBdUc.

BIBLIOGRAPHY

Nurin, Tara. "How Women Brewsters Saved the World." *Craft Beer & Brewing*, April 21, 2016. https://beerandbrewing.com/VNN4oCYAAGdLRZ-1/article/how-women-brewsters-saved-the-world. Accessed June 6, 2016.

Ocampo, Joshua, and Alex Delany. "We Tried the Weirdest Beers Out There—and We Mean Weird." *Bonappetit*, April 14, 2016. http://www.bonappetit.com/beer/article/weird-beer-flavors.

"Organizational Plan and Personnel Summary." Finance Resource. http://www.thefinanceresource.com/free_business_plans/free_microbrewery_business_plan.aspx.

Oubridge, Caroline. "Developing a Communications Strategy," DHA Communications, February 12, 2014. https://knowhownonprofit.org/campaigns/communications/communications-strategy.

"PA 101 of 2013—Growler Law." Michigan Liquor Law. July 16, 2013. http://www.michiganliquorlaw.com/3/post/2013/07/pa-101-of-2013-growler-law.html.

Palmer, John. "Brewing Water." *Craft Beer and Brewing Magazine*, January 29, 2016. https://beerandbrewing.com/VUKd4igAABcrKdWe/article/brewing-water.

Palmer, John J. *How to Brew: Everything You Need to Know to Brew Beer Right the First Time.* Boulder, CO: Brewers Publications, 2006.

"Part 9: Bottling." Brewers Association. YouTube. Last modified March 25, 2010. https://www.youtube.com/watch?v=_tqYGHqI9bs.

Patrick, Brian. "The Science Behind Hops Part 1—Alpha and Beta Acids." *Craft Beer Academy*. http://craftbeeracademy.com/the-science-behind-hops-part-1-alpha-and-beta-acids/.

"People." *Drake's Brewing*. http://drinkdrakes.com/the-brewery/the-people/.

Perleberg, Gregory B., and Jeffrey C. Obrien. "Ten Legal Steps You Need to Start Your Own Brewery." *Growler Magazine*, December 18, 2012. http://growler.mag.com/so-you-want-to-start-your-own-brewery/.

"Permits Online Customer Page." Alcohol and Tobacco Tax and Trade Bureau. https://www.ttb.gov/ponl/permits-online.shtml. Accessed July 14, 2016.

Peters, Erin. Personal phone interview. Palm Springs, CA: @TheBeerGoddess.

Prichep, Deena. "Wine Has Sommeliers. Now Beer Has Cicerones." *NPR: Weekend Edition*, August 24, 2013. http://www.npr.org/sections/thesalt/2013/08/24/214582851/wine-has-sommeliers-now-beer-has-cicerones.

"Processing Times for COLAs Online and Formulas Online Registrations." Alcohol and Tobacco Tax and Trade Bureau. https://www.ttb.gov/formulation/registrations-processing-times.shtml.

"Processing Times for Labeling Application." Alcohol and Tobacco Tax and Trade Bureau. https://www.ttb.gov/labeling/processing-times.shtml.

"Products and Services." Finance Resource. http://www.thefinanceresource.com/free_business_plans/free_microbrewery_business_plan.aspx.

"Product Approval." North Carolina Alcoholic Beverage Control Commission. http://abc.nc.gov/Product/Approval.

"Product Distribution." North Carolina Alcoholic Beverage Control Commission. http://abc.nc.gov/Product/DistributionMaltBeverage.

Pyatt, Billy. Personal interview. June 2016. Asheville, NC: Catawba Brewing.

Raley, Linda. "Beer History." Beer History, 1998. http://www.beerhistory.com/library/hold ings/raley_timetable.shtml.

Reinsvold, Eric. "Brewing with Mushrooms." *Beer and Brewing*, April 1, 2016. https://beer andbrewing.com/Vv2KjScAALouiXmi/article/brewing-with-mushrooms.

"Report Your Hop Usage." Brewers Association. http://www.brewersassocation.org/industry -updates/report-hop-usage/. Accessed August 12, 2016.

Roach, Dylan. "These 5 Beer Makers Own More Than Half of the World's Beer." *Business Insider*, February 9, 2016. http://www.businessinsider.com/biggest-beer-compnaies-in -the-world-2016-1.

Rosenfeld, Monica. "Developing an Effective Public Relations Campaign and Marketing Plan in 6 Easy Steps!" *WordStorm* (blog), December 29, 2015. http://wordstormpr.com.au/ blog/2014/12/03/developing-effective-public-relations-campaign-marketing-plan-6-easy -steps/.

Salazar, Lauren. Personal phone interview. Longmont, CO. New Belgium Brewing.

"Sedibeng Brewery: Executive Summary." *BPlans*. http://www.bplans.com/brewery_busi ness_plan/executive_summary_fc.php.

"Self-Distribution." Brewers Association. https://www.brewersassociation.org/government -affairs/laws/self-distribution-laws/.

Shea, Erica, and Stephen Valand. *Brooklyn Brewshop's Beer Making Book: 52 Seasonal Recipes for Small Batches*. New York: Clarkson/Potter, 2011.

Skelton, Andy. "Women Shaping the Brewing of Beer." *CraftBeer.com*, July 15, 2016. https:// www.craftbeer.com/craft-beer-muses/women-shaping-brewing-beer.

"SLA Announces 'One Stop' Contact for Craft Beverage Questions." New York State Liquor Authority. https://www.sla.ny.gov. Accessed July 28, 2016.

Slagter, Martin. "Three-Hearted Ales: Friends Share Unique Bond Over Beer, Open Heart Surgery." *MLive.com*, May 11, 2016. http://www.mlive.com/news/ann-arbor/index .ssf/2016/05/three_hearted_ales_friends_sha.html. Accessed May 11, 2016.

"Small Business Is Big Business in New York State: Information and Resources for Small Businesses." Empire State Development, 2016. https://cdn.esd.ny.gov/smallbusiness/data/ smallbizbrochure.pdf.

Smith, Brad. "Ten Tips Everyone Needs to Know Before They Brew Their Own Beer." *Home Brewing Beer Blog*. https://beersmith.com/blog/2015/12/08/ten-tips-wveryone-needs-to -know-before-they-brew-their-own-beer/. Accessed June 14, 2016.

Smith, Gregg. *Beer: A History of Suds and Civilization from Mesopotamia to Microbreweries*. New York: Avon Books, 1995.

Snider, Mike. "Women to Get Their Own Beer; Will They Want It?" May 28, 2016. http://www.usatoday.com/story/money/2016/05/21/women-get-but-want-their-own -beer/83857942/. Accessed May 28, 2016.

"Special Provisions Related to Beer." Alcoholic Beverage Control. Article 4. public.leginfo .state.ny.us/lawssrch.cgi?NVLWO. Accessed May 17, 2017.

Stack, Martin. "A Concise History of America's Brewing Industry." In *EH.net Encyclopedia*, edited by Robert Whaples. http://eh.net/encyclopedia/a-concise-history-of-americas -brewing-industry/.

BIBLIOGRAPHY

Staff of Entrepreneur Media, Inc., and Corie Brown. *Start Your Own: Microbrewery, Distillery, or Cidery*. Irvine, CA: Entrepreneur Press, 2015.

"Starting and Managing." Small Business Administration. https://www.sba.gov/starting-business/write-your-business-plan. Accessed August 2, 2016.

"State Craft Beer Sales and Production Statistics, 2015." Brewers Association. http://www.brewersassociation.org/statistics/by-state/. Accessed May 17, 2017.

Stetka, Bret. "8 Unusual Beer Styles You Need to Know." *Firstwefeast*, November 12, 2012. http://firstwefeast.com/drink/2012/11/8-unusual-beer-styles-you-need-to-know/15922.

Stevens, Mike. Personal interview. April 2016. Grand Rapids, MI: Founders Brewing.

"Supporting New York State Agriculture." Cornell Extension. http://cce.cornell.edu/sites/default/files/connecting_campus_and_communities_2015_annual_report_3.pdf. Accessed May 17, 2017.

"Sweet Milk Stout." *Zymurgy*, March/April 2012, p. 16. HomebrewersAssociation.org.

Symes, Steven. "How Is Research Important to Strategic Public Relations Plans?" *Chron.com*. http://smallbusiness.chron.com/research-important-strategic-public-relations-plans-15586.html.

"Talking Points and Resources." Brewers Association. http://brewersassociation.org/government-affairs/craft-beverage-modernization-and-tax-reform-act/talking-points-and-resources/. Accessed July 11, 2016.

"Tasting Beer." *Beer Academy*. http://www.beeracademy.co.uk/beer-info/tasting-beers/. Accessed May 17, 2017.

Teagarden, Danielle. "Can I Sell Homebrew? Can I Make Pro Brew at Home?" *Brewery Law Blog*, June 10, 2016. http://brewerylaw.com/2016/06/can-i-sell-homebrew-can-i-make-pro-brew-at-home.

Ten Eyck, Laura, and Dietrich Gehring. *The Hop Grower's Handbook: The Essential Guide for Sustainable, Small-Scale Production for Home and Market*. White River Junction, VT: Chelsea Green Publishing, 2015.

"Ten Key Legal Steps You Need to Take to Start Your Own Brewery." *Growler*, December 18, 2012. http://growlermag.com/so-you-want-to-start-your-own-brewery/.

Tiffany, Paul, and Steven D. Peterson. *Business Plans for Dummies*. 2nd ed. Hoboken, NJ: Wiley, 2005.

Tin, Ginger. "Ramping Up Server Training." Brewers Association. April 28, 2014. https://www.brewersassociation.org/articles/ramping-up-server-training/.

"Trade Practices." Alcohol and Tobacco Tax and Trade Bureau. https://www.ttb.gov/trade_practices/federal_admin_act.shtml.

"TTB's 'Growler' Policy." Brewers Association. https://www.brewersassociation.org/government-affairs/laws/growler-laws/ttbs-growler-policy/. Accessed May 17, 2017.

Ulrich, Laura. Personal phone interview. Escondido, CA: Stone Brewing.

"Union of Forward-Craft Thinking." Stone Brewing. http://www.stonebrewing.com/beer/stone-collaborations. Accessed June 9, 2016.

Vandenengel, Heather. "The Reality of Being a Woman in the Beer Industry." *All about Beer Magazine*, February 9, 2016. http://allaboutbeer.com/article/women-in-beer/.

Watson, Bart. "Diversity amongst Craft Beer Trends." Brewers Association, http://brewersassociaiton.org/insights/craft-beer-trends/.

Weger, Tessa. "3 Beer Brands Brewing Great Social Media Campaigns." *Content Strategist* (blog) Contently, June 6, 2016. https://contently.com/strategist/2016/06/06/3-beer-brands-brewing-great-social-media-campaigns/.

Wenzel, Michael (Mike). Personal Conversation. Albany, NY.

"What Are Carbohydrates?" *LiveScience.* http://www.livescience.com/51976-carbohydrates.html.

"What Is the Difference between Hop Pellets, Hop Plugs, Whole Leaf, and Extract?" Midwest Homebrewing & Winemaking Supplies. https://www.midwestsupplies.com/media/pdf-printouts/different_hops_1.pdf.

"What Is the Maximum Alcohol Content by Volume for a Malt Beverage?" *Frequently Asked Questions.* North Carolina Alcoholic Beverage Control Commission. http://abc.nc.gov/FAQ/Question/46.

"What Is Required for Product/Label Approval for a NC Brewpub Where the Product Is Piped to a Dispensing Tank?" *Frequently Asked Questions.* North Carolina Alcoholic Beverage Control Commission. http://abc.nc.gov/FAQ/Questions/46.

White, Christopher. "Flocculation Basics." http://www.whitelabs.com/sites/default/files/Flocculation_help.pdf.

Williamson, David. "UNC Chemists Figure out What Causes 'Skunky Beer'" *EurekAlert!* UNC News Services, October 18, 2001. https://www.unc.edu/news/archives/oct01/forbes101801.htm.

Wilson, Laurie J., and Joseph D. Ogden, *Strategic Communications: Planning for Public Relations and Marketing.* Dubuque, IA: Kendall/Hunt, 2015.

Wolfe, Allan. "Oats, Wheat and Rye: What Adjunct Grains Add to Your Beer." *Craftbeer.* http://www.craftbeer.com/craft-beer-muses/oats-wheat-rye-adjunct-grains-add-beer.

"World's Strongest Beer, 'Snake Venom,' Clocks in at 67.5% ABV." *Huffington Post: Taste,* October 29, 2013. http://www.huffingtonpost.com/2013/10/24/worlds-strongest-beer-snake-venom_n_4157580.html.

"Writing Effective Job Descriptions." https://www.sba.gov/starting-business/hire-retain-employees/writing-effective-job-descriptions.

"Wyoming: Alcohol Excise Taxes." *Sales Tax Handbook.* https://www.salestaxhandbook.com/wyoming/alcohol. Accessed December 20, 2016.

"Yeast Guide." *Beer Advocate.* https://www.beeradvocate.com/beer/101/yeast/. Accessed December 3, 2016.

"Yeast Pitch Rate and Starter Calculator," *Brewer's Friend,* http://www.brewersfriend.com/yeast-pitch-rate-and-starter-calculator/. Accessed December 27, 2016.

"Yeast Pitching Rates." *Northern Brewer.* https://www.northernbrewer.com/documentation/YeastPitchingRates.pdf.

"You've Heard about IBUs Before . . . But What Is an IBU?" *Beer Enthusiast.* http://www.thebrewenthusiast.com/ibus/.

Young, Michael T. Personal e-mail interview. November 24, 2016. Albany, NY.

Zainasheff, Jamil. "Classic American Pilsner: Style Profile." *Brew Your Own,* March/April 2012. https://byo.com/stories/issue/item/2424-classic-american-pilsner-style-profile. Accessed May 17, 2017.

Zeidler, Lauren. Personal interview. San Diego, CA: Ballast Point Brewing and Spirits.

INDEX

ABV. *See* Alcohol by Volume
alcohol. *See* biochemistry
Alcohol by Volume (ABV), xx, 17, 18, 31,
   51, 145;
  hydrometer, 31, 34, 35, 51
all-grain brewing. *See* brewing process
alpha acids:
 table, 20;
units, 32, 43, 51
American Grains Chart. *See* ingredients,
   primary
apps, 138–139;
  untappd app, xiv, xxiii, 38, 139
Armstrong, Emily, with Jeff Joslin. *See*
   Talking from the Tap
associations. *See* networking

Ballast Point Brewing and Spirits. *See*
   Zeidler
Barber, Tyler, 50
Beer Camps. *See* education
Beer Goddess. *See* Peters
Beer History. *See* History
Beer Judge Certification Program. *See*
   Education
beer types
  —ales, 18;
    IPA, India Pale Ale, 20

  —Common Beer Styles Table, 61
  —lagers, 18
  —"skunk" beer, 65–66
  —specialty beers, 18;
    ESB, Extra Special Bitter, 19.
  —*See* recipes
beverage containers:
  bottles, 35;
  crowlers, 22, 96, 98;
  growlers, 22, 45, 95, 98;
  growlets, 96
bines. *See* hops
biochemistry, 59–63;
  alcohol, 59;
  starch, 59;
  starch conversion, 63;
  sugars, 59
bottling, 35
Brewer's Friend, 55
brewing parts and equipment, 77–84;
  Hot Liquor Tank (HLT), 78, 82–84;
  keggle, 80;
  keezer, 82;
  manifold, 77, 79;
  mashtun, 77–78;
  mashtun cooler, 77–78.
  See also Alcohol by Volume
brewing process

ABOUT THE AUTHORS

Karen McGrath, PhD, has been researching and writing for over thirty years and has just recently coauthored a book with Regina Luttrell for Rowman & Littlefield entitled, *The Millennial Mindset: Unraveling Fact from Fiction* (2015). While her interests have been largely academic and popular culture–related, she has developed a strong interest in craft brewing. Karen was introduced to homebrewing through her partner, Sean. She has also developed an interest in the culture and history of craft beer as she continues to develop her palette via visits and tastings at local and regional craft breweries in the Albany, New York area, including western Massachusetts and northern Vermont. In fact, she brewed her first one-gallon brew, a German Blonde Ale (a Witte in taste and appearance), with her friend Cailin Brown, in September 2015. While she may be new to the beer culture and industry, she is currently expanding her network of homebrewers and craft brewers and anticipates attending the Brewers Association's "Great American Beer Festival" and other festivals in the near future to learn from brewers and enthusiasts across the nation while also sampling recipes and planning her own. Although not an expert, she is a budding novice who is developing her palette. She is willing to do what it takes to learn more . . . even if that means tasting more beer! Cheers!

Regina Luttrell spent the first portion of her career in corporate public relations and marketing. Her extensive background includes strategic development and implementation of public relations and social media, advertising, marketing, and corporate communications. She has led multiple rebranding campaigns, designed numerous websites, managed high-level crisis situations, and garnered media coverage that included hits with the *New York Times*, the *CBS Evening News*, and the Associated Press. Upon leaving corporate America she earned her PhD to teach public relations and social media at the university level. A contributor to *PR Tactics* and *PR News*, as well as peer-reviewed journals, Luttrell is a noted speaker frequently presenting at national and international conferences and business events on topics related to the current social media revolution, the ongoing public relations evolution, and Millennials within the classroom and workplace. She is the (co)author of *Social Media: How to Engage, Share, and Connect*; *The Millennial Mindset: Unraveling Fact from Fiction*; *Public Relations Campaigns: An Integrated Approach*; and *The Agency Handbook: A Practical Guide to Ethics in Public Relations*.

M. Todd Luttrell, a craft beer enthusiast, is an accomplished scientist and business professional with nearly twenty years of discovery and leadership experience. His fifteen years as an organic chemist promotes a philosophy of experimentation, which has led to many popular homebrews as shared within the community. He leverages a fundamental understanding of the science behind brewing to help unlock many of the hidden elements within the brewing process. Additionally, his many years of management, marketing, and business development expertise lend themselves in the execution of fundamental business strategies and successful business launches. He holds multiple patents and has also written various peer-reviewed articles.

Sean McGrath is a committed homebrewer with over twenty years of experience and many more years of enthusiasm regarding craft brews. He actively attends beer festivals and conferences in the New England region to further his knowledge of current craft brewing techniques and flavors. He currently serves as an assistant brewer on many occasions with Mike Wenzel and Michael T. Young at the Helderberg Mountain Brewing Company. Sean also has an interest in the detailed business and production sides of brewing, has developed a nuanced understanding of the industry, and is deeply committed to furthering and sharing his knowledge with others. Sean also dutifully served his country in the Navy and has been a service technician-senior for two global corporations for the past twenty-four years. He looks forward to continued brewing experimentation.